DONOR CONCEPTION FOR LIFE

Donor Conception for Life is one of a series of low-cost books under the title PSYCHOANALYTIC **ideas** which brings together the best of public lectures and other writings given by analysts of the British Psycho-Analytical Society on important psychoanalytic subjects.

Series Editor: James Rose

Recent titles in the Psychoanalytic Ideas Series
(for a full listing, please visit www.karnacbooks.com)

DONOR CONCEPTION FOR LIFE

Psychoanalytic Reflections on
New Ways of
Conceiving the Family

Edited by

Katherine Fine

KARNAC

First published in 2015 by
Karnac Books Ltd
118 Finchley Road, London NW3 5HT

British Library Cataloguing in Publication Data

A C.I.P. for this book is available from the British Library

ISBN 978 1 78220 203 5

Edited, designed and produced by The Studio Publishing Services Ltd
www.publishingservicesuk.co.uk
e-mail: studio@publishingservicesuk.co.uk

Printed in Great Britain

www.karnacbooks.com

CONTENTS

ACKNOWLEDGEMENTS

I would like to thank James Rose, Editor of the Psychoanalytic Ideas Series, for offering me the opportunity to edit this book. His interest in the subject of donor conception has been hugely appreciated, as has his feedback and encouragement during the preparation for this book.

I am very grateful to the contributors who have worked hard and with great commitment to write their chapters. I am delighted that we are all able to benefit from the wealth of thought and experience that is reflected in their work.

A special thanks to colleagues and friends who have helped me to structure my thoughts and consolidate my ideas. They have given generously of their time and their knowledge. I have been touched by the way in which they have responded to this project, offering me a sense of perspective that I have sometimes lacked. To Michele Roitt and Karen Nash a heartfelt thanks for their extraordinary friendship, professional insight, and selfless contribution. To Barbara Billings, Claire Cattermole, Gillian Barker, Michael Fine, Olivia Montuschi, Ora Dresner, Peter Swead, Rachel Daley, Susi Titchener, and Alison Vaspe, thank you for reading the drafts and offering your particular expertise: your comments were spot on.

Finally, I would like to thank my family who have endured my preoccupation with extremely good grace. Without them this book would not have been possible.

ABOUT THE EDITOR AND CONTRIBUTORS

Roberta Apfel is a semi-retired psychoanalyst and psychiatrist with a background in maternal and child public health. She is affiliated to Beth Israel Deaconess Medical Centre Massachusetts, a teaching hospital of Harvard Medical School. She has published widely.

Ken Daniels is Adjunct Professor of Social Work at the University of Canterbury in Christchurch, New Zealand. He has published extensively and been involved in research, policy development, and counselling for over forty years.

Diane Ehrensaft, PhD, is the Director of Mental Health and founding member of the Child and Adolescent Gender Center in California. She has published several books and articles in the areas of child development, gender, parenting, parent–child relationships, and psychological issues for families using assisted reproductive technology. She lectures and makes media appearances nationally and internationally on these topics. She has a clinical practice in Oakland, California where she sees adults, children, and adolescents in individual psychotherapy, both long- and short-term.

Katherine Fine is a psychoanalytic psychotherapist with the British Psychotherapy Foundation, working in private practice in London. She is a Clinical Associate of the Independent Psychology Service. A member of the Donor Conception Network since its inception in 1993, she has facilitated both 'Preparation for (donor conception) Parenthood' and 'Talking and Telling' workshops. She is a visiting lecturer, supervisor and adult psychotherapist at the Tavistock Centre in London and WPF Therapy in London.

Rheta Keylor is a doctor of clinical psychology practicing in the Newton area of Massachusetts. She is experienced in working with a wide range of relational, marital, and family problems. She has extensive experience in the field of infertility and parenting. She teaches at Harvard Medical School and has supervised students in many of the Boston area training programs. She has published in her field.

Tamsin Mitchell has a business background and now practices as a psychodynamic psychotherapist in a number of settings including private practice. She is a member of the Donor Conception Network and has been involved in the facilitation and development of their workshops. She has led 'Preparation for Parenthood' workshops since their inception, for heterosexual couples, lesbian couples, and single women.

Olivia Montuschi is the mother of two donor conceived adults. She and her husband Walter Merricks founded the Donor Conception Network with four other families in 1993. She has published widely in the field of donor conception, speaks regularly at conferences both in the UK and abroad, and has been part of the DC Network team that lobbied the government prior to the ending of anonymity for donors in 2005. Olivia trained as a teacher and counsellor and for many years worked as a parenting educator and trainer, writing materials and running parenting education programmes. She now works as practice consultant for the Donor Conception Network.

James Rose, PhD, is a Fellow of the British Psychoanalytical Society. He is a former chair of the British Psychoanalytic Council, which is the regulator for psychoanalytic psychotherapy in the UK. He has a private psychoanalytic practice and for many years worked in the

Brandon Centre, based in Kentish Town in London, an inner city charity specialising in the psychotherapeutic treatment of adolescents and young adults. He is the editor of the Psychoanalytic Ideas series published by Karnac.

Amy Schofield is a doctor of clinical psychology who has carried out research into male factor infertility and donor conception. She has worked with people facing infertility and using assisted reproductive technologies to build families and has helped run groups for children conceived via donor conception. She currently works as a psychologist with a charity that takes mental health services to the streets to help engage disadvantaged and excluded young people.

Susan C. Vaughan, MD, is on the Faculty of the Columbia Center for Psychoanalytic Training and Research at Columbia University College of Physicians and Surgeons where she teaches about gender and sexuality. A graduate of Harvard College and Columbia Physicians and Surgeons, she is the author of numerous books including *The Talking Cure: The Science Behind Psychotherapy* and *Half Empty, Half Full: Understanding the Psychological Roots of Optimism*. She maintains a private practice in New York City where she lives with her wife and two daughters.

STATEMENT OF CONFIDENTIALITY

This book is much concerned with personal issues that have been generously shared by people in the knowledge that they will not be personally attributable.

For this reason, the contributors have protected the identity of those whose experiences are being described or, where appropriate, the permission to publish has been sought from those whose circumstances are being specifically discussed.

FOREWORD

James Rose

The decision by a couple or an individual to create a family through donor conception often follows the discovery that they cannot have a baby in the conventional way. This might be as a result of infertility in one or both partners of a heterosexual couple; the absence of a partner for a single person; or of a partner of the opposite sex in lesbian and gay relationships. The use of donor gametes offers these couples and individuals an amazing opportunity: the chance to become involved in every aspect of the creation of a family, from choosing a donor if this is an option, through conception, pregnancy, birth, and raising children. The narratives of donor-conceived families referred to in this book suggest that despite the difficulties encountered on this journey, the joy of having a family amply justifies the decision. It is inevitable, however, that the inclusion of a third party in this intimate aspect of the lives of the assisted parents will stir up complex psychological and emotional challenges. As the title suggests, the involvement of a donor does not stop at the moment of conception but remains an ongoing fact: genetically, psychologically, and relationally, in the lives of all who are involved. UK legislation introduced in 2005 removed the anonymity of donors and gave donor-conceived children the right to trace their donors once they reach adulthood. This raises additional issues for consideration for all concerned; the long-term implications of this legislation will not start to become clear until after the first children with donor identifying information reach adulthood in 2023.

Donor Conception for Life brings together papers by authors with diverse clinical, research, educational and personal experience in this field. It offers a rich insight into the psychological experiences of women and men who have used donor assistance to create their families. The different sections consider: psychological and psychodynamic factors related to assisted reproductive technologies; issues that face couples and individuals undertaking donor conception; and the impact on children of knowing that they are donor-conceived. The final section questions how changes in the realities about where babies come from might, in the future, impact on social attitudes and challenge established psychoanalytic understanding about the development of the internal world. The authors in this book all argue that it is ultimately healthier for the psychological well-being of parents, children, and families, for donor conception to be talked about openly. This contradicts earlier professional and social advice. It may seem counterintuitive to the understandable fears and anxieties that some assisted parents may have about disclosure. The position the authors adopt may feel like an additional burden, but the authors discuss how talking openly can be done effectively.

From a psychoanalytic perspective, authors explore the powerful conscious and unconscious fantasies that can be aroused by the journey towards and through donor conception and how these may reawaken earlier anxieties and developmental struggles. They consider the emotional impact on the assisted parents as individuals, as well as on their couple relationship and the way in which they bond with their babies. How these emotional challenges are negotiated is likely to become reflected in the approaches they take to parenting their children as well as to whether and how they choose to speak to their children about their donor origins. The authors also apply psychoanalytic theory to illuminate clinical and research findings. There is still much to understand psychoanalytically. This book offers a useful contribution to this relatively new field that will hopefully encourage other clinicians and researchers to explore further.

This moving and thought-provoking book addresses people who are involved personally and professionally in the field of donor conception. It will be of help to those who have direct experience of donor-assisted conception or are contemplating using it to create a family, as well as to their friends or relatives wishing to understand more about the process. For many, the journey to becoming a donor-assisted parent can still feel a lonely one and the descriptions of the personal experiences of others referred to in the book may be supportive and illuminating. For clinicians and researchers of all kinds who work with infertility, assisted reproductive technologies and donor conception, this book offers a deeper understanding of those whose lives have been affected by donor conception.

PART I

AN OVERVIEW OF THE PSYCHOLOGICAL ISSUES RELATED TO REPRODUCTIVE TECHNOLOGY

CHAPTER ONE

Introduction:
how do we conceive the family?

Katherine Fine

The title, *Donor Conception For Life*, seeks to emphasise that this book is not just about procreation, but is about raising a family of donor conceived children. Some recipients may assume that in using donated gametes, that is a sexually reproducing organism, especially an ovum or sperm, they are simply acquiring a factor of reproduction, with no further implications. This assumption does not take account, however, of the genetic history and psychological legacy of the donor's family, such that the donor becomes part of the reality of the family for life: genetically and psychologically.

The book seeks to identify some of the significant issues that people encounter. In this introduction I will briefly outline the development of the thinking and practice of building families with the assistance of donor conception. In an effort to capture a very contemporary set of circumstances, I will describe a discussion I had with two fifteen-year-old girls who discovered five years ago that they are half-siblings; born into two different families, they share the same sperm donor. I will end this introduction by giving a short preface to Parts I to IV, to introduce and frame each of the contributions and define the structure of the book.

If you were to open a newspaper or a magazine these days, you would not be surprised to see an article about a family created using a donated egg or sperm, nor to read about some of the wider associated issues. Recent examples are stories about tracing the donor, families with same sex parents, women successfully postponing childbirth by using egg freezing or egg donation, or the fact of sperm as a marital asset. Twenty years ago, the idea that fertility treatment using donor gametes would have made such a leap into public consciousness would have seemed extraordinary, given the culture of secrecy that was supported and advocated by the majority of fertility clinics.

Advances in reproductive medical technology and in DNA testing have had a dramatic effect on the sorts of issues that confront prospective parents of donor conceived children, donor conceived families, and, most importantly, the donor conceived children and adults themselves. At the first national meeting of the Donor Insemination Network in Sheffield in 1993, attended by only sixty people, the main preoccupation of members was about whether to be open and tell donor offspring about the way they were conceived. In 2000, the Donor Insemination Network was renamed the Donor Conception Network to reflect the diversity of gamete donation, sperm, egg, embryo, and double donation. By 2013, the Donor Conception Network (DCN) membership stood at around 1,700, mainly UK based family members.

It seems fair to say that all parenting stirs up conscious and unconscious fantasies. As in other forms of psychological investigation, by looking at the more unusual aspects, in this case an alternative way of conceiving a child, one can throw light on our understanding of all processes of reproduction. We all have to come through these fantasies and processes in growing up, in having a relationship with our parents, both in our mind and in reality, and, ultimately perhaps, in becoming parents ourselves. Involving a donor as an external party to procreation raises many complex psychological, social, and relational issues. This challenges our fundamental preconceptions about "who is family" and "how babies are made".

Background

An increased understanding of the physiology of conception and reproduction has revolutionised the means of medically treating problems of infertility, conception, pregnancy, and childbirth. This knowledge and technical expertise has had far reaching social, individual, and family consequences. The notion that a sexually active heterosexual couple is a necessary condition for either conception or parenting no longer holds true. This has provided the opportunity to parent for individuals who are not in a position to create a family in the conventional way.

With the ending in 2005 of donor anonymity in the UK, the rights of the donor conceived child in this country have been acknowledged and changed. At the age of eighteen, donor conceived individuals will be able to access identifying information about their donor. This right will only become a reality for those conceived after 2005 and effective therefore from 2023 onwards, when the first children affected by the legislation reach the age of eighteen. The anonymity of the donors of those conceived between 1991 and 2005 will be maintained and their identity will never be disclosed, unless they have subsequently decided to waive their anonymity by "re-registering".

One can see how this combination of circumstances has inevitably led to a sea change in thinking and a much wider interest in donor conceived families.

Psychoanalytic ideas

In many ways, an understanding of the processes of procreation and child rearing embraces the whole body of psychoanalytic theory and practice. In introducing this book, I cannot summarise all of these ideas. An appropriate starting point however may be Winnicott's fundamental notion that any understanding of an infant is inextricably linked with the individuals upon whom the baby depends.

> "There is no such thing as an infant", meaning, of course, that whenever one finds an infant one finds maternal care, and without maternal care there would be no infant. (Winnicott, 1960, p. 39)

Ehrensaft (2000) develops this theme by saying you cannot have a donor conceived family and turn a blind eye to the donor. Over the last twenty years, there has been a revolution in thinking and in application, so that being open and honest about what Ken Daniels describes in this book: "as the family building history and the involvement of a donor", if it is well managed: "leads to healthy and well functioning families". The implication is that the journey is incomplete if the role of the donor as one of these parties is not acknowledged or more fully understood.

Thinking about the psychological implications of assisted reproductive technology has the potential to influence every parent, not just those who embark on fertility treatment. The technical possibilities offer the prospect of altering our fantasies about reproduction, conscious or unconscious, as well as impacting on the folk myths about how children can or should come into the world.

It may be essential to mourn the loss of one's fertility or the loss of an ideal family before being truly able to accept that conventional child bearing is not an option. In a strange way, we are now no longer innocently held hostage to fortune, given the opportunities for such procreative possibilities and outcomes through the use of donated gametes, be it through egg donation, sperm donation, double donation (egg and sperm), embryo donation, or surrogacy, to assist conception.

The oedipal myth is used in psychoanalytic theory to understand the process by which a child works out the relationships between themselves and those who care for them. The presence of the donor inevitably complicates this process, both consciously or unconsciously, for all participants in the donor conceived family.

Becoming a parent is a massive psychological challenge for everyone. Research suggests that all parents benefit from having an opportunity to explore the psychological implications for them, of becoming a parent (Cowan et al., 2009). Such analysis of thoughts and feelings may be even more important for people engaging in assisted reproductive technologies, such as donor conception.

Linda and Susie

I would now like to introduce you to Linda and Susie, who are half-siblings, because they were conceived through the same anonymous sperm donor, but to different mothers, in different families. Fifteen when I met them, they were born a few weeks apart, but did not know of each other until they were ten years old. I wanted to hear about their experience of having found each other. I hope that I am able to capture the essence of their particular sibling bond and how their being donor conceived seems to have been integrated into their sense of "family", as it has continued to evolve.

The girls talked about how they had both grown up, always knowing they were donor conceived; there never having been a "sit down at the table moment . . . of revelation". They told me about school, the curiosity of their peers and I was impressed by how they seemed to have managed this with great self-assurance. What stayed with me was the girls' fearless curiosity and their maturity. While for me this seemed an extraordinary story, for them this was ordinary life and in no way remarkable.

Linda and Susie call each other sisters, "because it's easier". Half-sister sounds "a bit detached and clinical". Both only children in their respective families, the girls seem to have grown up with a precocious sense of what is involved in handling the interest of others.

Susie is in a family with her single mother and had long been aware of the possibility of having half-siblings. Her mother had placed a notice in the DCN Sibling Link to register an interest in tracing any other children who might have been conceived using the same anonymous sperm donor. Susie knew that she probably had a minimum of nine half-siblings as the donor had contributed to nine other families, but she had never expected to meet one. Susie told me she has her grandparents who are like second parents; she feels part of a big extended family to whom she is close. Susie was never particularly bothered about siblings and now she and Linda have each other she is happy with that. She thinks less about the donor because of her sister from "that side of her family", which has satisfied her curiosity.

Linda is in a family with two mothers in a lesbian partnership. She had previously imagined that the anonymous man had donated only once, for her. When she was ten years old, Linda's mother was looking for a mentor for her daughter as she prepared for secondary school transfer. She thought it would be helpful for Linda to talk to someone else about being donor conceived and to consider the inevitable curiosity about her family and birth circumstances. If she were given the opportunity to meet the donor Linda said she would, although she would not like it if he were disappointing as a role model, or if he was not interested in her. Linda felt that if she had grown up with a brother or sister in her family, she probably would have been less curious about Susie, because she would have had someone of a similar age with whom she could talk about being in her family.

Donor conception for life—making contact

In sharing information about their respective donor, his distinctive hobbies and physical characteristics as far as they knew them, their mothers realised that the sperm donor was one and the same man. Proposing contact between the two families and the girls meeting each other, the mothers recognised that this was not a relationship that could be dropped if the girls did not get along; they would be in each other's families and lives forever. They were cautious, as Linda put it: "We are a happy family and didn't want to jeopardise it."

Finding out about each other was to be a fact of family life, even if it transpired that the girls were to regard each other as a sort of distant cousin with whom they would have limited contact. In the event, Linda and Susie told me they get on so well that they want to spend time together. They go away on holiday, both girls with each of their families, for their summer break. They both feel very accepted by each other's grandparents, staying overnight and going away with them too.

Susie felt that at ten years old, their discovery of each other was exciting, not confusing. Linda said it was really bizarre to see a picture of someone to whom you were genetically related. She clearly remembers the afternoon she was told by her parents that she had a half-sister:

> I felt my head was going to explode because you don't even consider the possibility of a sibling—hang on, you have a half-sister . . . I spent all afternoon asking questions.

Their first meeting

Linda felt that it mattered a lot because they wanted to start the relationship well, but bonding was not going to be automatic, as Susie put it:

> We never expected to meet anyone, we were so lucky to meet one another. Obviously this is a person you have never met before, you have to build a relationship with them but as you have this [genetic link] . . . it is a good starting point and thinking of the future we are going to be friends for a long time because we are related.

They remembered meeting each other as being incredibly awkward. They had been worried that they would be very different and would have to force their relationship, but they were pleased that they seemed to share common interests—they both liked *Dr Who*! Linda remembers Susie's mum answering the door and catching her first sight of Susie and thinking "there's my half-sister". She explained:

> You don't know what to do it's like a completely alien experience . . . you don't know whether to say "what do you do in your free time?" or "hey you're my sister" . . . we both wanted to make it work . . . it was only the two of us . . . we were thinking this is going to affect us for the rest of our lives.

They told me they feel lucky to be so comfortable with one another. Becoming friends quite quickly, they both remarked on the value of going through puberty at school and having someone to share it with.

How does the fact of the donor shape their sense of family?

They seemed at ease with the (anonymous) donor not being a part of their lives and unlikely to be known to them in the future. Appearing to take this in their stride they were receptive to the notion of him, but more in the sense of general curiosity, particularly now that they had each other. They both imagined the donor was probably married and had children of his own, although neither seemed to consider that if he had any, the donor's own children would be their half-siblings. In their discussion with me they seemed to be reflecting on the nature of his "gift" and what his motivation might have meant in terms of exploring his fit in their family. As Linda put it:

> You'd have to decide how much you would make them part of your life, would you have Christmas dinner together? Also, he has his own life, he's probably married and has kids of his own.

Linda would not think of calling her donor "dad" or anything like that. When she was little she used to think about the donor as the ideal dad sort of figure, whereas now she does not really want to know who he is because:

> . . . chances are he is not going to be that ideal figure that I have in my mind and I have a happy life and I have a half-sister that I really love

... I don't have the need to meet him, I don't feel that my life is any less for not having him in it.

Susie said she had thought about the donor, but less so since meeting Linda. They both feel they would only meet the donor if both of them were happy about it. Their relationship comes first, according to Susie:

> I wouldn't object to meeting him because what he did was so selfless out of compassion and wanting to help people ... if he was willing to meet then you know he wants to know more about you.

Linda used to think it was a compassionate donation when she was little, but now she has:

> ... a more pessimistic view, I mean he got paid to do it, that was his motivation.

Susie clarified that the donor did not get paid, but only got expenses; Linda concurred that he probably did do it as a really nice gesture but that she does not think about it anymore:

> It's not like you had a dad and he left and you have to adjust, you've never had one, you can't compare it, some people have a dad, some don't ... You don't need a dad to be happy ... It doesn't feel like an interesting story just [my] life ... I am grateful to him I don't feel I need the donor in my life. [I] managed fifteen years without him I can manage the rest of my life without him. When I was little I might have needed a dad more.

Implicit here is the recognition that having a donor is not the same as having a dad. Their donor is seen as having his own life and perhaps that is why they do not seem to claim his children as their half-siblings in quite the same way.

The implications of telling others for all the parties involved

Both girls remembered it as quite hard work having to explain the nature of their conception to friends at primary school. Susie recalled that other children would say:

. . . "you must have a dad everyone has a dad" and then other children didn't really understand how babies are made.

Linda felt that same sex relationships are more common now and more normalised in society as people have different sorts of families. In Year Eight though, she decided to make a presentation on donor conception, because she was tired of having to talk about her sister and having to explain herself:

> It was good, there were lots of questions and answers and people got to understand it.

They wondered if their donor made his donation when he was single and if he is with a partner now, as they assume he probably is, whether he has been open with his partner. They were sensitive to the significance of this task imagining how he might put it:

> "Oh, by the way there is something that I haven't told you that I have got nine to ten kids". It's going to be difficult for him; he might have told his wife but may have been quite young [when he donated].

They seemed well attuned to managing and satisfying the interest of others.

Their sense of an evolving family

Both girls felt that it was a bit "weird" that something so normal in their lives would be completely new to some people who are going to read this book. Linda commented:

> It makes French and Spanish oral a bit more complicated, I just say "my sister".

Susie wondered if their parents think about it much more than they do:

> Adults worry about it a lot more. They ask, how do you tell young children? They ask me how do I cope, "what is it like not having a dad?" I ask, "what is it like having a dad?"

They are grateful to the donor because they are alive. But they do not wake up every morning and say "wow I have a sister, it's . . . just life". Yet both girls are sensitive to the nuances of a family that may continue to expand given that there are a number of untraced siblings. They are not actively looking but if they found further siblings: "that would be amazing". They felt it might be difficult for the new sibling because Susie and Linda are so close. In a larger group of say four or more, they worried that there would be pairing off and perhaps they would lose the intimacy. But if someone else wanted to be in contact they would not say no because as Linda put it:

> ... it meant so much to us and we are family. It would be upsetting to say no to another sibling, we would be very hurt if someone said no to us—but it would be difficult to take more people along with you on holiday.

I think they are saying that family is about love, care, and commitment, it is not just about biology. Linda has never thought of her second mum, her non-biological mother as any less than her family, even though she is not genetically related. "I love her like she is my mum." It did not matter that she was not her birth mother; she is still the one who was picking her up from school and still the one who is making her dinner. She was acting like a mum would and should. Susie endorsed this:

> It doesn't matter so much about genetics, what matters is if they love you or look after you.

I was struck by the significance of their finding each other just as they were discovering their puberty and were encountering their own reproductive powers and futures. They had truly found sisters. I was left wondering whether it felt to them like finding someone they had not realised they had lost? I was touched by an over-riding sense of their discovery and curiosity, their immense strength and growth. They have clearly taken the knowledge of their donor conception (DC) and the challenges of meeting each other in their stride.

No doubt this interview will have provoked considerable interest and, perhaps questions about the experience of DC. We all gather an understanding of the "facts of life" through the prevailing conventions of the society in which we live. The impact of this "wisdom" is well illustrated by the testimony provided by Linda and Susie. For example, they make reference to other children saying: "you must have a dad everyone has a dad" and then finding that other children did not really understand how babies are made.

They have rejoiced in finding each other, as have their respective families. One can readily imagine the determination of their respective mothers to have a family and the emotional journey travelled to actualise this. We see the benefit to both Linda and Susie of their mothers being open with them about their histories. Their discovery of each other that came about as a result, would not have been possible without this knowledge.

Linda and Susie's curiosity about their genetic father and his background—for example, does he have a family? and what were his motives in making the gift of his sperm?—is a reflection of enormous changes in society's feelings about gamete donation in creating DC families. As Ken Daniels puts it in his chapter in this book: "this is perhaps most marked in the way we now think about the three main parties, the parents, the donor, and the offspring". As readers we can readily identify with a new openness to enquiry and be amazed at the experience of those people seeking to be parents in this way.

In this book, I have sought to bring these ideas to life through the contributions of some people who have been thinking about the emotional impact of donor conception for many years. They have written chapters specifically for this book, vividly describing experience and providing an overview of some of the significant issues. I have also included three previously published papers, both to enhance the psychoanalytic perspective and because in my view they capture beautifully the essence of the psychological challenges and opportunities presented by reproductive technologies.

Accordingly, this book has been divided into four parts, which I will now briefly describe.

Part I of the book offers an overview of the psychological issues related to reproductive technology. Two recently published papers are reproduced here as they make an invaluable contribution to the thinking and discussion. Chapter Two, by Roberta Apfel and Rheta Keylor, provides a thorough and sensitive overview of the emotional difficulties of people who encounter infertility. It begins by proposing that psychoanalysis, long interested in infertility, and a valuable treatment for men and women suffering with this affliction, has also helped to create and support a myth that the cause of infertility is solely psychogenic. But there are multiple causes of infertility existing across a physiological–psychological spectrum. Advances in assisted reproductive technologies provide treatments that can create emotional stress and outpace psychological preparedness of both patients and analysts. These can produce conflicts that reach into the deepest layers of the individual psyche, invade the interpersonal space, and radiate into the cultural surround and its definition of family. An analytic case illustrates some of the ways psychoanalysis can be a treatment of choice for people using assisted reproduction. A deep human understanding is seen as invaluable to the task of resolving the myriad ethical, medical and psychological dilemma in what is described as "the marriage of infertility and technology".

Chapter Three, by Susan Vaughan, augments the one above by outlining some of the reproductive choices available to same sex couples. In the vanguard of what she describes as an unprecedented "gayby boom", Vaughan begins by detailing the plan she and her female partner put to their infertility specialist back in 1997, whereby the author proposed becoming pregnant using her partner's egg and an anonymous donor sperm. An untested and novel idea, their subsequent experience of *in vitro* fertilisation (IVF) treatment was, as she describes, in marked contrast in a practice familiar with heterosexuals whose conventional reproductive attempts had been unsuccessful. The chapter explores different permutations of available assisted reproductive technology and their possible emotional meanings for the participants, in the light of growing de-stigmatisation of homosexuality.

Part II of this book addresses the issues that confront prospective parents of donor conceived children, families with donor conceived offspring, and, most importantly, the donor conceived children and adults themselves. Two of the chapters have been written specifically for this book by people long interested in the field of donor conception. The first of these, Chapter Four, by Katherine Fine and Tamsin Mitchell reflects on the emotional journey of over two hundred participants who have attended the Donor Conception Network "Preparation for Parenthood" workshops. Thinking of using donor conception to create their families, either as a result of years of failed fertility treatment, of being same sex couples, or single women, this chapter describes how, in having to make difficult decisions over a number of very important issues, people often feel isolated, under pressure, and overwhelmed with information. Striking a balance between the needs of their, as yet, unborn child and their own intense feelings, it seeks to explore the common anxieties and preoccupations that consistently emerge for individuals and for couples.

Chapter Five, by Amy Schofield describes a research study of men's experiences of infertility and donor conception and of disclosing donor conception to children, partners, and wider social systems. It considers the impact of the discovery of infertility by men and their realisation that donor conception is for life. Further, it considers how changing legislation, that has removed donor anonymity and thus given adult donor-conceived offspring the right to identify their biological father, impacts on assisted fathers and their relationships with their children. Also discussed, are men's experiences of the donor conception treatment process and support services.

Chapter Six, by Diane Ehrensaft, which has already been published, uses clinical examples from her work with parents and children in assisted-conception families. It explores the anxieties, conflicts, and psychological defences of parents as they intersect with the developmental tasks and emotional experiences of the children. Coining the term "birth other" to refer to the outside party in conception—donor, surrogate, or gestational carrier—the resurfacing of early primal scenes and oedipal dramas on the part of parents is connected to psychological strategies and defences, particularly denial, to ward off anxieties generated by introducing an outside party into the most intimate arena of family life, conception of a child. The parental negotiation of conflicts is then associated to three developmental tasks for the child. An interest in the existence of these innovations need not be confined to users of reproductive technologies. Society as a whole is effected by any departure from the conventional means of having a baby. Readers may well find themselves emotionally reacting to the ideas and experiences that are described in this part of the book.

Part III of this book explores the question of how to incorporate the fact of the donor within a new family boundary, as discussed in Diane Ehrensaft's Chapter Six above. Two of the chapters in Part III have been written specifically for this book by people who are world experts in this field. The move away from a stance of benign denial of the donor's existence, has resulted in a recognition that the donor is a person and not just a gamete. Further, this person's impact will remain in the family long after the resultant child has been born. The fact of donor conception being recognised in UK statute law with the lifting of donor anonymity has meant that secrecy about the means of conception is now untenable. In Chapter Seven, Olivia Montuschi, who has played a significant role in the changes and development of donor conception in the UK, traces the change in the climate of openness about donor conception, which is examined in the context of the fears that many parents have about sharing information with their child and with others. She reflects on the increasing culture of openness that led to the ending of anonymity and, with donors now stepping out of the shadows, the recognition of donor conceived people's needs for information. She discusses the implications of medical advances such that every person is likely to feel entitled to know their genetic history. The establishment and maintenance of secrets in the family may well be deleterious to secure and contented family life.

In Chapter Eight, Ken Daniels argues that, while recipients of donated gametes may think they are simply acquiring a factor of reproduction, actually they are receiving the genetic history of another family. This fact has to be absorbed, somehow into the recipient family. His chapter centres on the information and research that is available to donor conceived families as the parents share information about the infertility journey and the involvement of the donors in their family. The sensitive management of these relationships is considered in relation to establishing healthy and well functioning families.

Part IV of this book considers possible implications and speculations about the future. Chapter Nine by James Rose, considers the assumptions we can make, conscious or unconscious, about how children come into the world and how they should be looked after. These matters often evoke strong moral feelings that can create in society an uneasy reception of the possibility of donor conception, which risks complicating how people using donor conception come to feel about the process, before, during, and after. Having read the book, the reader may see the potential opportunities presented to people and, inevitably how these will be absorbed into how society understands reproduction and childcare. Probably there will continue to be some resistance in accepting these changes and it behoves us as a society to understand all the real and imagined implications of these remarkable innovations.

Psychoanalysis can make a contribution because it offers a perspective on the emotional experience of conventional reproduction and thus, potentially, on the experience of assisted reproduction. Further, it offers a perspective on the development of the child. There is a problem that this perspective can come to be seen as normative. This has the implication that deviations from the norm may be seen as potential causes of difficulty later in life. Psychoanalysis has much to learn from the accumulating experiences of assisted reproductive technology. However, this learning will not be easy because we may be much more wedded to our old certainties than we realise.

References

Cowan, P. A., Kline Pruett, M., Pape Cowan, C., Pruett, K., & Wong, J. J. (2009). Promoting fathers' engagement with children: preventive interventions for low-income families. *Journal of Marriage and Family*, 71(3): 663–679.

Ehrensaft, D. (2000). Alternatives to the stork: fatherhood fantasies in donor insemination families. *Studies in Gender and Sexuality*, 1: 371–397.

Winnicott, D. W. (1960). The theory of the parent infant relationship. In: *The Maturational Processes and the Facilitating Environment*. London: Hogarth [reprinted London: Karnac, 1990].

CHAPTER TWO

Psychoanalysis and infertility: myths and realities*

Roberta J. Apfel and Rheta G. Keylor

P sychoanalysis, long interested in infertility, and a valuable treatment for men and women suffering with this affliction, has also helped to create and support a myth of psychogenic infertility. Multiple causes of infertility exist across the physiological–psychological spectrum. There is no simple psychodynamic causality. Advances in assisted reproductive technologies provide treatments that create emotional stress and outpace psychological preparedness of patients and analysts. This chapter is based on the experience of a unique study group in Boston. An analytic case illustrates some of the ways analysis can be a treatment of choice for people using assisted reproduction. In fact, analysis offers a unique opportunity to elaborate fully the complex realities and dilemmas faced by people and their therapists throughout the infertility experience. More generally, this study of the concept of psychogenic infertility explores a valuable role for psychoanalysis in the treatment of medical conditions.

Half a century ago, analysis was the treatment of choice and indeed the last resort for infertile men and women. Today, assisted

*First published in 2007 in *Journal of Infant, Child and Adolescent Psychotherapy*, 6: 141–155. Reproduced with the permission of Taylor and Francis Press.

reproductive technologies offer a more direct route to parenthood. In addition, the proliferation of short-term therapies, support groups, and mind/body programmes offers a wide range of psychological interventions to the besieged couple. Many infertile sufferers try all of them simultaneously or in succession. Support groups, in particular, actively keep hope alive while countering emotional isolation and the sense of core defectiveness so hurtful to many. What then does analysis or intensive psychotherapy offer to the infertile man or woman that cannot be found elsewhere?

For some, the need for intensive treatment arises long before infertility is diagnosed. Patients are frequently in conflict between career goals and desires for parenthood while years of higher education delay parenthood as an agenda. Developmental difficulties, intrapsychic conflicts and ongoing needs frequently culminate in the failure to establish an intimate love relationship in which a secure sense of self-as-parent can flourish. Many persons are already engaged in treatment when the problem of infertility surfaces due to the time-consuming need to work through various levels of emotional conflict. The analyst–patient dyad is often alarmed when confronted with the painful paradox of having finally arrived at a readiness for parenting only to discover that conception is a problem. The crisis that ensues as the imagined future recedes out of reach once again threatens to undermine the gains people have worked hard to attain. Without warning, and often without preparation, both analyst and patient must now become experts on the very real details of the daily infertility experience, while not foreclosing on the analytic space the patient requires to encounter and integrate its past and present unconscious meanings. Many patients are profoundly aware of the value at such a time of an already established and holding therapeutic relationship through this disturbing crisis.

For many years, psychoanalysts have been involved in the treatment of women with infertility. From 1951 to 1997, case reports and papers about "psychogenic infertility" have appeared in the psychoanalytic literature. Conclusions based on these case-by-case attempts to advance the psychoanalytic knowledge of infertility and consequent psychological disturbance were then generalised to all other infertile women. Lacking other explanations for this angst-filled condition, psychoanalytic theories over time have attributed the cause of infertility to several psychological factors. Themes, believed to be causal, emerging from the psychoanalytic treatment of infertile women have included: unconscious fears and conflict over sex and pregnancy, rejection of feminine/maternal identification and one's reproductive destiny, rivalry and ensuing guilt toward male family members, wishes to remain dependent, identification with the father, envy of masculinity, guilt and hostility toward a disabled and/or deceased male sibling, and insecure or disorganised primary attachment. Certainly all these dynamics contribute to ambivalence about mothering, and may deter some women from childbearing until an age when infertility would become increasingly likely. However, it must be noted that these themes are also very familiar and present in analyses of women who have no difficulty conceiving, whether accidentally or planfully. Still other women with very serious psychic problems conceive with ease.

While analytic data are emotionally evocative and fascinating, and revealing of emotional truth for the particular analysand, they cannot easily be used to discern what is aetiological from what is secondary. Analytic theories of causality based on phenomenological data are difficult to translate into research utilising experimental and control groups and measures that can be replicated. When such research is done, the truth of analytic data cannot necessarily be validated as significant through the commonly used statistical research methods (Fisher, 1973). The tendency to over interpret and over generalise from individual cases has cast doubt on the scientific nature of analytic forms of knowledge. Unfortunately, many people who could potentially benefit from seeking psychoanalytic treatment, have been dissuaded from doing so due to the public misperception of psychoanalysis as antiquated and disproved.

Infertility is a deeply emotional experience for each affected couple. Psychological conflicts involving infertility reach into the deepest layers of the individual psyche, invade the interpersonal space of the couple, and radiate into the cultural surround and its definition of family. Old conflicts are frequently revived which may challenge the integrity of the marital relationship. A couple's pain is then compounded beyond their involuntary childlessness by invasive procedures and ethical dilemmas created by recent technological opportunities. Available psychoanalytic formulations do not provide a useful guide for analysts and patients through the labyrinthine dilemmas faced by the couple. At the same time, physiological infertility is frequently less emotionally central to the patient than is the psychological experience of it and the psychic explanations attributed to it by the patient. The subjective experience of infertility is central to psychological treatment and need not be compounded with physiological causality or treatments.

To address this problem and study the gap between reality and theory, a workshop on assisted reproductive technologies (ARTs) was started in 1992 at the Boston Psychoanalytic Society and Institute (BPSI).[1] Topics studied have included: multiple psychological meanings of infertility, the psychological experience of infertility, the relationship between therapist and patient during infertility, how assisted reproduction redefines the word "family", and what kind of psychological interventions are most beneficial. The workshop then surveyed the entire BPSI membership for its attitudes and experience with infertility. Colleagues with less personal contact with ARTs tended to express more allegiance to intrapsychic causality and to the concept of "psychogenic infertility", whereas those with direct experience held a more complex understanding of infertility and its causes. The workshop members also reviewed the literature, both psychological and analytic, on the topic of "psychogenic infertility". While the psychological research literature has shown a consistent trend towards rejection of the concept, even recent psychoanalytic literature has emphasised unconscious psychological causality.

History of the concept of psychogenic infertility

Prior to the wealth of recent information about physiological aspects of infertility, psychoanalytic writers (Benedek & Rubenstein, 1942; Deutsch, 1945; Jacobson, 1946; Knight, 1943) postulated that infertility in women reflected unconscious repudiation of femininity and motherhood, and fears of sexuality. Working through these issues in analysis presumably allowed women to embrace their femininity more fully. The psychosomatic literature at one time speculated that it was lack of orgasm, a corollary of frigidity, caused by masturbation, which impaired the process of insemination (Kelly, 1942). Benedek (1952) was the first to suggest that functional sterility (i.e., unexplained by organic aetiology, therefore psychogenic) might be more complicated. In order to show how preparation for pregnancy takes place on a psychic level (mediated via hormonal effects on brain and behaviour), she linked monthly hormonal changes with psychoanalytic clinical observations. While her women patients in their thirties were consciously seeking pregnancy, she noted unconscious fear of procreation and aggression against children. She concluded that infertility was a somatic defence that protected the self and unborn children while permitting the women consciously to be unambivalent about wishes for motherhood. Psychologically weaker women might have a spontaneous abortion or hyperemesis. Both Benedek and her discussant, Flanders Dunbar, noted that there is never a static equilibrium between psychic defences and biology or reproduction.

In a classic paper, Benedek et al. (1953) studied six women with infertility, whose husbands had extremely low sperm counts (only one as high as 11 million, others in the 1 million to 6 million range). The women were referred for psychoanalysis to resolve ambivalent relationships with their mothers while the men were left untreated. Not surprisingly, the only woman of the group who conceived had the husband with the highest sperm count. Regardless, this conception was attributed to the therapeutic action of the analysis. Benedek speculated that these women had unconsciously chosen infertile men to marry as a defence against pregnancy. In fact, the psychoanalytic literature has contained very few case reports of men with infertility especially with respect to psychogenic impotence (Noy, Wollstein, & Kaplan-Denour, 1966; Rothman & Kaplan, 1972).

During the nineteen fifties, awareness of these theories made some infertility clinics routinely include psychiatric evaluations (Sturgis, Taymore, & Morris, 1957) in order to discriminate functional from organic infertility patients. Some (e.g., Ford et al. 1953) tried to develop a "psychogram of functional sterility" which reflected cultural attitudes of the time about feminine role. This self-report test included such items as "Would you rather work or keep house?" Such questions implied a direct causal relationship between overt feminine role compliance, culturally defined, and infertility.

With the discovery of more physiological causes of infertility in the ensuing decades, functional sterility decreased in prevalence. Now, fewer than 5% of couples have no clear physical reason for their infertility, and that small number is decreasing continually. We are not suggesting that psychic states do not contribute at all to physiological functioning, but only that this relationship is enormously complex, unknown as of now, and is far from the simple, linear, direct causal relationship that was previously espoused. This has been demonstrated in other medical conditions as well, to wit, the peptic ulcer which now is treated with antibiotics. While the psychodynamic theory of rageful dependency may be aetiologically implicated for some patients with ulcers, other patients express these affects without such ulcers, and still others develop ulcers without such a dynamic. There seem to be many intervening variables.

Soma affects psyche and vice versa. Psychotherapeutic treatment affects the body and its functions and dysfunctions in complex ways. The older literature is replete with efforts to translate bodily states directly into the language of emotions. Pelvic vascular congestion is equivalent to blushing; endometrial hyperplasia, to many frustrated menstrual cycles; tubal spasms, to a physical expression of choked feelings; irregular uterine motility, to psychological tension (Marsh & Vollmer, 1951). In our time we are rightly less confident of such one-to-one correspondences as we contemplate the bi-directional influence of mind and body, or of any important relational dyad, including the therapeutic relationship.

Many research studies utilising interview data and/or psychological testing have searched for variables which can distinguish women with unexplained infertility from those with a biological basis for infertility and from women who are fertile controls. None has demonstrated significant and replicable psychological, personality or diagnostic differences between the groups. Several studies reviewed by Seward et al. (1965) and Denber (1978) are prime examples of poor research, which fails to demonstrate a pathological personality for infertility but nevertheless concludes one must exist. Even when greater disturbance in the functional groups was shown on Rorschach protocols (Eisner, 1963) causality could not be demonstrated, since the Rorschach data were generated after the infertility had been diagnosed. Noyes and Chapnick (1964) critically evaluated 75 references that presumed that psychological factors (some 50 factors) influence fertility and found the evidence scanty, poorly organised and badly analysed. What they did find conclusive is that frigidity does not decrease fertility and adoption does not increase it. Despite these studies, we adhere to the idea that infertile women are more psychologically pathological somehow. Even the medical language we use illustrates this underlying belief. For example, the term "hostile cervical mucus" refers to the condition of antibodies to partner sperm being present, as if this reflects a woman's conscious or unconscious hostility (Christie, 1994).

Another widely held cultural belief is that adoption enables infertile women to relax and conceive and that this can be construed as further evidence for psychogenic infertility (Orr, 1941). This belief implies that psychological tension over non-conception directly leads to infertility so that relief from tension due to childlessness via adoption will restore fertility. While this may appear to be true for some couples anecdotally, the research does not statistically support it. When conception after adoption was specifically studied, it was found to be no more frequent for infertile couples who adopted than for infertile couples who chose not to adopt. We might conclude that infertile couples can sometimes conceive against expectation if they are not using birth control, whether or not they adopt, but adoption does not make this statistically more likely. Paradoxically, these studies showed that more non-adopting couples (35%) conceived following primary infertility than did adopting couples (23%) (Tyler, Bonapart, & Grant, 1960; Weir & Weir, 1966).

There are no valid research data to support a view that resolution of psychological conflict, via treatment alone, or together with adoptive parenting, can result in pregnancy. Moreover, there is ample evidence testifying to the fact that adoption does not remove grief over infertility and its damaging impact on a woman's sense of self, which can continue for years. In fact, mourning for a child who never existed has proven to be difficult to resolve for many women. Even the existence of one biological child in the family does not protect a woman from the acute stress of secondary infertility or from the damage done to one's identity (Klock et al., 1997; McMahon, 1999). Adoption and infertility are quite different psychological events. In any event, while adoption reduces the secondary stress of *in vitro* procedures, it cannot be assumed to overcome ambivalence about motherhood or to heal the sequelae of infertility.

Recent literature on the psychology of infertility

More recent psychoanalytic theorising about infertility has focused primarily on two salient and problematic dynamics. First is the failure to adequately mourn a previous loss. Christie (1997, 1998) reviews several cases that suggest a psychobiology of infertility correlated with early separation from a parent and un-mourned parental death. This observation argues for the usefulness of a period of psychological treatment for an infertile couple in which to explore these life events before beginning assisted technologies. Allison (1997) has described three cases of unexplained infertility in which guilt over the death or defectiveness of a male sibling appeared to be central to the meaning made of the infertility; resolution of these powerful feelings seemed to help prepare for motherhood, but it is a stretch to conclude that analysis cured infertility. Pines (1990) has also argued cogently for more preparation of the psyche for the ARTs, since the infertility itself, and the treatments for it, reactivate previous losses and dormant conflicts.

The second and related dynamic of concern to modern analysts concerns the absence of ambivalence and disavowal of negative feelings about pregnancy and motherhood that is frequently seen among infertile women. While this is understandable in some women who downplay any negative feelings about the infertility or about the treatments as they focus on their powerful goal of motherhood, some see this disavowal as an aspect of "psychogenic infertility" (Christie, 1998). Others feel it to be a defensive response to the infertility experience that, in turn, may make it additionally difficult to conceive. Kemeter and Fiegl (1998) believe this intolerance of ambivalence leads to a frantic effort to control fertility, through repression of negative thoughts and feelings that might, in turn, have a physiological suppressing impact on fertility. While they do not specify a particular bio-psychological mechanism, they suggest that the "hard labour of infertility" negatively effects fertility, reactivates all previous separation–individuation conflicts, and creates an endangered sense of self that leads to more and more rigid efforts of defence. Research support for this thesis (Bolter, 1997) is found in a study of coping styles. Women in this study who were most actively engaged in efforts to control the infertility, and who were most preoccupied with it, showed both the highest levels of anxiety, depression, distress, self-punishment, and the lowest levels of self-esteem. The author suggests that the futile effort to control what is uncontrollable increases emotional stress and is undermining to a sense of well-being.

If psyche and soma mediate to each other, then how do we tease apart the variables and make sense of a welter of contradictory data?

For example, a study of women presenting for infertility treatment, while already demoralised, did not rate their satisfaction level with their partners or their sexual relationships significantly differently from controls. At the same time, 8.5% of infertile women, compared to 2.9% of controls, met criteria for major depression (Downey et al., 1989). While generally happy with their marriages and sexually well-adjusted, infertile women are very unhappy, even clinically depressed, about their infertility. However, Visser et al. (1994) raised the caveat that, while questionnaire data may be valid, infertile women may be motivated to give what they perceive to be desirable responses to test questions when they believe that access to infertility treatment, and hence to a baby, can depend on their answers.

Numerous cross-sectional investigations of the psychological profiles of couples seeking IVF (*in vitro* fertilisation) indicate no more need for psychiatric intervention than for fertile couples who are coping constructively with life challenges (Garner, Kelly, & Arnold, 1984; Paulson et al., 1988; Visser et al., 1994). A prospective longitudinal study of 180 Finnish women, begun prior to the onset of childbearing attempts (Vartiainen et al., 1994), tried to determine whether pre-morbid factors, psychosocial or work-related stressors or personality configurations would influence infertility. Analysts interviewed women and followed them through conception and pregnancy. No significant association was found between later fertility problems and personality factors. Few multi-generational studies of infertility and psychological factors exist. However, Kipper and Zadik (1996) demonstrated that the mothers of functionally infertile women in Israel express more conflict about femininity, both consciously and unconsciously, than do mothers of organically infertile women. These authors caution that intergenerational intervening variables may be operating invisibly, possibly in a bi-directional manner. Nevertheless, the grandmother's attitudes play an important role in creating the familial psychological surround. A member of our workshop, Eva Appelman, is at present researching the attachment style of infertile women, both to their mothers and to their babies born to them after infertility treatments.

Stress from infertility, however, is painfully conscious. Whether the stress is related to unconscious conflict or not, numerous longitudinal studies demonstrate that infertility stress has a reliable and deleterious impact on both physical and mental health (Abbey, Andrews, &

Halman, 1995; Beaurepaire et al., 1994; Benazon, Wright, & Sabourin, 1992; Berg & Wilson, 1990; Domar et al., 1992; Lalos et al., 1985; Slade et al., 1992; Thiering et al., 1993). Although infertility patients and controls do not differ on self-reports of sexual functioning, partner satisfaction or prior history of depressions, those undergoing infertility treatments report significant changes in both mood and sexual functioning which are indistinguishable from major depression. When the duration of infertility and time spent in IVF programmes are taken into account, it is clear that coping ability deteriorates over time, reflecting the erosive effect of years of infertility and of organising life around technological conception. As one patient wrote, "pursuit of pregnancy can be an exhaustive encounter with doctors and needles and hope and rage, leavened by shared marital indignities and comic schemes to beg, borrow, or steal an embryo" (Fleming, 1988, p. 104).

In fact, women with chronic infertility have psychological test profiles similar to women with cancer, heart disease, hypertension, chronic pain and HIV (human immunodeficiency virus) infection (Domar et al., 1993). Coping with infertility is like coping with major medical illness. Those like the biblical Hannah[2] who despair from infertility also resemble women experiencing other devastating life events, such as the loss of a life partner. With every failed cycle, more patients become increasingly depressed (Hynes et al., 1992). Furthermore, the stress factor is most apparent in women who have a hormonal basis for their infertility. Those with an anatomical basis, for example, blocked tubes, do not show the same extent of measurable stress (Wasser, Sewall, & Soules, 1993). This indicates that women with greater hormonal dysfunction leading to infertility may also have increased hormonal responsivity to stress. This specific subgroup is one in which emotional responses may both contribute to the infertility and to the desirability of psychological intervention. Psychological help, including psychoanalysis, may have the greatest impact within this subgroup of clinically depressed women. Possibly these women comprise those described in the recent analytic literature whose infertility losses reactivate early unresolved grief for someone who is unconsciously entangled with the fantasised child (Doria-Medina, 1999; Leon, 1996). Further research about this subgroup might help clarify why the psyches of some people become overwhelmed while others cope better. Clearly, the new technologies can create additional trauma and new emotional challenges of their own for therapists to confront (Bernstein, 1993; Levin, 1993; Pines, 1990; White, 1998).

Which psychosocial or psychological intervention to choose, how best to alleviate the stress of ARTs, and how the hormonal picture can be altered to allow for conception without wreaking havoc with psychological functioning are all unresolved questions. The fact that brief and/or long-term psychological assistance may contribute to a better sense of well-being, and even foster conditions which hopefully enhance the likelihood of conception secondarily, does not prove that psychological factors caused the infertility to begin with.

We know also that hormonal change alters psychological functioning and sense of well-being. This is demonstrated again during the course of infertility treatments when mood shifts occur with the use of hormonal drugs. What is less clear and more complex is the a priori effect of emotional state on endogenous hormones. Both animal and human studies have looked at the effect of stress on endocrinology and, in humans, on psychology (Reichlin et al., 1979). Research on rodents (Barnea & Tal, 1991) has demonstrated that stress-related hormones affect placental hormonal secretion, compromise uterine circulation, impair the metabolism of the decidua through direct humoral factors and modify placental function. The period of greatest stress coincides with the first trimester, when rodents have a high rate of foetal re-absorption, and humans have the highest rate of pregnancy loss. Yet stress is difficult to define in humans and depends on coping and defences. Demyttenaere et al. (1991) have tried to develop a more specific construct on coping for women undergoing IVF. Highly driven and depressed women, less able to modulate their emotional involvement with the ARTs, show high anticipatory cortisol concentrations that can have a predictably negative influence on IVF outcome. Again, preoccupation and excessive efforts to control infertility may have negative consequences.

Facchinetti et al. (1992) reviewed psychosomatic factors related to female fertility, specifically excluding anecdotal and psychoanalytic hypotheses, and proposed an integrated model. In this model, they consider an unfulfilled wish for a child to be a stressful life event for any couple. The intensity of the stress experienced depends on the personal context, relational and intergenerational, for any given couple and should be appraised. Secondarily, each individual's different way of coping with the stress of infertility needs to be assessed. The interaction of each couple's context and style will determine how effective the coping will be and how depressed the individuals will become. In turn, this will influence fertility outcome through psycho-endocrinologic (prolactin, cortisol, gonado-tropin releasing hormone) and psycho-immunologic stress responses. Some physiological barriers to conception can be directly circumvented by IVF. Conditions such as eating disorders and medications that impair the ovulatory mechanism inevitably interfere with fecundity (Robinson & Stewart, 1996).

The longer the duration of infertility, the more protracted the medical intrusions, the higher the anxiety about eventual outcome, the greater the distress, which in turn affects a woman emotionally and physically (Greil, 1997). Marital relationships suffer; couples report increasing levels of generalised somatic complaints the longer they pursue IVF (Hynes et al., 1992). Those who use avoidance and self-blame seem to be at highest risk (Morrow, Thoreson, & Penney, 1995). Baseline psychological make-up is difficult to assess after a long period of stress and concomitant regression. After some time in an IVF programme, infertile couples list significantly more somatic complaints related to fertility, such as menstrual disturbances and sexual dysfunction (Kemeter, 1988). The language of chronic warfare is used in one study where those undergoing first-time IVF are called "inductees" (15% clinically depressed compared to a community average of 12%) and all others are "veterans" (25% depressed) (Thiering et al., 1993). What is the effect of fatigue and loss of the usual restorative mechanisms? What is physiological per se? What has to do with tension in the marital relationship (Edelman & Connolly, 1986)? Gender is a significant variable since women experience and report their distress more often than do men (McCartney & Wada, 1990).

Yet, male-factor infertility accounts for a minimum of 45% of all cases. When male-factor infertility is primary, studies have shown that marital instability and strife significantly increases (Connolly, Edelmann, & Cooke, 1987). Men who are infertile show higher levels of distress and guilt about the infertility. Despite how infertility affects both genders, research and intervention have focused almost exclusively on the female partner for historical and medical reasons as well as the greater willingness of women to take any and all steps necessary towards motherhood (McEwan, Costello, & Taylor, 1987). Findings underscore the need for psychotherapeutic help for men as well as for women undergoing infertility and the usefulness of that treatment, particularly in the reduction of immediate stress, psycho-somatic symptoms and maladaptive behavioural defensive strategies (Guerra, Llobera, & Barri, 1998). This will be the subject of a future paper (Apfel, 1999; Keylor & Apfel, unpublished manuscript).

Where does this all leave us? We propose an integrative psycho-biological model of infertility. The unfulfilled wish for a child is a stress that undermines the psyche, the body, intimate relationships and the social fabric. Fertility may be further decreased by negative affects and by negative lifestyle behaviours in either partner, or both (sexual avoidance, smoking, nutrition, excessive exercise), and by alteration in psycho-endocrinologic pathways (prolactin, cortisol or testosterone) (Demyttenaere et al., 1989). Interventions at any point in this cycle or at multiple points can then augment fertility, but not guarantee it. The broad brush of psychological distress covers a vast area that must be delineated in more detail. Specifically, we need to learn how hormones respond to developmental derailments, particular relationships, and to certain behavioural triggers. Perhaps, in the future, there will be a new diagnosis of psycho-physiological infertility in a more definable subgroup of infertile women, after specific correlations of psychic states with body chemistry, structure of reproductive function and hormonal shifts have been demonstrated.

Our clinical experience

Years of working with infertile women and men have shown us that all cases are individual and complex. In common are feelings of grief, anxiety, despair, depression, rage, envy of others with babies, futility and magical thinking, all of which follow from being deprived of parenthood while enduring painful and humiliating medical procedures. The loss of parenthood is multifaceted and involves more than the loss of fertility; there is loss of spontaneous sexuality, of the pregnancy experience itself, of children and genetic continuity. There is stigma and isolation. Real-life and family situations are enormously variable and complex, necessitating the most open-ended, non-judgemental psychoanalytic treatment. Some patients come with such medical problems that parenthood would have been out of the question in the pre-ART era. Ideas of parenthood that had been laid to rest earlier are now being revisited.

The analyst's own feelings and beliefs about what would be best in certain circumstances can be at odds with those of the couple, thus requiring great restraint of a wish to offer oracular advice and overly certain formulations rather than to continue non-judgementally to explore the ambiguous emotional terrain. For these very vulnerable patients, psychodynamic formulations intended to interpret unconscious conflict, contain, or provide insight into defences may be experienced as destructive or conflictual. Very often the patients and therapists together are confronted with dilemmas and decisions which are entirely original to both and, in fact, have never been posed before the past few years of history. One of us, for example, was telephoned one night because the woman had to decide by the next morning how many of the three to eight embryos that had been fertilised to implant! Nothing in our analytic training truly prepares us for such a moment. And yet, the analytic relationship and the training in listening may be crucially helpful at such a time in our patient's life.

Another critical dimension in treatment is the analyst's reproductive situation. If the analyst is in a contented place with his/her own parenthood, there is sometimes guilt and yearning for the patient to have a similar experience. If the analyst is also dealing with fertility problems, both pregnancy and pregnancy loss in her clients is fraught with difficulty. A broad terrain of events and dynamics confronts any therapeutic dyad working with the crisis of infertility, whether the infertility is the reason for seeking treatment or a problem that emerges in the course of an analysis. Analytic work under these circumstances cannot be rigidly strict and traditional at all times. Sometimes it becomes necessary to see another family member; sometimes treatment must be suspended temporarily or a period of more supportive psychotherapy is advisable. Useful short-term psychotherapeutic goals of relieving dysphoria and enhancing self-esteem (Rosenthal, 1992), are not necessarily contradictory to an overall psychoanalysis. Whether analysts or therapists, it is of utmost importance for the professional to be knowledgeable and non-judgemental about infertility and the ARTs. As technology continues to change and the experience of infertility is thus altered, psychological treatments become experimental as well.

The following analytic case will demonstrate some of the complexities and difficulties as well as the rewards of working with infertility in an analysis.

Usefulness of psychoanalytic treatment and thinking in a case example

The following case discussion highlights the more dramatic events and dynamics related to infertility as they unfolded in one treatment. However, the analysis was quite ordinary in many respects. The process of change was incremental without any single turning point. There was regression and progression and a good deal of transference with transference interpretation. While the patient brought many dreams to the analysis, there were no pivotal "breakthrough" dreams and no sudden revelations. In most respects, this was a typical analysis with a steady background of daily work that provided the essential stability throughout the turmoil of the infertility experience.

Mrs P was referred for treatment for severe depression following an early pregnancy miscarriage and a stillborn baby at five months' gestation. Mourning these losses, she found taking care of her 3-year-old son difficult. She also felt guilty for harbouring rejecting feelings towards him that were reminiscent of her mother's rejection of her as a small child. Her gynaecologist suggested group therapy for her infertility, but she felt too ashamed of herself as a mother, too defective in her femininity and confused about mothering to tolerate exposure to others. Recently moved from Europe because of her husband's business, she missed the availability of friends and familiar surroundings though she was pleased to have some distance from her family. Soon after her marriage, her father had been killed under ambiguous circumstances. At the time she had wondered whether it was suicide but had soon become pregnant with her first child who was born within a year of her father's death. She grew quite depressed postpartum and sought help from a European analyst who recommended that she continue once she arrived in the US. Her husband was supportive, but largely unavailable due to extensive travelling for his work. He encouraged the idea of analysis particularly because he could not tolerate the long intimate conversations she craved. She soon dedicated herself both to the infertility procedures and to her analysis.

Mrs P was born seven years after her older siblings, two brothers and two sisters, who had a special camaraderie with the parents, since they were all bora (*sic*) during the war and had survived those perilous years together. A heavy price was paid by the family during the liberation of Europe when mother's favourite brother was killed in combat.

Also, a year prior to Mrs P's birth, her mother delivered a full term, stillborn daughter who was intended to replace and memorialise the heroic brother. Eager to conceive again, mother took diethylstilbesterol (DES) to maintain her next pregnancy. Mrs P, named for the dead uncle, was a double replacement for the deep family losses.

As her mother's special child, she was seen as most like her mother in many ways: less intellectually gifted than father and siblings, sickly, more a pet than a person. Mother was depressed for long intervals, leaving Mrs P in the care of a cranky older family nanny. As little was expected of her as a student, she was left to struggle through school as best she could. Later, in her twenties, she sought education and work as a special needs teacher for emotionally and cognitively challenged young adults. This cherished professional identity became the antidote to her self-image as too dumb to achieve anything substantive. An important aspect of the analysis was working through the paradox of living up to the heroic legacy of her dead uncle at the same time that she was considered one of the "dummies" of the family. While her mother had a bond with father, she was unable to foster his connection to young Mrs P. Old hopes for her father's love, attention and approval, rekindled by her marriage, died with his tragic death. She then sought affirmation through her marriage, but her infertility reawakened powerful feelings of specialness, inadequacy and powerlessness.

Mrs P discovered her exposure *in utero* to DES for the first time during her treatment for infertility. In fact, her gynaecologist hypothesised the drug to be a likely cause of her secondary infertility. In her fantasy about the DES, Mrs P began to believe that her mother had taken it to prevent her from being able to reproduce; her infertility became the evidence of her mother's hatred toward her. Although her first child had been conceived and delivered without difficulty, the secondary infertility and the news about DES revived her old feelings of female inadequacy. As a child she had felt chronically unwanted and defectively feminine. As a woman, she felt undesirable and unprepared to be a mother. She blamed her mother for her feelings and even became convinced, for a while, that she was never meant to be born. In a nightmare, from which she awakened terrified, a "doctor" told Mrs P that she had AIDS (acquired immune deficiency syndrome). Trembling she sat up in bed saying to herself "No, it's DES I have, not AIDS!" When the hystero-salpingogram (a routine procedure in evaluating infertility) showed a bicornuate uterus, Mrs P fantasised that there was good side and a bad side. The good side was both large and nourishing enough to grow a baby, but the bad side would starve and desiccate the foetus. This compelling image provided a metaphor for the reactivation of defensive splitting as her previous level of integration was undermined by a threatened sense of self.

During this period, Mrs P focused on the inadequacies she felt "in millions of things", and on the bad aspects of her mother which were linked to her experience of herself as a bad mother. In the analyst's judgement, however, her actual mothering was "good enough". The ongoing stress of hormonal infertility treatments, the effort to co-ordinate fertilisation with her husband's travel schedule and the daily care of a pre-schooler heightened her need to use her analysis as a safe haven. The analyst, who was familiar with the havoc infertility procedures can produce in the analytic rhythm, admired Mrs P's motivation, effort and desire to keep her sessions sacrosanct. The experience of the analyst's undivided attention provided the container she needed to be able to explore and understand her inner world. On occasion, when flexibility was needed, the analyst was willing to accommodate. Mrs P's diligence and rigidity about her analysis at the expense of other responsibilities were also analysed and understood.

For a time, the analyst, offering only non-toxic (non-DES-like) interpretations, was preserved as the good mother. Sometimes Mrs P used the analysis to work on improving her mothering skills, frequently responding with greater empathy and attentive listening to her child after a session. The analyst understood this as an active effort to strengthen her internalised good object mother. Transference shifts for the most part took place gradually, with Mrs P accepting and rejecting interpretations in an active manner. For example, when the analyst suggested that the stillbirth had made her re-experience her powerlessness, she felt misunderstood and clarified that she had actually felt more respected and powerful in managing that delivery than she had during the Caesarean birth of her son, although she felt some shame in acknowledging this since the baby died.

After almost two years of analysis and hormonal intervention, Mrs P conceived. To maximise her chances of carrying to term, complete bed rest was recommended. Mr P drove his wife to a single face-to-face session after this recommendation and asked to be included in the session. The analyst decided to act as the couple's counsellor for that hour, as they talked about the implications of the bed rest for the family and for the analysis. Either a sudden inter-ruption of the analysis, or a change in the frame posed problems for the treatment that neither patient nor analyst wanted. Yet Mrs P was unprepared for even a temporary termination. Her fears of miscarriage, her previous losses and her confinement deepened her dependency on the analyst. To preserve the relationship was seen as a priority by everyone and telephone sessions continued for the duration of the pregnancy.

Telephone sessions from bed were associated with enforced naps in her childhood, when Mrs P had felt banished to her room. She yearned for the company and warmth of her mother (analyst) in the next room, but was required to remain in isolation. She resented the bed rest, the people who recommended it and everyone who supported it (husband and analyst). Memories of her father's return to the house for the midday meal and "naps" with mother revived painful feelings of exclusion from their relationship. She also felt excluded from her relationship with her active 5-year-old, who preferred the company of the live-in nanny. Worse still, she felt a childlike dependency on this same young woman who also took care of the household tasks. With no family nearby, few friends and an absent husband, she relied on the analyst for emotional support. Mrs P developed a different view of her mother's use of DES when she herself needed to take hormones to sustain her pregnancy. She realised that she must have been a deeply wanted child for her mother to have done likewise. She became more forgiving of herself and her mother in light of this new understanding. A more positive identifi-cation with her mother developed as she felt relief, pride and repair to her self-esteem in holding on to the pregnancy. She gave birth to a baby boy close to term.

When Mrs P delivered in the same hospital where her analyst had an office, she called to say she was there and invited the analyst to visit. The analyst reflected on the meaning of the invitation, then decided to visit and to analyse the decision later. The analyst was also invested in this hard-won delivery, had not seen the patient in months, and wanted to see the patient and her baby together. However, this brief visit to mother and baby initiated a wave of negative transference in the form of the patient's perception that the analyst's warmth and admiration of the baby had not matched Mrs P's expectations. As the analyst took on the role of bad mother, Mrs P's resentment about the months of exclusion and separation during the telephone contact found expression. Logistically and realistically, it was difficult to resume analysis, but crucial to do so.

Ambivalence about bringing the baby *vs.* leaving him with a sitter provided the first focus. The desire to share him and receive maternal advice ultimately lost to her need to preserve her private dyadic relationship from his intrusion. Finally, Mr P, concerned that his wife was becoming depressed, insisted that the analysis be re-established when the infant was 6 weeks old. She was furious, and, having achieved her goal in motherhood, felt empowered to express her full rage. The analyst was Jewish, only middle class, an old crone, smelly and had bad taste in furniture. With the analyst's containment of her rageful attacks, Mrs P worked through her disillusionment and loss of her formerly idealised analyst, becoming more accepting of the human limitations of them both. She came to understand that her bad analyst mother in the hospital room represented her collective anger at separation, her retaliatory wishes towards her depriving mother, her fear of being a bad mother herself, and her oedipal anguish.

The analyst's hospital visit was also condensed in the patient's mind with a visit by the paediatrician about the same time. He told Mrs P that her new son had a defect in his penis which would require surgery in the first year to correct a hypospadias. The news of his genital imperfection devastated her and reminded her of her own feelings of defectiveness. She feared that the DES and the hormones she had taken were responsible. Again, analysis served a stabilising function, allowing the fantasies to be examined while she considered the best possible treatment for her baby. Without the analytic space, her guilt and rejection of the infant could well have repeated her infantile psychological experience and her mother's postpartum depression. A significant concern for her was that the circumcision which would be necessary as part of the surgery would make this baby different from his uncircumcised father and brother and be a concrete manifestation of his genital defect. Once again, her concern about her own reproductive defects arose. She felt relieved to have had a son rather than a daughter, feelings that were analysed over subsequent years. More immediately, she was fearful about what to tell her older son, who was asking curious questions about anatomy. The analyst encouraged her to talk to him at his level in a matter-of-fact manner.

Much to her relief and surprise, the child's response was "Oh, my baby brother will have an American penis like the boys at school." Her child's cheerful reframing of the meaning of the circumcision helped her to regain her understanding that subjective reality is not identical to objective reality, while analysis helped avert the transmission of neurotic anxiety to a third generation.

During the surgery, Mrs P was able to comfort the baby. She found herself singing Italian lullabies she had learned from her own mother, revealing yet another dimension of that loved and hated figure. She found she was enjoying being a mother and feeling competent at it. The infertility was now understood as a metaphor for her impaired sense of self and a vehicle for the projection of dissociated bad internal experience. Verbalising her fantasies of inner badness in her analysis permitted her not only to deal with an infertility crisis and recover from a serious depression, but to mourn the losses and conflicts of her childhood and arrive at a new level of reintegration. In the ensuing years, Mrs P consolidated her identity as a woman, returned to graduate school to seek an advanced degree, aborted an unexpected pregnancy because her family felt complete, appropriately terminated her analysis and moved closer to her own mother, geographically and emotionally.

Discussion

The case above illustrates how analysis can integrate traditional analytic goals with the vicissitudes and dynamics of infertility. In our experience, much of the immediate stress from infertility may be alleviated at the site of the problem, in the body and in the IVF clinic. Before, during and after the intervention, patients have strong psychological needs that may be minimally acknowledged by those performing the procedures. Seibel and Levin (1987), interviewing infertile couples at seven phases of the IVF process, found each stage of intervention was fraught with anxiety. Mitigating anxiety at the IVF clinic is most effective through a combination of education, in-house counselling and collaboration with outside therapists during the course of treatment and throughout any subsequent pregnancy (Seibel, 1997).

There are wide variations in sensitivity and empathy among doctors and nurses conducting the procedures at these highly emotional moments for patients. Even minor interventions of a psychological nature may make a significant difference. For example, Sarrel and Decherney (1985) showed that a single psychiatric interview of an infertile couple in the presence of the fertility specialist could identify areas of marital conflict, fears of procedures and pregnancy, and conflictual internal object relations. Eighteen months after this brief intervention, six of the ten women in the couples interviewed had conceived compared to one in a control group. Although this is a very small sample, it is an interesting finding with regard to the potential benefits of reducing stress at the ART site. Explaining it is another matter. Did the couple feel supported and understood or accompanied in a way that was helpful? Did the doctor contribute to the staff's understanding of the particular couple? Does a clinic that has such a procedure feel safer? Did the interview make the couple more cooperative or reduce marital discord?

The staff of most IVF programmes tend to be optimistic and heavily invested in maximising positive outcomes, that is, pregnancies. While nurses are often aware of patients' emotional and physical distress, sometimes even more that the patients themselves, doctors consistently underestimate both (Kopitzke et al., 1991). Patients in IVF programmes frequently complain about the lack of support services, education and self-help groups that could assist them in coping with the cycles of emotions that parallel the course of treatment. Perceived coldness or insensitivity in the staff amplifies already intense anxiety, humiliation, rage and despair. Daniluk (1997) urges physicians to have respect for the emotional time required to process feelings about failed cycles before considering whether or not to proceed with the next step. Even brief (six-month) cognitive-behavioural therapy can make a difference by helping couples to time intercourse more reliably (Tuschen-Caffier et al., 1999).

Support groups, such as those sponsored by RESOLVE, have been useful in combating isolation as well as offering mutual support and information sharing. As with other self-help organisations, these groups help normalise, validate and empower their members. McQueeney, Stanton, and Sigmon (1997) have shown that groups which focus on sharing affects about infertility significantly enhanced the sense of well-being in infertile women, an effect that continued to increase after the group had ended, whereas problem-solving groups aimed at sharing information and promoting self-assertion did not.

Nor did they mobilise feelings of greater control. Helping couples and women regain aspects of their lives that have been abandoned during the long struggle with infertility is an important goal in all therapeutic domains. Domar et al. (1993) discovered that mind/body group therapy aimed at recovering one's life redirects attention away from disability (infertility) and back on to work, pleasure and other relationships in one's life. The self is rediscovered in its multiple dimensions; other goals take centre stage, while the dream of parenthood moves temporarily to the background. Relaxation exercises and meditation, which may be beneficial to the immune system, can also be powerfully healing in concert with group discussion and cohesion. A disadvantage to these groups is the extrusion of women who do become pregnant and whose pregnancy causes pain to the other members. Loss of membership in the group due to longed-for pregnancy can be a painful price for success in conceiving. While some women wish to "forget" their infertility experience once they are pregnant, others need continuing support since the normal anxieties of pregnancy are greatly amplified in formerly infertile women. Nor is the pain of infertility so quickly forgotten by many. A patient once said, following the birth of her second ART baby, "I will always be an infertile woman." Groups based in a religious context have helped those with roots in those communities. Even women not affiliated religiously may experience infertility as God's curse and might need some religious authority to absolve them when peers and therapists cannot.

Helplessness engendered in both patient and analyst by infertility makes us all reach for explanations. The difficulty of tolerating the condition of not knowing makes us susceptible too often to the temptation to say that psychological treatment has "worked through" something when the outcome is favourable and pregnancy is achieved. Conversely, we tend to say that something is insufficiently analysed when desired pregnancy does not occur. It is the "something" that demands much more careful research into the bi-directional influence of the internal psychological world and the biochemistry of the body. *Post hoc ergo propter hoc* (after which, therefore because of) reasoning is irresistible to us all, but very often false. When applied to infertility, psychoanalysis has made many such claims that require revision. The theory of psychogenic infertility is, at best, a questionable truth, certainly not universal, and is definitely unhelpful as a construct in treating people with infertility.

When Benedek et al. (1953) pioneered in this area, they were asking a centrally important question about how the human psyche impinges in human reproduction, a question that could not then, and cannot now fully be answered, although progress in that direction is being made. As Benedek noted, cows become pregnant following artificial insemination nearly 100% of the time, whereas the rates for women are considerably lower. Presumably cows are far simpler creatures with respect to their psychology, while the complex hearts and souls of women affect their physiology. How this happens, how it is mediated, and where individual psychological variability affects the outcome remains a puzzle. Mind-body research is an increasingly sophisticated area of inquiry towards which psychoanalytic data can importantly contribute. As psychoanalysts, if we can let go of our certainty about the causes of infertility, and thoughtfully consider how our rich and compelling phenomenological data can be translated better into questions for bidirectional research, we could make more of a contribution to this interdisciplinary inquiry.

Analysis (or psychoanalytic psychotherapy) is at its best, and can be most helpful for infertile people, as a reflective craft. The analytic space and relational containment can provide a welcome refuge and antidote to the seeming omnipotence of the IVF clinic, and a safe autonomous place for the ongoing discovery and repair of the self. This space offers the opportunity to heal from the fragmentation and numbing experiences of infertility interventions, to recover, for example, the feeling that one's body is part of the self and not a thing to be manipulated or even an adversary to be hated. While couples may not have enough fertile time to engage in a long treatment prior to a decision about parenthood or assistance with reproduction, there is still more time than is often believed to pace interventions, and chart a course in a thoughtful manner with respect for emotional time. In some countries, where infertility programmes are state-supported rather than profit-making, there is a mandated wait of one or two years which provides a window of time for useful therapeutic work. The UK now requires some psychological intervention for all couples undergoing infertility treatments. The patient or couple who comes to an analyst's office seeking help for the first time because of the infertility, may find there a perspective and larger frame. At a time when medical interventions are undermining a sense of integration, analytic space and time permit an opportunity to consider the whole self.

Realistically, however, infertility treatments can become totally involving of body, mind and spirit. For those individuals, unfortunately, infertility collapses potential, leaving them unavailable for any in-depth analysis. Analytic treatment then can still help keep animated other aspects of life, and of the self, and can encourage and promote self-righting capacities. Providing a venue for the consideration of the risks as well as the potential benefits of the ARTs is an increasingly important aspect of the therapeutic role as well.

The ARTs necessitate that analysts comprehend novel and complicated family structures and family creation experiences. This is emotionally, ethically and intellectually challenging for the analytic dyad. In many ways, these new realities are materialising faster than the psyche can process them. The luxury of solely concentrating on intrapsychic or even co-constructed transferential reality must be foregone at times for a full consideration of questions that were unimaginable a short while ago. The availability of egg donation, surrogacy, family participation in sperm and egg donation, choices about what to do with extra frozen embryos after conception, or post-divorce, require the analyst to be cognisant of all the realities of the patient's social-emotional environment as well as the details of the procedures being undergone.

Attributing psychic causation or assigning blame for the infertility is not only potentially harmful, but, more importantly, may even be irrelevant.

More to the heart of the matter is the question of how the analyst himself or herself can remain steady in order to help overwhelmed patients negotiate a deeply emotional pioneering voyage. At the same time, decisions taken and realised are redolent with symbolic meaning which, through *Nachträglichkeit* reorders and reworks internal experience towards a new integration. The exploration of fantasies and feelings is more mutative than the search for any purported intrapsychic root causes of infertility. Support through the trauma and anxiety of the procedures, maintaining perspective and, sometimes, helping a couple decide when to stop and why, are aspects of our real connection with our patients which are vitally needed.

How can we honestly accept the fact that many things like infertility can neither be explained nor fixed by us? We should not hold out a false promise that we can "cure" infertility any more than we can cure cancer. Nor do we require such omnipotence when the help we can offer is so profoundly needed and useful. It is time to retire the term "psychogenic infertility" as simplistic and anachronistic. As analysts and therapists we must stay open-minded and receptive to learning from those who endure ever-changing treatments for this old and complex problem, welcome greater research on mind/body aspects of infertility and collaborate openly with our colleagues in other disciplines whose medical technologies assist with reproduction. Above all, let us continue to provide the deep human understanding on multiple levels of reality that we have always offered to our patients. We need to work together to find resolutions, case by case, to the myriad and growing number of ethical, medical and psychological dilemmas that are so exemplified by the marriage of infertility and technology, with which we are continually confronted.

Note

1. In addition to the authors, workshop members include: Adrienne Asch, PhD, Eva Appelman, PhD, Darlene Bojrab, MSW, Mara Brill, MD, Sandra Steward Horne, MSW, Deborah Issokson, PsyD, and Susan Levin, MSW.

2. ... to Hannah he would give one choice portion, for he loved Hannah, and the Lord had shut up her womb. And so he would do year by year, as often as she went up to the house of the Lord, so she would anger her, and she wept and would not eat ... Hannah, she was speaking in her heart, only her lips were moving and her voice was not heard, and Eli thought her to be a drunken woman. And Eli said to her: "Until when will you be drunk? Throw off your wine from upon yourself." And Hannah answered and said: "No, my lord, I am a woman of sorrowful spirit, and neither new wine nor old wine have I drunk, and I poured out my soul before the Lord". (Samuel 1, 1: 6–15; Hirschler translation, 1990).

References

Abbey, A., Andrews, F. M., & Halman, L. J. (1995). The role of perceived control and attribution of meaning in members of infertile couples' well-being. *Journal of Social and Clinical Psychology, 68*: 455–469.

Allison, G. H. (1997). Motherhood, motherliness, and psychogenic infertility. *Psychoanalytic Quarterly, 66*: 6–17.

Apfel, R. J. (1999). Shooting blanks: male infertility. Presented at American Psychoanalytic meetings, "Workshop on Fatherhood", New York.

Barnea, E. R., & Tal, J. (1991). Stress related reproductive failure. *Journal of In Vitro Fertilization & Embryo Transfer, 8*: 15–23.

Beaurepaire, J., Jones, M., Thiering, P., Saunders, D., & Tennant, C. (1994). Psychosocial adjustment to infertility and its treatment: male and female responses at different stages of IVF/ET treatment. *Journal of Psychosomatic Research, 35*: 231–243.

Benazon, N., Wright, J., & Sabourin, S. (1992). Stress, sexual satisfaction and marital adjustment in infertile couples. *Journal of Sex & Marital Therapy, 18*: 273–284.

Benedek, T. (1952). Infertility as a psychosomatic defense. *Fertility & Sterility, 3*: 527–541.

Benedek, T., & Rubenstein, B. B. (1942). *The Sexual Cycle in Women: the Relation Between Ovarian Function and Psychodynamic Processes.* Washington, DC: National Research Council.

Benedek, T., Ham, G. C., Robbins, F. P., & Rubenstein, B. B. (1953). Some emotional factors in infertility. *Psychosomatic Medicine, 15*: 485–498.

Berg, B. J., & Wilson, J. F. (1990). Psychiatric morbidity in the infertility: a reconceptualization. *Fertility & Sterility, 53*: 654–661.

Bernstein, J. (1993). Psychological issues in infertility: an historical overview. In: M. M. Seibel, A. A. Kiessling, J. Bernstein, & S. R. Levin (Eds.), *Technology and Infertility*–287). New York: Springer-Verlag.

Bolter, D. T. (1997). Defenses and adaptation to infertility. Doctoral dissertation, Boston University.

Christie, G. L. (1994). The psychogenic factor in infertility. *Australian and New Zealand Journal of Psychiatry, 28*: 378–390.

Christie, G. L. (1997). The management of grief in work with infertile couples. *Journal of Assisted Reproduction and Genetics, 14*: 189–191.

Christie, G. L. (1998). Some socio-cultural and psychological aspects of infertility. *Human Reproduction, 13*: 232–241.

Connolly, K. J., Edelmann, R. J., & Cooke, I. D. (1987). Distress and mental problems associated with infertility. *Journal of Reproductive and Infant Psychology, 5*: 49–57.

Daniluk, J. (1997). Helping patients cope with infertility. *Clinical Gynecology and Obstetrics, 40*: 661–672.

Demyttenaere, K., Nijs, P., Everskeibooms, G., & Konickx, P. R. (1989). The effect of a specific emotional stressor on prolactin, cortisol, and testosterone concentrations in women varies with their trait anxiety. *Fertility & Sterility, 52*: 942–948.

Demyttenaere, K., Nijs, P., Everskeibooms, G., & Konickx, P. R. (1991). Coping, ineffectiveness of coping and the psychoendocrinological stress responses during in vitro fertilization. *Journal of Psychosomatic Research, 35*: 231–243.

Denber, H. C. (1978). Psychiatric aspects of infertility. *Journal of Reproductive Medicine, 20*: 23–29.

Deutsch, H. (1945). *Psychology of Women, Vol. II, Motherhood*. New York: Grune & Stratton.

Domar, A. D., Broome, A., Zuttermeister, P. C., Seibel, M., & Friedman, R. (1992). The prevalence and predictability of depression in infertile women. *Fertility & Sterility, 58*: 1158–1163.

Domar, A. D., Broome, A., Zuttermeister, P. C., Seibel, M., & Benson, H. (1993). Psychological improvement in infertile women after behavioral treatment: a replication. *Journal of Psychosomatic Obstetrics & Gynecology, 14*: 445–452.

Doria-Medina, R. (1999). Panel reports on the new reproductive techniques. *International Journal of Psychoanalysis, 80*: 163.

Downey, J., Yingling, S., Mckinney, M., Husami, N., Jewelewicz, R., & Maidam, J. (1989). Mood disorders, psychiatric symptoms and distress in women presenting for infertility evaluation. *Fertility & Sterility, 52*: 425–432.

Edelman, R. J., & Connolly, K. J. (1986). Psychological aspects of infertility. *British Journal of Medical Psychology, 59*: 209–219.

Eisner, B. G. (1963). Some psychological differences between fertile and infertile women. *Journal of Clinical Psychology, 19*: 391–395.

Facchinetti, F., Demyttenaere, K., Fioroni, L., Neri, I., & Genazzani, A. R. (1992). Psychosomatic disorders related to gynecology. *Psychotherapy & Psychosomatics, 58*: 137–154.

Fisher, S. (1973). *The Female Orgasm: Psychology, Physiology, Fantasy*. New York: Basic Books.

Fleming, A. T. (1988). Babies over 40. *Lears*(Sept.–Oct.): 104–115.

Ford, E. S. C., Forman, I., Wilson, J. R., Char, W., Mixon, W. T., & Scholz, C. (1953). A psychodynamic approach to the study of infertility. *Fertility & Sterility, 4*: 456–465.

Garner, C., Kelly, M., & Arnold, E. (1984). Psychological profile of IVF patients. *Fertility & Sterility, 41*: 575.

Greil, A. L. (1997). Infertility and psychological distress: a critical review of the literature. *Social Science & Medicine, 45*: 1679–1704.

Guerra, D., Llobera, A., & Barri, P. N. (1998). Psychiatric morbidity in couples attending a fertility service. *Human Reproduction, 13*: 1733–1736.

Hynes, G. J., Callan, V. J., Terry, D. J., & Galloi, C. (1992). The psychological well-being of infertile women after a failed IVF attempt: the effects of coping. *British Journal of Medical Psychology, 65*: 269–277.

Jacobson, E. (1946). A case of sterility. *Psychoanalytic Quarterly, 15*: 330–350.

Kelly, K. (1942). Sterility in the female with special reference to psychic factors. *Psychosomatic Medicine, 4*: 211–222.

Kemeter, P. (1988). Effects of emotional stress on fertilization and implantation in in-vitro fertilization. *Human Reproduction, 3*: 341–352.

Kemeter, P., & Fiegel, J. (1998). Adjusting to life when assisted conception fails. *Human Reproduction, 13*: 1099–1105.

Keylor, R. G., & Apfel, R. J. The untold story of male infertility: a review of the psychoanalytic and research literature. Unpublished paper.

Kipper, D. A., & Zadik, H. (1996). Functional infertility and femininity: a comparison of infertile women and their mothers. *Journal of Clinical Psychology, 52*: 375–382.

Klock, S. C., Chang, G., Hilley, A., & Hill, J. (1997). Psychological distress among women with recurrent spontaneous abortion. *Psychosomatics, 38*: 503–507.

Knight, R. P. (1943). Functional disturbances in the sexual life of women: frigidity and related disorders. *Bulletin of the Menninger Clinic, 7*: 25–35.

Kopitzke, E. J., Berg, B. J., Wilson, J. F., & Owens, D. (1991). Physical and emotional stress associated with components of the infertility investigation: perspectives of professionals and patients. *Fertility & Sterility, 55*: 1137–1143.

Lalos, A., Lalos, O., Jacobsson, L., & Von Schoultz, B. (1985). The psychosocial impact of infertility two years after completed surgical treatment. *Acta Obstetricia et Gynecologica Scandinavica, 64*: 599–604.

Leon, I. G. (1996). Reproductive loss: barriers to psychoanalytic treatment. *Journal of the American Academy of Psychoanalysis and Dynamic Psychiatry, 24*: 341–352.

Levin, S. (1993). Psychological evaluation of the infertile couple. In: M. M. Scibel, A. Kiessling, J. Bernstein, & S. Levin (Eds.), *Technology and Infertility* (pp. 289–296). New York: Springer-Verlag.

Marsh, E. M., & Vollmer, A. M. (1951). Possible psychogenic aspects of infertility. *Fertility & Sterility, 2*: 70–79.

McCartney, C. F., & Wada, C. Y. (1990). Gender differences in counseling needs during infertility treatment. In: N. Stotland (Ed.), *Psychiatric Aspects of Reproductive Technology*. Washington, DC: American Psychiatric Press.

McEwan, K. L., Costello, C. G., & Taylor, P. J. (1987). Adjustment to infertility. *Journal of Abnormal Psychology, 96*: 108–116.

McMahon, C. A. (1999). Does assisted reproduction make an impact on the identity and self-esteem of infertile women during the transition to parenthood? *Journal of Assisted Reproduction and Genetics, 16*: 59–62.

McQueeney, D. A., Stanton, A. L. & Sigmon, S. (1997). Efficacy of emotion-focussed group therapies for women with infertility problems. *Journal of Behavioral Medicine, 20*: 313–331.

Morrow, K., Thoreson, R. W., & Penney, L. L. (1995). Predictors of Psychological distress among infertility clinic patients. *Journal of Consulting & Clinical Psychology, 63*: 163–167.

Noy, P., Wollstein, S., & Kaplan-Denour, A. (1966). Clinical observation in the psychogenesis of impotence. *British Journal of Medical Psychology, 39*: 43.

Noyes, R. W., & Chapnick, A. B. (1964). Literature on psychology and infertility: a critical review. *Fertility & Sterility, 15*: 543–558.

Orr, D. W. (1941). Pregnancy following the decision to adopt. *Psychosomatic Medicine, 3*: 4441–4446.

Paulson, J. D., Haarmann, B. S., Salerno, R. L., & Asmar, P. (1988). An investigation of the relationship between emotional maladjustment and infertility. *Fertility & Sterility, 49*: 258–262.

Pines, D. (1990). Emotional aspects of infertility and its remedies. *International Journal of Psychoanalysis, 71*: 561–568.

Reichlin, S., Abplanap, J., Labrum, A. H., Schwartz, N., Sommer, B., & Taymor, M. (1979). The role of stress in female reproductive dysfunction: a panel. *Journal of Human Stress, 5*: 38–45.

Robinson, G. E., & Stewart, D. E. (1996). The psychological impact of infertility and new reproductive technologies. *Harvard Review of Psychiatry, 4*: 168–172.

Rosenthal, M. B. (1992). Infertility: psychotherapeutic issues. *New Directions Mental Health Sciences, 55*: 61–71.

Rothman, D., & Kaplan, A. H. (1972). Psychosomatic infertility in the male and female. In: J. G. Howells (Ed.), *Modern Perspectives in Psycho-Obstetrics* (pp. 31–52). New York: Brunner/Mazel.

Sarrel, P. M., & Decherney, A. H. (1985). Psychotherapeutic intervention for treatment of couples with secondary infertility. *Fertility & Sterility, 4*: 897–900.

Seibel, M. M. (1997). Infertility: the impact of stress, the benefit of counseling. *Journal of Assisted Reproduction and Genetics, 14*: 181–183.

Seibel, M. M., & Levin, S. (1987). A new era in reproductive technologies: the emotional stages of in vitro fertilization. *Fertility & Embryo Transfer, 4*: 135–140.

Seward, G. H., Wagner, P. S., Heinrich, J. F., Bloch, S. K., & Myerhoff, H. L. (1965). The question of psychophysiologic infertility: some negative answers. *Psychosomatic Medicine, 27*: 533–545.

Slade, P., Raval, H., Buck, P., & Lieberman, B. (1992). A 3-year follow-up of emotional, marital, and sexual functioning in couples who were infertile. *Journal of Reproductive and Infant Psychology, 10*: 233–243.

Sturgis, S. S., Taymore, M. L., & Morris, T. (1957). Routine psychiatric interviews in a sterility investigation. *Fertility & Sterility, 8*: 521–526.

Thiering, P., Beaurepaire, J., Jones, M., Saunders, D., & Tennant, C. (1993). Mood state as a predictor of treatment outcome after in vitro fertilization/embryo transfer technology (IVT/ET). *Journal of Psychosomatic Research, 27*: 481–491.

Tuschen-Caffier, B., Florin, I., Krause, W., & Pook, M. (1999). Cognitive-behavioral therapy for idiopathic infertile couples. *Psychotherapy & Psychosomatics, 68*: 15–21.

Tyler, E. T., Bonapart, J. & Grant, J. (1960). Occurrence of pregnancy following adoption. *Fertility & Sterility, 11*: 581–589.

Vartiainen, H., Saarikoski, S., Halonen, P., & Rimon, R. (1994). Psycho-social factors, female fertility and pregnancy: a prospective study—Part I: fertility. *Journal of Psychosomatic Obstetrics & Gynecology, 15*: 67–75.

Visser, A. P., Haan, G., Zalmstra, H., & Wouters, I. (1994). Psychosocial aspects of in vitro fertilization. *Journal of Psychosomatic Obstetrics & Gynecology, 15*: 35–43.

Wasser, S. K., Sewall, G., & Soules, M. R. (1993). Psychosocial stress as a cause of infertility. *Fertility & Sterility, 59*: 685–689.

Weir, W. C., & Weir, M. D. (1966). Adoption and subsequent conceptions. *Fertility & Sterility, 17*: 283–228.

White, R. S. (1998). Public forum addresses assisted reproduction. *American Psychologist, 32*: 29.

CHAPTER THREE

Scrambled eggs: psychological meanings of new reproductive choices for lesbians*

Susan C. Vaughan

Introduction

L et me begin by explaining the origins of the title of my chapter. Back in 1997, when my partner and I were proposing to our own Ob-gyn, an infertility specialist, our plan for me to become pregnant using her egg and anonymous donor sperm, this was an untested and novel idea. After thinking about it for a moment, she smiled, gave a bemused shrug, and said: "It takes three things to make a baby. An egg, sperm, and a womb. Any combination, you tell me." As we were going through IVF (*in vitro* fertilisation), we were just about the only cheerful and upbeat patients in the office for our near daily visits and became friendly with the staff, who found us a breath of fresh air in a practice filled with heterosexuals whose conventional reproductive attempts had failed and who were demoralised about their ability to conceive. In contrast, we were just at the beginning of an exciting venture. The staff was open-minded but unused to lesbian couples in their infertility practice at that point, and they sometimes had trouble keeping our names straight. One day one of them dubbed

*First published in 2007 in *Journal of Infant, Child and Adolescent Psychotherapy*, 6: 141–155. Reproduced with the permission of Taylor and Francis Press.

us "the scrambled egg ladies," and the name stuck. Perhaps, I thought, the idea of my partner and I cooking together was not such a bad image for making a baby.

We have only to look around us on the streets of New York to confirm that we are indeed in the midst of an unprecedented "gayby boom." While accurate statistics are hard to come by, the 2000 census estimated that 25% of same gender unmarried partners were raising children, including 34% of female couples and 22% of male couples. Extrapolating from these numbers, Tasker (2005) estimated that 2 to 14 million children in the United States today are living with same-sex parents. Despite the recent trend of gay men and lesbians having their own biological children or adopting children in the context of a committed relationship, the majority of children being raised by a gay or lesbian parent or parents are still in step-families or blended families in which their gay or lesbian parent had their biological children in a former heterosexual relationship, then came out and perhaps even created a new family with another partner later on. Thus, from the beginning we're dealing with two complex and different groups of kids raised by gay parents. In some cases children have been through the divorce of heterosexual parents with its many psychological considerations about custody and living arrangements as well as the psychologically complex situation of the coming out of a parent. Only recently have there been an increasing number of kids born or adopted into already stable same-sex couples or into various familial configurations or co-parenting arrangements that have been decided up front. Advances in reproductive technology have intersected with the growing destigmatisation of homosexuality in the United States to produce choices about how to have children unimaginable only a few years ago. Given the state of things today, it may surprise you to know that before 1985, many physicians were reluctant to inseminate single women of any sexual orientation, believing that children should be raised in households of heterosexual couples. Single women now account for about 30% of all women who use donor sperm. In addition to increased access to donor sperm, advances in artificial insemination and egg donation as well as surrogacy have also opened new doors to lesbian couples.

Today, I hope to do three things to highlight the psychological meanings of the reproductive choices lesbians make. First, I will highlight some of the concerns that lesbians may bring to parenting and that may inform the choices that they make and the issues they struggle with in making those decisions. Second, I will take one issue—that of the choice of a known *vs.* an unknown sperm donor—and demonstrate the myriad psychological considerations from multiple patients that go into this one of many decisions along the often complex lesbian path to parenthood. Third, I will present case material from three different individuals and couples with whom I have worked in psychoanalysis and psychotherapy as they sorted out the psychological implications of their reproductive choices and the way these mirrored important psychodynamics within themselves and with their partners.

Let's begin by taking a look at the concerns that some lesbians may bring to parenting. Even for lesbians who have been out for many years, are in happy and stable relationships and have reached the point of planning a family, lingering issues of internaliased homophobia are likely to surface in the form of concerns about parenting. Parenting is really the final frontier in gay and lesbian development in the sense that it pushes one to be as out and as comfortable as possible with one's identity. If you are not, your children will be only too happy to out you, usually in a crowded elevator in a conservative midwestern city.

The concerns I'm about to outline arise from the internalisation of and also reflect concerns about lesbian parents in society at large. I will review them briefly now because I believe they are important to have in mind as well as potentially to watch for in your own counter-transference reactions to lesbians planning families. While on first blush we may wish to believe that these concerns are the purview of politically and socially conservative, religious elements in American society, I believe that they cannot be dismissed so easily as out there and not in us all to some extent.

A first, fundamental concern lesbians may have is about whether or not they will be unfit as a parent simply by virtue of their sexual orientation. As one patient put it "I can't even believe I'm having this conversation (about having children) with you. For one thing, for so long, I always told myself I'd never be a mother because it simply wouldn't be fair to the kids. They'd be teased and ostracised and end up hating me and thinking I was weird and abnormal. Now I can see that that's me talking about myself." The same patient continued:

> Also, part of my burgeoning lesbian identity growing up and part of the way I tried to distinguish myself from my mother and sister was

that I'd be a career woman and I'd never get married and have children. I really had convinced myself I didn't want them and even that
I hated them until I was around 30. It's like the first way I was trying
to tell people I was different, that I was gay, before I even knew what
that was myself. Don't expect me to be a normal woman who gets
married and has kids. And that was secretly combined with the belief
that I couldn't or shouldn't because it wouldn't be fair.

Second, as is prevalent in society, lesbians themselves may conflate
of gender and sexuality. They may see themselves as more masculine
by virtue of their lesbian orientation itself or based upon gender atyp-
icality in childhood and this perceived masculinity may lead in turn
to two concerns about parenting. First, they may fear they will not be
adequately maternal since mothering is taken to be a stereotypically
female trait. Second, they may fear that their daughters will not be
feminine enough due to lack of an adequately (i.e., stereotypically)
female role model. As one patient noted with anxiety, "All that time
my sister spent playing with dolls I spent climbing fences. I never
even held a baby or babysat until my sister had children. Maybe I
haven't been practicing all this time. Maybe I won't know what to do."
Sometimes this concern can be assuaged by the presence of another
female in the couple who may have a different perceived blend of
masculine and feminine traits. For example, one lesbian in psychotherapy had been discussing her fears that she would be unable to
parent a girl who "Liked frilly dresses and all the things I abhorred as
a child." She returned home one day after a session in which we had
been discussing her concerns of not being able to understand what she
termed a "girlie girl" and found that her partner had bought a gift for
a friend's child. The gift was a one-month supply of stick-on earrings,
which were sparkly and undeniably "girlie." "I guess we have our
bases covered after all," my patient concluded with evident relief,
though this relief later turned into a concern that if she had a daughter her partner and her daughter would bond around "girlie" activities while she would once again feel "the odd man out," recapitulating
the childhood traumas she had experienced as a tomboy who felt she
was not quite right as a woman. This same patient later revealed a
fantasy that she had been sex-reassigned at birth and was secretly
male and that this would be discovered around the couple's attempts
to have children when she would be found to not be female or able to
conceive.

Related to the concern that one will not be able to make a child of one's own gender "right" is the notion that a child of either gender will suffer due to the lack of a paternal and a maternal influence. A patient I treated in psychotherapy was concerned about whether, if she and her partner had a daughter, that daughter would be at a disadvantage for not having had a relationship with a father. "I think little girls are supposed to get a sense of their attractiveness and femininity from their fathers, so I wonder where our daughter will get that sense. And about family romance, can she use one of us as her prince?" Yet this patient was equally concerned whether, if she and her partner had a boy, they would be able to impart an adequate sense of masculinity to him. She said, "I was pretty good as a little league player myself and played just after girls were first allowed in, but can a boy get just as much masculinity from his gay mother as from a father?" "After all," she quipped, "if his teammates tell him he throws like a girl they'll be right!" "I just wonder how being a gay couple shakes up all the usual issues of gender, sexuality and attraction within a family," said one astute lesbian patient. "I think it's a real question, but I also wonder if it's a continuation of feeling bad about myself for being gay that makes me worry about it so much." As we worked through lingering aspects of her homophobia, my patient came to feel that shaking things up and having them be problematic were two different things.

I do not mean to imply that all lesbians have these beliefs and I think it is worth highlighting that when internalised homophobia and issues about gender and sexuality are worked through, lesbians can relish and embrace the girlie girl they never were or the identifications with their sons around sports or the ability to impart traits traditionally thought of as masculine or feminine to their opposite gendered children so as to break down cultural stereotypes about gender. They can respond to triangulation and family romance and can stand in for either gender depending on the needs of the child and can do so with a sense of fun and excitement. But often getting to this point requires good clinical work around the issues I have outlined.

Let me move on to my second way of exploring psychological meanings of reproductive choices by examining patients' variable to the choice of a known *vs.* an unknown sperm donor. This is only one of many choices to be made along the path to parenthood, and probably has as many variations on a theme as there are individual patients, so what I present here is by no means intended to be exhaustive or to imply any fixed set of issues that comes up in all lesbian patients.

For many couples, the choice about donor sperm is relatively uncomplicated and they elect to use anonymous donor sperm. Statistically this is the most common choice in two recent studies and many women find it the safest and least psychologically complicated choice, at least initially. The potential legal threats and psychological issues that result from having a known biological father are permanently laid to rest.

For some lesbians, the choice of the donor can represent the chance to choose the perfect man who should have been, the one Mum would have wanted you to bring home to meet her. Because donor profiles allow prospective recipients to so specifically choose physical attributes and intellectual interests and achievements, as one patient put it "I didn't know if I was building the perfect man or practicing modern eugenics. You want your kid to have every advantage, but you start to design the perfect baby, whatever that is in your eyes. But really, here we are this rather radical lesbian couple and who are we picking as the donor? Mr. Pre-Med Prom King." There may be tensions about choosing this "perfect" man over choosing traits in a donor that match those of the partner whose egg is not being used in an attempt to make the baby look like both members of the couple. What is clear is that during the decision-making process, the donor is usually very much alive, a felt presence within the couple. One couple even celebrated their final choice of a donor with a third glass of champagne for the donor himself. "An Elijah's cup" as they put it.

Choosing an unknown donor can also trigger a mourning reaction within couples about their de facto infertility and inability to have children together. The process of picking a random stranger can highlight the loss of the known and loved partner as a mate for making a biological child. One patient said,

> Of course I always knew we couldn't have children together, but the whole process of choosing a(n) (anonymous) donor made me so sad. I think I dealt with it by joking a lot about what someone's favourite animal was and choosing men that liked the colour purple or liked cats, especially big, wild ones like cheetahs or mountain lions. I know it sounds absurd on my part, but that's how I tried to decide whether someone is a nice person or not. If I thought about it more seriously,

I'd cry, because that's not such a good reason to choose a man to have a baby with. We settled on a man whose audiotape made him sound likeable, sane, and thoughtful.

Yet despite the reasonableness of this approach to making a choice, this patient ultimately discovered in psychotherapy that the main problem was that this unknown donor was not the person with whom she would like to have a child and that she was simultaneously choosing a donor and mourning the loss of her partner as a biological mate.

Another issue that arises around an unknown donor is the realisation that the child born of his sperm will one day look at his profiles and listen to his audiotape. Therefore, patients may muse about what kind of mental representation these materials might allow a child to construct about this potentially important figure to whom the child owes half his or her genetic makeup. In turn, lesbians may feel they are making an indirect statement to the child about what they value in a man and what type of man they might like enough with whom to have a child. For the children of lesbian parents, the vast majority of whom will be straight, a kind of proto-heterosexual relationship of his or her lesbian mother can be constructed from information about this unknown donor. The area is ripe for fantasy on the part of both parent and child.

In contemplating a known donor, whether a male friend or relative and whether gay or straight, different but no less complex issues arise. Some of these are centred around the issue of the relationship between donor status and parenting status. How involved is the known donor and what are his rights as a parent, if any? As a patient put it,

If our friend John is less involved, then there's less advantage to having him *vs.* having an anonymous donor. Then we're running all sorts of risks for nothing. And if he's really involved, then how will we negotiate what his rights are and what ours as a couple are. It'd be nice to allow our child to know his father, but it's hard to predict what might go wrong; on the one hand I have fantasies in which he's known but totally uninvolved and our child feels abandoned by him and at other points I imagine that he's too involved and actually comes between me and Laura. I don't want to be part of a threesome. We're a couple. And I'm quite concerned about whether I'll seem less of a parent if both biological parents are involved. It's hard enough being a lesbian couple, with everyone quizzing us about who the real mother is all the time. I even think it would lessen the legitimacy of the relationship I've built with Laura in my family's eyes to suddenly have John on the scene.

She continued,

I know it seems silly, given that they can test for it, but I do still worry about HIV [human immunodeficiency virus]. John is negative and has safe sex, but he is a gay man and Laura and I otherwise have no HIV risk at all.

This concern and her seemingly disproportionate anxiety about it ultimately seemed to represent a sense that John would be contaminating, intruding upon and even infecting her relationship with her partner. This patient also expressed concern about choosing a gay known donor. "There's the feeling I have about my kid having a gay father; sounds dumb since I'm lesbian myself, but somehow I feel that having a gay father undermines the reasons for involving a man we know." I think this devaluation of John as a gay man is another example of the lingering kind of internalised homophobia—the conflation of masculinity and homosexuality, as if John is lacking as a man by virtue of being gay—that can come into play as lesbians make decisions about having children. With further exploration with this patient in psychotherapy, it became clear that another meaning of her dislike of John as a gay man was that she really wanted her child to have a straight parent and to form a union with a man that was like the one she had been expected to form growing up. This giving up on the myth of the straight couple as the ideal parents allowed this patient and her partner to opt for an anonymous donor as they began to recognise that some of their reasons for wanting an involved known donor and father had to do with lingering resistances to the idea of themselves as a couple being adequate as parents.

I hope these sketches of some of the psychological issues that arise around one choice in the process of becoming a parent highlight the psychological complexity of the process. Let me now turn to my clinical vignettes, which demonstrate how deciding whether and how to have a child can be understood in terms of the psychodynamics of the individual patient as well as her dynamics with her partner.

Ann was 34 when she presented for psychotherapy for work related concerns. An investment banker, she was tired of the hours and work and having trouble getting herself motivated to continue. As we worked in psychotherapy it became clear that Ann was using her heavy work schedule to avoid her own questions about her sexual orientation. She'd had three brief relationships with women and had slept with men in high school and college, but her fantasy life when she masturbated revolved around images of women. She was extremely concerned about what her conservative parents would do if she came out, and they all seemed happy to avoid the discussion, never asking about boyfriends or encouraging her to marry but never asking about whether she might be lesbian either. Don't ask, don't tell seemed to prevail in the family. Meanwhile, Ann was very involved with her older sister's children and envied the "normality" of her sister's marriage and family. As she progressed in therapy and began to be more comfortable with herself, Ann met Beth, a 39-year-old woman who ran her own successful small business. The two soon fell in love and moved in together, to the chagrin of Ann's family, with whom Ann's relationship remained strained for several years but who did not disown or disinherit her as she had feared. For the first two years of their relationship, Beth pushed the idea of children but Ann felt she wasn't ready. Finally, the two decided to both try to get pregnant at the same time using the same sperm and see who got pregnant first since they claimed not to care who carried the child. They chose to use donor sperm after a long negotiation with a close college friend of Beth's that she had once dated. They tracked their cycles and dates of ovulation, awaited the FedEx delivery man with glee and tried to make their mutual inseminations a part of sex with one another, joking about how they were both having an affair with the same man. Because Beth was now 41, after 3 failed cycles, she began an ovarian stimulant and had her insemination attempts done at the doctor's office rather than at home while Ann, now 38, continued to try without the drugs. During this period of time, Ann spoke about their method in her treatment, which had become analysis after two years in twice a week therapy.

> It's like a race to see who can do it first and now it seems almost unfair that she has the drugs and I don't. It's not like my ovaries are so young, you know. It reminds me of my sister and competing with her when I was younger for my mother's attention. Mom was always so busy socialising and doing her various charities and stuff that there

wasn't enough of her to go around. So when I'd get her attention, my sister lost out and vice versa. I even wonder if I'm getting equal numbers of sperm to Beth or is she somehow getting more. I wonder if mine are from the bottom of the sample and are the heavy female sperm while hers are from the top and are the fast, really super viable male sperm. I guess that goes back to my feeling in the family that boys are better and worth more and here I'm going to come out on the short end of the stick and have a girl, whereas if Beth gets pregnant first, she's going to have a boy. I don't know if two women should even raise a boy, but if we do I'm sure Beth's going to be the better mother and father since she's the athletic one who'll be playing catch. You're lucky because I bet you have a normal family and got pregnant the old fashioned way with a man who loves you and your family is all happy about it.

Ann had been in my practice during my first pregnancy and had assumed without ever asking me or the referring clinician that I was straight.

I hope this material gives you a sense of the competition that was going on, at least in Ann's mind, between Ann and her partner at this time and also cropping up in the transference. In fact, while Ann and Beth had planned to stop trying as soon as one of them got pregnant, once Ann was pregnant Beth decided she really wanted to keep trying. The two got pregnant five months apart and had a boy and a girl, now about two and one-and-a-half. Ann gave birth to the boy first then Beth had the girl five months later. The fact that she had a boy and had him first gave Ann a guilty sense of accomplishment at having beaten Beth as well as a continued feeling that she was ahead in the race because by dint of his age, her boy was always ahead of his little sister, though that gap continued to close as the children get older. It seemed to me at times when the children were younger that Ann and Beth functioned like two single mothers who just happened to live together and each took much more care of her "own" baby rather than the other partner's child. I referred them to couples therapy to address this issue and it has recently changed, marked also by the fact that the two decided to go through with second-parent adoptions for both children. To highlight for purposes of later discussion, Ann and Beth really are Mothers of Invention—they have two children who are non-twin half-sibs related through their father who are less than nine months apart in age—a situation we would never have seen before without lesbians and IVF. When their son began to speak, he tended to refer to his birth mother Ann as mummy and his other mother as Mama Beth. Beth's daughter did the reverse, calling Beth Mummy and Ann either Mama Ann or simply Ann. More recently, Ann's son calls her Mummy and Beth Mama and their daughter does the reverse, suggestive, I believe, of further healing of the split within the family as couples work has continued and as the mothers have re-established themselves as the primary unit within the foursome.

Let me move now to a second vignette. Carol was 32 and had been in an 8-year relationship with Diane when she presented, extremely anxious, with the unusual complaint that after years of disinterest, she was suddenly and intensely attracted to men. Her "symptom," as she termed it, had come about during a summer vacation in which she and her partner were at the beach, and she had surreptitiously masturbated to images of having intercourse with men. Her partner Diane had been tapered off an antidepressant and had a rough summer, being depressed, irritable and withdrawing from Carol. As we worked to understand the context of Carol's sudden interest in male bodies and penetration by penises it became clear that Carol felt Diane had withdrawn from her amidst this depression and the couple, who normally enjoyed daily sex while on vacation, had not been having sex. Diane had also been attacking the core of the couple's relationship, claiming it was a mutually co-dependent mothering relationship in which they were both trying to grow up. Diane also attacked Carol's refusal to merge the couple's finances completely as evidence of lack of commitment. Once back on antidepressants, Diane's depression remitted and her perspective changed and she was eager to repair the damage to the relationship and continue with the couple's previous discussions about having children. As Carol and I continued to explore what had happened that aroused her interest in men, it seemed Diane's unavailability and also Carol's perspective on sleeping with men as a potential retaliation against her for this unavailability were in the fore. Carol quickly revealed her sexual longings for men to Diane just after starting therapy in a guilty and self-destructive way and proposed that the couple consider having a threesome with a man so she could "get rid of her feelings." While initially hurt and angry, Diane soon capitulated and the pair began exploring various venues for meeting a man with whom they might have sex. As the couple's mutual participation in this escapade continued, Carol was markedly less anxious and noted that her longings for men had begun to disappear. In the end the couple never had the proposed three-way encounter. Around this time in therapy, Carol casually mentioned that Diane had been tapering off her antidepressants to try to get pregnant and that the couple was planning to do IVF because of a childhood ovarian condition of Diane's. The couple were planning to use a known donor, a gay man named Dave who was a mutual friend, and in fact had already frozen his sperm just before summer vacation because it had to be quarantined for six months so that he could be retested for HIV at the end of that time. When I pointed out that it was interesting Carol should casually mention this now, she grew defensive and asked what I meant. I noted that we hadn't explored what role Diane becoming pregnant might have played in Carol's emergent sexual interest in men nor had we discussed the role that having a known donor might play. Carol grew quiet and sad and said in a resigned way,

> But it's going to be their baby, not mine. Diane's going to be the mother, not me. I'll be the other mother. Diane and Dave will grow closer because, I mean, she's having his baby even though he's signing over parental rights to us. And then once the baby is born there will really be no room for me, too. I feel like I'm gaining a kid who isn't really mine and losing the love of my life in the process.

I inquired about how the couple had decided upon this course of action and was told that because of Diane's childhood condition,

> It was really important to her to get pregnant, and I don't really care. In fact, I'm afraid of the pain of it and of resenting the baby for what he or she does to my body. I don't even know if I want children. Even though I'm committed to Diane, I like the idea that I'm not tied down. I'm free to leave because there isn't that much that really holds us together. Once we have a baby that all changes.

I remarked that it was interesting that she was finding the notion of a man's erect penis and intercourse fascinating at the same time that she was adamantly opposed to becoming pregnant herself and saw it as Diane's domain, especially given that pregnancy was a potential outcome of such an encounter with a man. In the session following this discussion, the patient reported the following dream:

> I'm at a basketball game and all these celebrity lesbians (who were then currently pregnant) are in the stands, cheering. I'm on the court and I'm the shortest one of all but somehow I keep making all the baskets. There's a coach on the sidelines egging me on; she looks pregnant but she has a big bulge where a penis would be.

Diane associated to me as the coach who had it all—the eggs, the sperm, the uterus, and the baby—while she was coming up short in the baby game. She spoke of the pressure she felt within the lesbian community and from her own family to have children as "a lesbian conspiracy—what if I don't really want them? I always did hate basketball anyway. A big lesbian sport that I was never good at. I'm not going to go buy season tickets for the Liberty just because I'm a dyke!" As we explored the dream, it seemed Carol feared that she was neither man nor woman enough to be a parent, that she came up lacking. But why then, I wondered, did she keep scoring in the dream? Her associations to this question were all to my use of the word scoring and making the baskets. She reported that she feared that having a baby would make Diane and the baby close and "I'll lose control and go start having affairs and wreck our relationship. I'm thinking about how having a baby with her is like putting all my eggs in one basket and it was fine as long as it wasn't permanent, but now it feels different." The way in which Carol's parents' marriage had come to a crashing end around the issue of her father's affair with her mother's best friend after her youngest sister was born came to light. As we explored these issues in treatment, Carol grew more comfortable with progressing with the planned pregnancy with Diane, who became pregnant on the second round of IVF and the couple developed a new plan: If they decided to have a second child, Carol would be the one to get pregnant. As the pregnancy continued and the couple's daughter arrived, Carol and I continued to watch in therapy for any sense of separation or lack of involvement on her part, and Carol made special efforts to switch to a more freelance style of work so she could be home. The couple's daughter is now five and understands that you need a man and a woman to make a baby and that Diane and Dave are her biological parents but Carol "is my mother because she loves me and she takes care of me." The relationship with the donor has been easy and seemingly uncomplicated to date, and the couple's daughter spends the night with him and his boyfriend on a weekly basis, affording

Carol and Diane some private time. Carol used AI (artificial insemination) to become pregnant with the couple's second child using Dave's sperm.

Let me move on now to a third vignette. Erin and Faye, a couple of five years, were in their mid-30s when they came to see me for couple's therapy as part of their discussion about having a family. Both had had individual treatment in the past with other therapists, and both other therapists declined because of this to treat them as a couple. Both women favoured having children, but Erin was concerned that their already shaky and infrequent sexual life would suffer further if they were to have children. Much time was spent in couple's therapy on setting up specific times to have sex and trying to rekindle Faye's interest, which did improve remarkably once she was tapered off of an SSRI prescribed by her internist for dysthymia and anxiety. Faye was worried about the financial aspects of having a child and affording private school in New York City, and the two differed in their perspective of how important private school was to them. Faye also worried that she would feel left out if Erin were to get pregnant by AI using donor sperm as they had discussed and that she would be forced to work longer hours in her career, which was more lucrative than Erin's work. This, she feared, would mean that she repeated the dynamic within her own family in which her father was always at work or travelling and child care was left entirely to her mother.

Not long after we began treatment, the couple learned of the way my partner and I had become pregnant through a mutual acquaintance in the lesbian community with whom they were chatting at a party. They brought it up in the following session, thought it was a "cool" solution, and decided they would like to try it. Faye felt that she might feel more involved and less likely to be like her father if Erin got pregnant using her egg. The couple began to use their sessions to question me about real-life practical things, such as what clinic my partner and I used and what lawyers in the gay and lesbian communities did second-parent adoptions. At this point all attempts to introduce an exploration of their individual or joint transferences to me were met with "Don't be so Freudian with us!" I finally agreed to give them the names of three qualified lawyers and three IVF clinics I knew of that had a proven track record of working well with lesbian patients of mine but not disclose the professionals I had chosen. Meanwhile, they began to joke between sessions about me and my partner and family, a light-hearted banter that became quite useful in revealing their mutual concerns about having children and how to go about it. Specifically, they imagined my feeling that my partner was impregnating me when I received the embryo that had come from her egg. They pictured her as a tall, butch lesbian who was perhaps a Broadway stagehand, carpenter, or set designer (as they had also gleaned from the mutual acquaintance that I lived in the theatre district and liked theatre). She was male and I was Mum. Or I was the breadwinner and she was a lipstick lesbian who was an actress. In fact, maybe she was even Cherry Jones! Did I feel put upon being pregnant and the breadwinner both, like I was doing all the work while she got her nails done? Did I feel like an absent parent since I worked? Did the baby look like my partner, or did we try to choose a sperm donor that would make the baby look like me? Was the one of us with the genetic link to the child going to feel like more of the real parent as the child grew up? Speaking about these issues in displacement in relationship to me and my partner seemed to make the discussions less tense and more free-flowing between them than directly addressing their concerns with each other and the possible pregnancy. As they were talking about the meaning of these sorts of things, still uncertain about whom was going to get pregnant, they went to a fertility clinic and both had workups so that either could serve as the egg donor for the other one if they so decided. However, in the course of this workup Faye was discovered to have cervical cancer and had to undergo a hysterectomy and chemotherapy. Her prognosis for a complete cure was deemed excellent, over 95%, but the couple was understandably crestfallen and anxious about this turn of events. The cancer scare and treatment also seemed to intensify their sense of being a solid couple as they performed well under pressure, dealing with Faye's illness as well as severe, life-threatening illnesses of Erin's father and sister during this time. With this intensification of their sense of coupledom came an intensification of their desire to have a baby. In fact, their attitude toward the baby was that the baby had saved Faye's life, as her cervical cancer might not otherwise have been detected in time. Thus, they had a quite tangible kind of love and appreciation for this as yet unconceived child. It was decided that given the medical situation, Faye would serve as an egg donor for Erin, and the couple underwent three rounds of IVF for this to happen. Erin gave birth to a healthy baby boy. At this point, Faye actually seemed to develop a kind of postpartum depression, highly envious and angry that Erin had had the experience pregnancy and of giving birth while she had not. This fact, complicated by Erin breastfeeding seemed intensely threatening to Faye, who withdrew. With work around the issue that she was repeating the very dynamic of withdrawing that she had feared and with restarting Faye's antidepressant, the situation came to stabilise and the couple planned for each to work half days and care for their son the other opposite half. This equal "Mummy" time seemed to help make both aware that there really was room for two mothers. The couple has continued to struggle to find time and space to have an intimate sexual relationship, but their concerns about finances have largely resolved secondary to Faye's father becoming very involved with his grandson and offering to pay for his education as well as buying the couple a new apartment. Faye's father seems to be making up for time spent away during Faye's childhood by being extremely involved, supportive, and helpful. It seems that in addition to working and travelling during her childhood, he also felt excluded from her relationship with her mother and that her mother was highly protective of her role as primary parent. The couple's son is now three. Interestingly, he calls Faye's father Daddy, though he has been told that this is Grandpa, not Daddy. Nevertheless, he persists for now and tells friends he has two mommies and a daddy. Of note, the couple subsequently decided to become pregnant again and their IVF physician had retired. A new associate in his former practice suggested that now that Faye's eggs were 39, almost 40, perhaps they should consider an egg donor to improve chances of success. Faye's outrage at this suggestion heightened my sense that her genetic link to their son held important psychological meanings and had also helped repair the damage done to her sense of femininity by the hysterectomy. The couple have since had twin boys using Faye's eggs, Erin's womb, and the same donor sperm they used to conceive their first son, making the children full siblings.

Conclusion

Let me end by saying that even though many of the reproductive options and psychological considerations I've outlined are unique to lesbian parents, the decision to become a parent is a significant one for anyone, gay or straight. In fact, the experience of becoming a parent may be a life-altering experience that both trumps and transcends the issue of straight or gay. In the playground I find I have more in common with my straight counterparts than ever before, as we trade ideas on how to get a 2-year-old not to take his diaper off and play with his penis at dinner or how to convince a 4-year-old that yes, it really is time to get out of the pool after all. On a deeper level, becoming a parent returns us to being a part of the life-cycle—to what my 7-year-old daughter, under the sway of the Lion King, would call "the circle of life"—in a personally meaningful and very direct way. I think this is crucially important because before the sea changes in our culture, gay men and lesbians often felt they had to choose between being openly gay and being closeted and married in order to have children. Now that there is growing cultural freedom to be both, we can be both if we have the internal freedom to do so. Yet for so many of us, arriving at this internal freedom still means getting good psychodynamic treatment, and that is where all of you come in. Your patients will rely on you to help them see that even if their eggs are scrambled, their basic human longings and desires are not. Perhaps when we speak of mothers and fathers of invention today, what we are really speaking about is helping our patients to have the psychological flexibility and freedom to invent themselves as genuine and unique individuals. As my favourite story of the *Velveteen Rabbit* suggests, once we are real, we can have the joy that comes with the full use of our hind legs and can jump into the joys and challenges of parenthood along with everyone else.

PART II

DONOR CONCEPTION: AN EXPLORATION OF SOME OF THE ISSUES FACING INDIVIDUALS AND COUPLES

CHAPTER FOUR

Donor conception: family of choice?

Katherine Fine and Tamsin Mitchell

Introduction

Thinking about having a baby using donor gametes[1] frequently catapults people into unknown territory, psychologically and physically. There are some very real practical decisions that need to be made: where to have treatment, be it in the UK or overseas, whether to use an anonymous or identifiable donor, whether to use gametes from a known donor such as a family member or friend, or whether to egg share or to co-parent.[2] The advances in reproductive technologies have opened up a new frontier, producing an industry with a significant and commercial profile, but exposing potentially vulnerable consumers to considerable pressures.

In this chapter we hope to distil our understanding of the common anxieties and preoccupations that affect individuals and couples as they endeavour to think through the issues and to decide whether donor conception (DC) is the right way for them to have treatment and to create their family.

The Donor Conception Network (DCN)[3] adapted weekend "Preparation for Parenthood" workshops from those pioneered in Germany by Ken Daniels and Petra Thorne (Daniels, Thorn, &

Westerbrooke, 2007). Run for the last six years in the UK, the workshops are for those who are currently contemplating or having treatment. They are for heterosexual and same sex couples, or single women who are considering egg, sperm, or embryo donation as a way of building or adding to a family. At the time of writing only one male couple has attended, but that is expected to increase. Ten male couples joined DCN in 2013. The aim is to help individuals and couples to think through the issues and explore the emotional meaning of using donor conception. Through observations made in facilitating these workshops we hope to convey a real sense of the experience for participants attending.

Given that a total of 1,756 donor conceived children were born in the UK in 2009 alone, the last year for which statistics were available from the Human Fertilisation and Embryology Authority (HFEA),[4] the people who attend these workshops cannot necessarily be held to be representative of all prospective DC parents. That said, the workshops give a unique insight and, over their duration, a fairly consistent picture has emerged of what it is people encounter when thinking about whether DC is the right way for them to have a family.

In finding a balance between the needs of their as yet unborn child and their own intense feelings, people often feel isolated and overwhelmed with information while having to make difficult decisions. Of course, this emotional maelstrom is not the same for everyone, as Susan Vaughan shows in her chapter in this book. As she and her partner embarked on *in vitro* fertilisation (IVF)[5] treatment, they considered themselves the only "cheerful and upbeat patients" in the clinic. As a lesbian couple, she describes how they were just at the beginning of an "exciting venture" as compared to the heterosexuals, whose conventional reproductive attempts had not been successful.

The workshops take place in the context of enormous social change from the culture of secrecy that was supported and advocated by the majority of fertility clinics, even as recently as twenty years ago. Thinking and practice has developed at such a pace that involving a donor as an external party to procreation can now be thought about much more openly. But for many people contemplating DC and attending these workshops, the assumption still seems to be that they are simply acquiring a factor or gamete of reproduction necessary for them to have a baby, Daniels (2012). For many of those wrestling with the implications of having a baby in this way, it may be challenging to recognise that in using DC they will be receiving the genetic history of another family, which means thinking about the place of the donor in the family he/she is helping to create.

There may be a question as to how far a weekend workshop can hope to provide an understanding of the link, at whatever level, between the families of the recipient and the family of the donor. Perhaps it is most helpful to see this as the start of a rather long process and one that will need to be re-visited at various stages in a family's lifespan.

"Preparation for Parenthood" workshops

An introduction

The "Preparation for Parenthood" weekend workshops provide an opportunity to gather information, hear from parents of donor conceived children and, via film, the children and young people themselves. Sharing experiences and stories with others contemplating family creation via donor conception, participants are encouraged to discuss thoughts, feelings, and experiences with qualified speakers who have worked in the field of clinical and psycho-social aspects of donor conception, treatment, and subsequent family raising. If participants can deepen their understanding of some of the issues and the feelings that are likely to arise, it is hoped they will be in a better position to make well informed decisions. By working in small groups and sharing an evening meal together, there is a chance to break the isolation felt by many individuals and couples considering donor conception.

Setting the scene: who are the participants?

Given that DC involves a number of family types—namely, solo mums, heterosexual couples, and same sex couples—the experiences they bring will be very different. These experiences can be very emotionally challenging and painful. The reader may find that, in reading this chapter many of their values and assumptions about procreation are challenged and that they are likely to have strong emotional reactions. It is inevitable that one of the challenges of a chapter like this is to try and do justice to the diversity of issues raised and to try and integrate all of these into our thinking.

Many, although not all participants come with a history of infertility. In the past this was largely considered the woman's problem, but, according to Notman (2011), increasing sophistication of diagnosis has demonstrated that 40% or higher in some data of infertility is due to male or male/female combined factors. In the twenty-first century, fertility treatment has become mainstream and the use of donated gametes through egg, sperm, double (egg and sperm), or embryo donation to assist conception is becoming more commonplace.

It can be hard to describe the painful impact of many years of infertility and treatment on a person and their relationship. This can also apply as a result of secondary infertility, that is where a family may already have a child born of their own gametes but a subsequent pregnancy is proving to be elusive. It is difficult to bear the ignominy of investigative procedures, desperately hoping that there is nothing wrong, while at the same time wanting/needing a reason to explain the failure to conceive and the harrowing absence of a baby. It has long been understood that infertility evokes an internal sense of inadequacy in couples and individuals. For heterosexual couples with years of failed treatment behind them, it can feel, as Dinora Pines has described it, like:

> ... an enormous personal crisis—a powerful blow to the individual's narcissism, a diminution of pride in the mature body ... To the sexual relationship which may seem to become mechanical, especially if fertility techniques place constraints on its spontaneity ... (Pines, 1990)

Apfel and Keylor capture the essence of the emotional experience of infertility, in their chapter in this book. They observe that psychological conflicts stir up the deepest layers of emotional resonance such that: "old conflicts are frequently revived which may challenge the integrity of the marital relationship." The pain is then compounded, they suggest beyond an: "involuntary childlessness by invasive procedures and ethical dilemmas created by recent technological opportunities."

Managing the emotional upheaval of fertility treatment has the added complication of organising and negotiating work schedules around a punctilious demand for medical procedures, scans, blood tests, and consultations. How can privacy and a sense of dignity be maintained under these circumstances? Feeling under pressure to reveal the reasons for unexplained absences often leads to a reluctant and rather resentful involvement of work colleagues in this most intimate part of a person's life.

One woman in the workshop described the effects of IVF treatment in this way: feeling discombobulated with the influx of hormones into her body, she could not bear anything to touch her, her skin seemed so fragile and sensitive. She became very tearful as a result of the drug regime and described herself as having felt hyper sensitive physically and psychologically. Yet, as she continued to go to work, this seemed invisible to those around her. She could not believe that no one even seemed to notice her fragility.

For single women and lesbian couples who attend, the issue is the absence of a male partner to form a family. It is less usual for them to have experienced the lengthy medical infertility journey that many heterosexual couples have endured. For a few, their first visit to a clinic may reveal infertility, presenting them with similar challenges of not being genetically related to a subsequent DC child. For most, the decision to explore the possibility of donor conception feels a positive step forward.

Single women, however, encounter a different sadness and sense of inadequacy. Without a partner and for some already struggling with issues of self-esteem, feelings of rejection and the failure to form a lasting fertile relationship, this means confronting the grief and mourning of this loss. The prospect of a childless future seems to bring a different sort of fragility, when many other parts of life such as careers, financial security, physical fitness, and emotional maturity can be at their peak.

Deprived of the family that they may have dreamt about, to be childless may, as Pines (1990) ascribes it, induce feelings of guilt at not being able to continue the family line and give grandchildren to their parents. Wanting to be supported or be supportive, but not wanting to face one's own envy or the imagined triumph of the fertile other, childlessness can produce a sense of being isolated in a bubble of desperate pain, anguish, and self-reproach.

For everyone, no matter what their background and situation, when thinking about procedures such as IVF, egg or sperm donation, and surrogate motherhood, all are compelled to consider difficult medical, moral, and ethical issues. The new techniques in reproductive medicine continue to challenge, particularly given that as Zalusky (2000) suggests, these techniques have not yet for the most part, been integrated into a shared social consciousness.

Structure of the "Preparation for Parenthood" workshops

As mentioned, the workshops devised by the DCN were modelled on preparation workshops pioneered by Ken Daniels and Petra Thorn (Daniels, Thorn, & Westerbrooke, 2007) that were initially run in Germany. These German workshops, determined largely by fertility treatment available at that time, catered only for heterosexual couples needing sperm donation. In 2008, with the help of a government grant, the DCN developed their own workshops with some significant differences; they are open to any prospective parent thinking about using egg, sperm, or embryo donation. Rather than being facilitated by professionals, they are led by two facilitator members of the DCN, all but one of whom are themselves parents of DC children. The one facilitator who is herself a parent but not of donor conceived children, is a donor conceived adult who was told about her genetic origins at the age of thirteen. The aim is always to have one facilitator who is *not* genetically related to their own child(ren).

These workshops were designed to mirror the journey travelled, starting with a recognition of the likelihood of remaining childless from the conventional route, to a position of being able to embrace donor conception as a treatment of choice, rather than as a last resort. Initially, the groups of up to a maximum of eighteen people were composed heterogeneously to include same sex or heterosexual couples and single women. On the one hand the diversity enhanced the groups, but given the disparity of their experience, it became apparent that single women and lesbians sometimes preferred and appreciated separate provision from heterosexual couples. The needs of these two former groups are not exactly the same, but they are sufficiently different from the needs of heterosexual couples to distinguish the specialist workshops: either for heterosexual couples or for same sex couples and single women.

Beginning the workshop

Acknowledging that people may be at different stages in their journey so far, facilitators invite a shift in thinking away from donor conception as a fertility treatment, to thinking of it as a way of creating a family. Some participants may have already decided that this is the way forward for them, but many will be thinking of this as a last chance treatment, perhaps the only way that they are going to achieve their longed for family.

Inevitably, there is enormous anxiety about even being at the workshop, given the nature and the rawness of experiences to be assimilated. This may be the first time participants have faced a social situation other than in the waiting room of the fertility clinic, which either identifies their fertility circumstance and their need of assisted reproduction, or defines them as a single person seeking parenthood but not being part of a couple. It is as if in attending, they have crossed the threshold of being recognised as such in a public domain.

Moving into the introductory exercise, all participants are asked to choose a participant whom they do not know and, for ten minutes or so, to discuss not only their fertility history, but the particular issues that they may be concerned about and that they hope will be addressed at the workshop.

Challenging the secrecy, which for some is an inevitable consequence of the unrequited desire for a family, frequently this is the first opportunity people have had of talking one to one with a stranger about these matters. For some single women, this may be the first time they have overtly expressed their desire and intention. It is not uncommon for it to be a nurtured secret, tangled in with feelings of shame or sublimated in a wealth of scientific medical facts and statistics. For other participants, this workshop can represent the start of something exciting, an inspiration for them to move ahead with their plans to have a family.

During this exercise, facilitators frequently notice an incremental change in the atmosphere in the room. From one of apprehension and a sort of frozen look on the faces of many, to a sense that people are really starting to engage with each other in discovering that they share common ground. The volume of discussion seems to go up as people, talking in their pairs, become more animated in a space that allows for the revelation of very personal anecdotes, or a previously well hidden and private pain.

Briefly introducing their working partner back to the reconvened group, this is a big undertaking, or a real ice breaker for many and tears are not unusual. Listening to one's story being retold by someone else may well be the first time it has been heard or has been told out loud. It can be very raw to hear oneself described as infertile, or partner-less, or even as a partnership that has not been able to achieve a family in the conventional way.

Facilitators record issues arising from the personal stories. Typical of the issues that may come up are: the impact of treatment in the UK *vs.* overseas, the implications of cultural differences, the choice of an anonymous or a known donor, the question of a donor child emotionally bonding with its non-genetic parent(s), the way to talk to family and friends, and the consequences of a child not resembling anyone else in the family. Lesbian couples and single women may be concerned about public perception of their decision and how this will affect their child, as well as the need for male role models. Single women sometimes bring practical problems about finance or childcare that will not be addressed in the workshop, but are anxieties that need to be acknowledged. Clearly it is useful to have this information as a reference point for the whole weekend and for outside speakers to have, at a glance, a quick overview of the group.

On another level though, it seems that this is an opportunity for the group to move from being a set of isolated individuals and to start to weld itself together, through recognition of common themes and areas of struggle. The significance seems to lie in the fact that amorphous feelings of conflict and pain can be shared and explored together. Beginning the workshop and assisted by the facilitators, stories articulated by strangers create a promise of mindfulness and deep thinking. It is at this stage that having revealed something of their pain and anguish through the narrative process, the significance of the task emerges as one of processing something intensely and deeply personal. This is analogous to a good experience that takes something internal and overwhelming and offers to contain and help bear the feelings.

Anxieties discussed and thought about set the tone of a space where issues move from silent and secret to named and known. For people who have come as a couple, where each may have felt they are the only port in the storm, there is a chance to separate out and differentiate their respective positions. A couple relationship might well have been strained while struggling to contain a whole host of feelings of anger, shame, and being out of control. In addition, the partner who is not infertile may be going to some lengths to hide their own feelings of triumph, projecting their own vulnerability into their partner, the one who is seen as being in need of treatment. Ken Daniels in his chapter in this book suggests:

... that a more useful way of conceptualising this is to think of the infertility arising out of the two partners. The desire is that *the couple* wish to have a child/children and it is *the couple* who cannot realise this goal without assistance.

One woman at a workshop spoke of her deep sense of shame following her first (and unsuccessful) treatment with anonymous sperm donation. She felt she could not face her partner, nor look him in the eye and felt deeply remorseful as if she had been unfaithful to him. As she described it, she wondered if she was also protecting her infertile partner, taking up his feelings of shame at not being able to give her what she so desperately wanted.

In another couple who were considering egg donation, the emotions that were being carried by each of the partners noticeably altered during the course of one of the workshops: Mr E appeared reluctant to attend; this was endorsed by Mrs E who spoke openly about their circumstances saying that happily, she had come to terms with egg donation. During one of the later break-out sessions, Mrs E became very upset with a woman who was proposing to use donated sperm and was therefore going to be genetically related to her child. Mrs E rather irritably questioned how the other woman could possibly know what it felt like to her, given that she would not be genetically related to her child? Later on in the main group, contained by the facilitator and the rest of the group, Mrs E broke down and cried copiously. Meanwhile, her husband, actively and for the first time, started to engage in the exercise and visibly seemed to relax. It seemed that as Mrs E had expressed her fears about her proposed non-genetic child, Mr E's resistance had dissipated and he no longer felt the need to protect his vulnerable partner.

The group listening to each other's stories becomes a testament to what people have had to endure. One single woman said "I thought, he's left me, and I'm nearly forty, he's taken so much, I'm not going to let him take away my chance to be a mother." It is not only the facilitators, but members of the workshop themselves who clearly hold the individual narratives in mind, as evidenced over the weekend discussions. Particular interests lead to bonds among individuals, which can be built upon during social periods, such as a reasonable lunch break, an overnight stay, and a group supper together. For single women, who have not attended with a partner, these bonds are all the more important and strong friendships can form very quickly. Listening to others', and talking about one's own, painful emotional experience can be very hard work. The setting and discipline of the workshop, indeed the DCN as an organisation comes to symbolise what is necessary to hold people through the process of assisted procreation. It might be other support groups or even the fertility clinics that become the structures containing powerful anxieties on behalf of individuals, as described by Menzies-Lyth (1960).

After the introduction exercise, participants frequently seem more receptive and more inclined to focus on the bodily realities and demands associated with treatment. Both the conceiving and non-conceiving partners engage with the "medical question and answer session" and seem largely comfortable with this exercise, which is led by fertility specialists, either a doctor or an embryologist.

"What does using donor sperm or eggs mean to me?"

Trying to conceive remains a deeply personal area of an individual or a couple's life. Introducing a stranger—be it a baby or a donor—it might be the case that for any pregnant woman the experience of carrying a new baby could have the potential for feeling her body has been colonised in some way by another being growing inside of her. The stirrings of feeling invaded by "foreign" matter, or an alien species, even if anticipated as a primal fear and possible in any pregnancy, is one with which some prospective DC parents are particularly likely to identify. This is also true for lesbian couples and single women in contemplating the introduction of an outsider and a "male" into their lives.

Having successfully conceived of the idea of building a family this way, it is timely to move into the next exercise: "What does using donor sperm or eggs mean to me?" This exercise was designed to provide an opportunity to examine the inevitable preconceptions and concerns that a contemplation of DC can involve. It is intended as an opportunity to talk with others of the same gender and share thoughts and feelings.

The participants do this in smaller break-out groups. For heterosexuals, men and women are divided into same gender groups. For the single women and lesbian partners the groups are generally self-selecting, one for those using double or embryo donation, one for the non-conceiving partners, and one or two for those using sperm dona-tion. Single lesbians will sometimes choose to be with other lesbians and those using egg or double donation (i.e., sperm and egg) will nearly always choose to be together, regardless of whether or not they are part of a couple.

Facilitators have consistently noted the change in atmosphere in the smaller groups. Although more exposing, they are also intimate and rather personal. There is often a relief for participants at being able to continue the thinking, comfortably, in their own style, with their own sex, in the knowledge that they are sharing with people with whom they can identify. For those in a couple, it might be a relief to feel free of the emotional constraints of protecting or disagreeing with their partner. Mourning the loss of their hoped for child, is common among all groups. This small group forum seems consistent in providing an opportunity to share the trauma of some of their past experiences. There is also the chance to explore the difficulties and obstacles anticipated in the future.

Following this, the groups reconvene in the large group to discuss what has emerged in their discussions.

Emerging issues and themes

As is to be expected, there are a great many issues and themes that emerge in the main group when it reconvenes to hear what has been discussed in the smaller groups. Key issues are consistently to do with loss and the choice of donor, family boundaries, and talking and telling. In describing these themes, it seems helpful to link them to the prevailing preconceptions in society about procreation and parent-hood. Ken Daniels in Chapter Eight describes what he calls the "pro-natalist view". This might be said to be a kind of ideal held by society. In brief, it can be described as a process in which a man and a woman meet and then procreate in the conventional manner. Once the child is born, that same couple become the parents of the child and are responsible for rearing the child to maturity. Any deviation from this norm can become a cause of judgement and potentially lead to a feeling of moral censure. The power of this norm creates the potential for a situation in which those using donor conception methods of procreation might be particularly vulnerable to a feeling that they will be censured.

At the point when DC becomes a treatment of choice there is then the question of the choice of a donor. At first, this may be seen by society and by participants in the process, as simply a question of obtaining the gametes necessary for procreation, or the creation of a baby. But the donor is a person and will inevitably be present in the new family long after the child's birth. This sense of "who we are" as it defines the family boundary is one that, having emerged, will continue to develop over time.

Let us now return to a description of the themes that emerge in the workshops. In the light of these discussions, we will address loss and choice of donor first, before thinking about the impact on both family boundaries and on talking about the fact of a donor within and beyond the family boundary.

Loss

A deep emotional motif running through all the workshops is one of loss. For women and men, many of whom have endured years of fertility treatment or disappointment in their relationships, indecision can still reign over the question of how to know when the time is right to draw a line, either knowing that it is time to stop treatment with one's own sperm or eggs, or to give up fertility treatment altogether.

Loss of personal space, privacy, and of a normal sex life is painful for many participants. The impact on a sense of femininity/masculinity is only emphasised by the monthly cycle of blame following menstruation. Participants are often utterly at one when complaining about being taken over by the demands of treatment. This inevitably means confronting a loss of (social) time, of a sense of good health, certainly of money and of relationships that are too painful or too difficult to maintain. Some infertile men who are contemplating sperm donation have described a sense of feeling alienated from a tangible connection to the physical reality of a pregnancy. This is unlike the situation for infertile women who, even with egg or embryo donation, will still carry the pregnancy, in their bodies, to term. The clinical nature of the process of conception taken out of the bedroom can leave single women feeling particularly sad, as if it compounds a sense of being unable to maintain a successful creative relationship with a man, or a woman. For single women a child does not replace a partner, nor a gamete a father, so an uncovering of defences can help to anticipate feelings that may return at a later date. Lesbians may feel a sense of loss at their inability to give their partner this one small but vital (male) gamete.

Time and again at these workshops participants comment on the intensity and level of pain of other participants; that giving up on either their own or their partner's gametes has become a blot on their internal emotional landscape. Experiences are shared of being informed of diagnoses, difficulties of treatment, of pregnancies lost through miscarriage, of relationships and partnerships lost to be replaced by single parenthood, or of age threatening to leave childbearing behind. Deprived of the joy of conceiving through lovemaking and the loss of an unthinking conception, it is not uncommon for couples to have had seven or eight failed IVF attempts with their own gametes.

The most obvious loss to many participants is born of the wish to conceive a much loved partner's baby. The end of the genetic line for those who are infertile can be a shocking concept, removing as it does a personal and cultural heritage of the "mini me", so called by many participants. This can be felt as acutely by the fertile partner in having to relinquish the fantasy of a baby born from the mix and combination of a much loved partnership. Older single women often report a deep sense of responsibility to try, even against the odds, to retain a genetic connection. Failing to give a genetically related grandchild to their parents has been described by those who are infertile as akin to a death of hopes and dreams and yet, there is no funeral and no body. It can be hard to understand the particular grieving for the child you will never have.

The workshop is attended early on in the thought processes of most lesbian couples and single women. Unlike heterosexual couples, there has generally been no lengthy fertility treatment and so these participants do not have to wrestle with a sense of a failing of their own body to conceive. For a few though, their first visit to a clinic may also have revealed infertility.

The prospect of not being genetically related to a resultant child for single women and lesbians using double donation and embryo donation, evokes similar conflicts as those for heterosexual couples. Being open about sperm donation where their own bodily functions are not held accountable, they imagine *not* telling the child, family, and friends about the egg donation where their fertility is implicated. Seeking to avoid either rejection of them by a resultant child, or a rejection by grandparents of a non-genetic child, group discussion frequently opens up the pain of infertility and the sense of shame and inadequacy.

Most lesbians and single women who attend these workshops talk of a childhood with a traditional model of a father and mother. Facilitators have observed how it seems more difficult for women who themselves have had an absent father, whether through divorce, death, or emotional withdrawal, to engage fully with the process of thinking about what it will mean to them to conceive using donated sperm. For those who have had a rich relationship with a father or grandfather, they seem more in touch with the sense of the loss of a father figure for their own prospective child.

Lesbian families often seem well attuned to their feelings of loss; creating a family through donor conception becomes something to be celebrated rather than mourned. Same sex couples, some of whom consider co-parenting, frequently bring anxieties around the exposure of their hitherto private relationships, whether it be to clinics, neighbours, work colleagues, or family and friends. There is concern that the arrival of a (DC) child will re-ignite homophobic feelings, even among the most accepting of their friends and relatives who they imagine will question the suitability of their family structure for child rearing.

Facilitators frequently find it deeply moving to witness how individual agony and collective pain is managed with extraordinary grace and compassion. Many value and enjoy each other's company, a degree of intimacy is achieved, and the main group acquires a sense of solidarity with a feeling of being heard and understood, perhaps for the first time.

Choosing a donor: are they simply gametes or a person?

Ehrensaft (2000) described the use of donated gametes as evoking and stirring up fantasies of a *ménage á trois,* that donation introduces a third person into the sexual couple relationship. Perhaps there is a wish to avoid knowledge, so that thinking of sperm as sperm or the egg donated similarly as an egg, negates the reality of a person having donated their gametes. In recent times, there has been a change in direction, away from a parent centred focus which supported keeping donation a secret and sought to protect the position of the donor and, by dint of that, the parent.

When the donation was seen simply as a means to an end, the "silent partner" in the family, or the "very kind man or woman", as they can be referred to by some, might on one level have been attributed with intimate familial type characteristics by recipient families, but inevitably, the donor as an actual person was kept at bay, the distance controlled by the anonymity.

As reported in the Introduction of this book, DC children conceived in the UK after 2005 will, at the age of eighteen, be able to access identifying information about their donor, thus ending donor anonymity in the UK.[6] Understandably, participants seem well informed about the changes in legislation, but their manifest response is often related to the practical implications for treatment. It is harder for many to imagine how the donor might be integrated into the family in the future, particularly where there is access to identifying information.

Choosing a donor raises difficult decisions that have to be confronted by many with a long infertility history and the continued deep longing for a child. Faced with the very real consequence of unsuccessful treatments and a woman's advancing age, participants often report feeling overwhelmed by the responsibility for the choice of donor. Legislative changes have coincided with considerable developments in the accessibility of fertility treatment overseas. The price of this immediate availability of an anonymous donation overseas means that the right to much information about the donor will be sacrificed. As a consequence, rarely will there be any access to identifying information for any resultant offspring. This clearly has enormous implications for anyone born through DC and makes the significance of the choice of the donor far reaching and lifelong.

European and American sperm banks are increasingly divulging more, albeit non-identifying information on donors that may include more detailed information about family background, hobbies, likes and dislikes, and lifestyle. Access to gamete providers such as the European Sperm Bank and sperm banks in the US allow a degree of donor selection not easily available before the legislative changes in the UK. Browsing photographs and pen pictures of donors is often a heated topic of conversation among the single women in the smaller groups. Some have compared the process to being one step further on from internet dating. One woman said: "If you are going to do it this way, you might as well have one that looks like George Clooney." On occasion, facilitators wonder whether this becomes a distraction from the pain of really knowing what it is they have lost.

Preferences may be expressed in terms of wanting donors with, say, specific hair colour, eye and skin colour, height and build. If using overseas donors, prospective parents are sometimes concerned about their donor offspring having features typical of the country of origin of the donor. They wonder whether or not this can be celebrated as a positive decision to go abroad. Those hoping to be private about their means of conception may have particular concerns about children's features that show evidence of ethnic roots not found in the raising family. Inevitably, anonymous overseas donation will leave unanswered questions about the genetic and cultural heritage of the child.

So often, those attending talk of their desire for a *baby* or a *child* and it can be hard for participants to imagine, at this stage in the process, that the longed for (donor) baby will grow up. With the DVDs of DC adolescents offering a psychosocial perspective of the impact of donor conception on older children, facilitators consistently see a transition over the course of the weekend. The choices made at the time of treatment and conception start to be seen as significant, particularly at the point when the child is conceptualised as growing into an independent adult with thoughts and feelings that may be different to their own.

Regard is often shown for the donor as a person amid ethical concerns expressed as to whether the donor should be paid, or be given other incentives. The European Tissues and Cells Directive, which states that EU donors should not be paid for donating but that they can be compensated for inconvenience, still leaves this a grey area. A single woman challenged the idea of a donation being altruistic during a medical session: "How do I know he is a kind man—I don't really know—I might know his hair colour but you can't really tell me what he is like, he might be awful." This brings the donor into very sharp relief as a real person. For those couples contemplating co-parenting or donation of gametes from a family member (often a sibling) or friend, there are different factors to be considered given the inevitable impact of this on relationships and future family dynamics.

In the safety of the group it becomes possible for many participants to acknowledge that, as Ken Daniels puts it in his chapter in this book: "Many parents liked and felt comfortable with the previously solid boundaries of using non-identifying donors, as it meant that the donor could almost become a 'non person' and not exist." Faced with the thinking of others in the group seems to open up the notion of a potentially deep regret if, as a parent, you are unable to meet a young person's desire for information about their donor, perhaps made worse by the knowledge that other DC people will be able to satisfy this desire.

Inevitably, the attitude of the donor can change from when a donation is made, depending on the donor's own experience and ongoing personal circumstances. Donors who are traced may be reluctant to have contact with donor offspring some twenty or more years after their donation, particularly if it means exposing their partners, children, and grandchildren to their decision. On the other hand, research has shown that donors often do wish to know the outcome of their donations. Ken Daniels (2004) refers to studies showing that many (male) providers: "do not provide their semen without an investment and interest in the outcomes". At some stage, he continues: "they will think about the children who may have been conceived, their features, their lives unfolding with their families and their happiness." These issues are explored further in later chapters in this book.

Family boundaries—what do we know for sure?

The identity of a family within society creates a family boundary such that all know, or are assumed to know, who is within this boundary and who is outside it. A donor crossing this family boundary may arouse potentially very strong feelings. Perhaps the drive for the anonymity of a donor can be seen in terms of a guarding and maintaining of this family boundary, or an effort to avoid someone crossing the line who is seen as threatening the integrity of the family boundary. It seems that some prospective parents find it harder to conceptualise the donor as a person, with whom resultant offspring may, or may not, wish to connect. Perhaps the donor being seen as someone who donates gametes, but not as a person, is a response to a very deep fear, as Ehrensaft describes it in her chapter in this book, that the donor will return to claim his/her children and thereby threaten the very future of the family.

Making decisions then, in relation to treatment, can be a particularly challenging task. Engaging with that challenge, let us imagine a scenario of the recipient family with children created with the help of the donation, and the donor with a family of his or her own. The donor is both within and outside the family boundary. How can this interrelationship best be managed? Even if they have decided to use donor conception, there may still be some anxieties and a number of feelings left hanging in the air. For example, the question of how to integrate the knowledge of such a potentially large number of siblings (from sperm donation) into family life, given that there could be nine or more half-siblings, born to different families. HFEA guidelines allow a donor to donate to up to ten families. Or, trying to imagine how the relationship between a newly created DC family and the family of the donors and their children would be played out in reality. The reader may also be left hanging, so it may be helpful to offer some perspective on these anxieties by reviewing the experience of two DC adolescents.

In the Introduction to this book, we heard from Linda and Susie, who are fifteen years old and half-siblings, conceived through the same anonymous sperm donor, but to different mothers, in different families. Both having grown up always knowing they were donor conceived, their positive experience of having discovered that they were sisters, seems to be testament to an outcome born of the girls' early knowledge of their DC and the comfort with which their respective families have discussed this. These impressive young women seem to have a very clear sense of the family boundaries and their donor's place within them.

Readers may recall that Linda has two mothers in a lesbian partnership and Susie is in a family with her solo mother. Both are only children in their respective families and perhaps this had a bearing on a wish to find a sibling; Linda seemed to think it did, although Susie felt not. It seems likely that greater awareness will lead many donor conceived people to assume this information is a birth right, even if they are not much interested in it themselves. This is quite a shift from the situation even as recently as fifteen years ago. Parents then who wanted to be open with their children saw their responsibility mainly in terms of informing them about the fact of the donor. It was not on the agenda for most at that time and many parents we have spoken to whose DC children are older, did not think about contact with half-siblings as being a legitimate part of DC family life. Meeting someone else having treatment at the same clinic at the same time inevitably raises the notion of the donor being the same, but formerly it was almost considered as contact by default.

Linda and Susie shared a sense of amazement and excitement at the prospect of discovering someone to whom they were biologically related. Both of them knew that: "this was going to affect us for the rest of our lives". It may be obvious but seems to attest to the lifelong implications of the choices made. Linda and Susie felt lucky to have found each other. Given the anonymous nature of the donation it was by no means a certainty that they would have been able to trace any of their half-siblings. Treatment overseas, where the vast majority of donors are anonymous and very little information about them is given to recipients, means that contact between half-siblings such as Linda and Susie is likely to continue to be very difficult to orchestrate. Outside of the UK, central registers of those involved in the donation triangle are held only in New Zealand and most states in Australia. In other countries each clinic holds its own records with no guarantee that they will be securely looked after should the clinic go out of business.

The girls thought less about the donor because, as Susie put it they have found each other from: "that side of . . . [their] family" and this has satisfied their curiosity. Perhaps it is reassuring to prospective DC parents that Susie says she does not think about it: ". . . not on a day to day basis, adults worry about it a lot more". They both seemed to feel replete in having each other as sisters and in the interview did not seem to be tantalised by the notion that there could be six or seven further half-siblings, at least. They did wonder about how the donor manages the information about his donation with his biological family, or if he tells at all? They considered whether he might have donated before he met his partner? If he had not told his family, how would he put it? Their concern shows that they think about the donor as a person and not as a function.

It is not clear whether Susie and Linda have acknowledged that their donor's own family children would be their half-siblings, but this reflects a family boundary that is very much still in process. Given that it was Linda and Susie's parents who initiated contact between the girls, one does not know if they themselves would have pursued it left to their own devices. Not all donor conceived young people are interested in sibling tracing. As a donor conceived teenager of fourteen, who lives in his family with his heterosexual parents and his fully genetic sibling said:

> I've never really thought about it—why would you care, they're not really siblings, its only biology. I'm not sure I've ever talked about it

[his donor conception] with my friends either. It's not that I'm insecure there is just no need . . . maybe if you're a girl but if you're a boy
you don't really talk about that stuff.

In this young man's mind, "biology" or the genetic link is not
equivalent to an emotional link. For him, family is defined by the relationships he has, with his mother, his recipient father, and his sibling,
who was conceived by the same anonymous sperm donor. His donor
and potential half-siblings are hazy concepts in his mind that he does
not think of as family and in whom, certainly at this stage in his life,
he has little interest. The emotional attachments he has to his family
and friends are what really matter to him, there seems to be no
contemporary relevance, at this stage in his life, to the notion of DC
half-siblings.

The concern of prospective parents that their non-genetically
related children may not love them as much and that there may be an
issue with bonding, is addressed by the girls in the interview. Linda
says she has never thought of her non-biological mother as any less than
her family, even though she is not genetically related. "I love her like
she is my mum." It did not matter that she was not her birth mother;
she is still the one who was picking her up from school and still the one
who is making her dinner. She was acting like a mum would and
should. Susie endorsed this, it does not matter so much about genetics
she said, what matters is if they love you or look after you.

We know that adoptive children who seek out biological parents
and siblings often wait until they are older, when they have families
of their own, after the death of adoptive parent(s), or in the aftermath
of family breakdown following divorce. We do not yet know whether
donor conceived young people will follow this pattern. The desire for
sibling tracing might be greatest among only children and those from
single parent families at the moment, but with greater awareness,
curiosity might become more mainstream. It seems likely that the
need to structure a sense of self, an identity, and to know the unknown
will continue to drive these connections.

Questions that remain open to thought and discussion

Actively engaging with fertility treatment means accepting what may
feel to be an inevitably gross and intrusive personal boundary violation

of privacy, as well as of the family boundary. How this affects an individual's fears, fantasies, and desires and where the bedroom is preoccupied with "baby-making sex" as Olivia Montuschi refers to it in her chapter in this book, is unfinished business for participants as the workshop ends.

There may still be questions about how to define a family that is conceived using another's family and how best to incorporate the other family. What is certain is that the position of the donor in the UK has now become legitimised and enshrined in a more public and legally constituted acknowledgement, through the 2005 legislation. With the advances in DNA testing and less stigmatisation born of greater general awareness, perhaps negation of the donor's existence will become less of an imperative to those who struggle with being open. It seems inevitable that secrecy will become increasingly difficult to sustain. The DCN have had some enquiries from donors wanting guidance on how to talk to their own children about their donation. This is no doubt a sign of things to come.

Olivia Montuschi in her chapter in this book describes the preparatory steps that she and her husband took in preparing for DC parenthood, many years before these workshops had even been thought about. She reports that: "separately and together, [we] moved towards a place where it was possible to make a decision about donor conception. Today we would recognise this as a grieving and ultimately healing process." She says that her husband's and her preparation was quite consistent, as it turned out, with the experience for many in these workshops. Perhaps one can then assume that the scenarios, experiences, and feelings described in this chapter are typical of what many people go through when contemplating DC parenthood, not just those who attend the workshops.

That said, the post evaluation feedback attests to participants feeling much better able to imagine the DC scenario in the light of any misgivings and consider the sorts of decisions that will have to be made along the way. Even so, it may be difficult to fast forward and focus on the things that typically are going to have to be thought about further down the line. A sense of belonging is an essential ingredient to a secure family life and the preoccupation that can so often follow the birth of a new baby, "doesn't he/she look like . . ." seems to demonstrate this. Perhaps voicing their fears about having to face up to having a child whose appearance does not resemble either parent or the wider family can helpfully be anticipated. There is an emotional adjustment to be made in this new style of family. In a mixed family of non-genetic siblings, there may well be children conceived from different donors, or in a family with DC child(ren) and child(ren) born with parent's own eggs and sperm, there may be a question as to whether the donor baby will be loved as much?

Informing and educating those who are not familiar with the implications of infertility and the treatments available, brings with it responsibilities of talking and telling. In the concluding session, one man spoke of his difficulties around telling his parents. He said that his body was failing to deliver on what he felt was a fundamental right to have a child of his own. Deeply ashamed and feeling inadequate, it was abhorrent to him to have to explain to his parents that he and his partner were embarking on fertility treatment. He felt sure that his parents, who were rather old, would never have heard of donor conception. Telling and talking and being open about donor conception has long preoccupied prospective parents. Even if parents expect to be open, questions remain, once children appear, of what to say and how to say it. Who else should be informed, grandparents, friends, and colleagues? In telling other people, reactions are likely to need managing. Perhaps overcoming each of these hurdles can be seen as preparation for a sharing with the wider community. This is fully explored in later chapters in this book.

Overall conclusion

Donor conception can be seen as a real opportunity for a family, but if prospective parents can work towards mourning their losses, it may be easier to relinquish the agony or the shame of their particular circumstances. This can open up the possibility of truly embracing what reproductive technologies can offer and of finding a new narrative for the whole family. The process of mourning can continue long after their family is complete, as a natural and inevitable response to psychic growth.

As Daniels (2004) says: "accepting the gift of donation is about embracing a whole genetic history." The question may now be one of how best to make room for others in the family? It is proposed that an acknowledgement of the donor is a natural corollary to the complete rethinking of the culture of secrecy. It is clear that Linda and Susie, the donor conceived young people interviewed for this book, have continued to actively think about their donor. Assuming that donor conceived people have increasing expectations of tracing their genetic relatives, is likely to continue to be a driving force for change. It may still be terribly hard though for some DC parents to think about the donor beyond the sum of the gametes they have donated.

At the workshops many people speak of a new dimension to their partnership and in other relationships, where the adversity and pain has in the end brought them closer, given what has been survived. New opportunities and doors opening through personal and relationship growth can lead to a sense of taking back control. Decision making can be hopeful, not necessarily ideal, but with purpose.

Reaching what Melanie Klein (1957) describes as "the depressive position" involves a real resolution, with a state of gratitude to the donor for the generosity of their egg or sperm. By this means, the potential of the donor to become a persecutor is reduced. Prospective parents might be able to use it to enhance their awareness that children are given to parents for safe keeping until they become independent, but they are never owned. Eventually, they will leave to create family boundaries of their own albeit within the family boundaries whence they originated. In creating new families, sons and daughters "in-law" cross the family boundaries created by the parents. They are not called "in-law" for nothing.

It is not a wish of this chapter to claim that this is the only way forward in preparing for DC parenthood. Clearly, given the HFEA statistics of the number of DC births annually, there are a very large number of DC families who are not represented here. But the workshop post evaluation questionnaires seem to attest to a positive outcome such that participants feel they leave with a notion that normal family life is possible, even when having to contemplate the fact that someone else's genes are mixed with their own or their partner's genes. The question remains whether taking account of different biological material as an unknown makes it harder to predict the impact on the relationship between parent(s) and/or with their child, or whether this is just in the nature of having children. One of the greatest compliments paid to the workshops as a testament to their success, is when a desire to be a parent moves from the position of considering the use of donor gametes as being a last resort, to a position of wanting a family created in this way.

Alternatively, finding a genuine feeling that it is possible to contemplate moving on in a life without children.

Notes

1. Sexually reproducing organisms, especially an ovum or sperm, which fuses with another gamete of the opposite type during fertilisation.
2. An agreement in which a donor will take an active role in child rearing and the child will have a relationship with them.
3. The Donor Conception Network is a support network of 1,700 mainly UK based families with children conceived with donated sperm, eggs, or embryos, those considering or undergoing donor conception procedures, and donor conceived people.
4. Human Fertilisation and Embryology Authority is the UK's independent regulator overseeing the use of gametes and embryos in fertility treatment and research.
5. IVF (*in vitro* fertilisation) is the joining of a woman's egg and a man's sperm in a laboratory dish.
6. Information on numbers and sex of half-siblings is available to parents (of donor conceived children) at any time and to donor conceived children from the age of sixteen. At eighteen, half-siblings who wish to make contact can be given details about each other by mutual consent. HFEA rules that a donor can contribute to a maximum of ten families.

References

Daniels, K. (2004). *Building a Family With the Assistance of Donor Insemination*. Palmerston: Dunmore.

Daniels, K. (2012). A family building approach to donor conception. Presented at the PROGRAR (British Association of Social Workers Project Group on Assisted Reproduction) Workshops at The Nuffield Foundation in London, July 2012.

Daniels, K., Thorn, P., & Westerbrooke, R. (2007). Confidence in the use of donor insemination: an evaluation of the impact of participating in a group preparation programme. *Human Fertility*, 10(1): 1–20.

Ehrensaft, D. (2000). Alternatives to the stork: fatherhood fantasies in donor insemination families. *Studies in Gender and Sexuality*, 1(4): 371–397.

Klein, M. (1957). *Envy and Gratitude*. London: Tavistock.

Menzies-Lyth, I. (1960). Social systems as a defence against anxiety. *Human Relations, 13*: 95–121.

Notman, M. T. (2011). Some thoughts about the psychological issues related to assisted reproductive technology. *Psychoanalytic Inquiry, 31*: 380–391.

Pines, D. (1990). Emotional aspects of infertility and its remedies. *Int. J. Psycho-Anal., 71*: 561–568.

Zalusky, S. (2000). Infertility in the age of technology. *Journal of the American Psychoanalytic Association, 48*: 1541–1562.

CHAPTER FIVE

"It takes a second to be a father but a lifetime to be a daddy." Men's experiences of infertility and donor conception

Amy Schofield

T he prospect of irreversible infertility pushes men and women, both individually and as couples, to evaluate both the strength of their desire to become parents and to question the very meaning of parenthood. Is being able to procreate and replicate your own genes the be-all-and-end-all of parenting? For some people it is, and the idea of adoption or of conceiving using another person's gametes is not something they would consider. If, however, parenthood is also about the wish to have and to raise a family, then for an infertile person to achieve this means they have to relinquish dreams of becoming a biological parent and allow others to intervene into what is usually a private and intimate concern.

The distress that women experience when faced with a diagnosis of infertility and in undergoing fertility treatment, is widely recognised. Men's feelings about being told they are infertile, however, or about choosing to engage in assisted reproductive technologies such as the donor insemination of their partners, are less well understood or publicly discussed.

In undertaking psychological research, I became aware of how the literature into infertility and donor conception (DC) biases very heavily towards the experiences of women. I was curious as to the reasons why men's voices had gone largely unheard. Was this because they were not being asked, or that men preferred to stay silent? My interest in trying to understand men's perspectives led me to carry out a qualitative study, to explore the lived experiences of eight men who had been diagnosed as infertile and who had subsequently become fathers through donor conception since 2005. It was in this year that legislation was introduced that lifted the anonymity of donors and afforded offspring the right to identify, from the age of eighteen, their donor and any potential half-siblings. My research was based on extended semi-structured interviews, to try and elucidate the common threads and themes that emerged from the men's narratives.

Many of the men told me that they had volunteered for this research in order to explore their own feelings, and so that the voices of men could be heard and understood more widely, and the stigma attached to this area be reduced. They have agreed to their words being used in this chapter, although their identities have been anonymised. Some have commented that they want their loved ones to read the findings of the study, so that they might gain a better insight into men's feelings and experiences.

Both the practical and emotional roads to fatherhood via donor conception are different for each man who embarks on this process. The men in this study spoke openly and movingly of their own very personal journeys. Their experiences cannot be taken as universally representative of all men who are either contemplating or experiencing parenthood via donor conception. I hope however, that describing their stories might provide some insight for others who are involved in donor conception and facilitate more open conversation between couples, families, and their wider social networks. It became clear that lack of public and private discourse around male factor infertility and donor conception left some of the men feeling very alone with their feelings. Many of them felt that medical and psychological services could have done more to understand and support them throughout the process. This chapter also makes suggestions for the structuring of such services.

I will begin by considering the cultural context in which a diagnosis of infertility and the achievement of parenthood by donor conception takes place, and will then draw on the stories of these eight men to trace their journeys from the point of discovery of infertility, to becoming a dad, and the early years of parenthood. The chapter outlines the losses, the grieving, and grievances this entailed; follows the paths they took and the changes that they and their relationships underwent. What emerged in most of their stories, was a gradual shift, from a profound sense of loss, to a feeling of becoming a proud father and a more robust man.

The cultural context of fatherhood

In Western culture, our representations of family life, as reflected in art, literature, advertisements, social policy, and even psychological and psychoanalytic research and theory, bias heavily towards the importance of motherhood, often seeming to render fathers somewhat invisible or irrelevant. Although recent decades have seen a revision of social attitudes in the West and attempts made to encourage, support, and make space for a more active involvement of fathers in childrearing, many men may be left somewhat at sea in understanding what "good fathering" entails. In social discourse, impregnation is portrayed as a demonstration of virility, and fatherhood can appear to become reduced merely to the passing on of one's genes. It could be argued the Christian story of the birth of Jesus presents a rather similar family model, and may have some parallels with the donor conception experience. As in donor conception, Mary's was a non-sexual conception, a gift donated by an unseen, omnipotent Being, who represents the absolute embodiment, or disembodiment, of fatherhood. The relationship between mother and baby is revered, while Joseph's part in the family narrative is, rather as some donor recipient fathers might feel, marginal.

The above is clearly a distorted and exaggerated portrayal. Yet I think that this model of parenthood, which appropriately emphasises the specialness of the mother–child relationship but glorifies the procreative father, while underplaying the role of the nurturing father on the ground, is deeply embedded in our cultural psyche. The subtle social messaging involved in this cultural iconography may encourage us to form an internal picture of parenthood as primarily a two-way, dyadic relationship between mother and child, rather than as a three-way, triangular relationship between mother, father, and child. This may be particularly unhelpful in view of the important role contemporary psychoanalysts believe fathers play in mental development by mediating between the more inward-looking intimacy of the mother–infant relationship and the outside world. This presence of the father offers the child a "third position" (Britton, 1989) that introduces to the infant an awareness that there is a separate external reality that exists outside of their relationship with their mother.

There is psychological research evidence that greater paternal involvement in childrearing is associated with benefits in all aspects of children's development: cognitive, educational, social, behavioural, and emotional (Lamb, 2004). Like mothering, fathering is not a single act of creation, but a life-long venture.

The focus in post-Freudian psychoanalytic research and theory has also centred on the mother–infant relationship, although more recently, there has been some interest in thinking about the importance of the father in the development of the child's internal world (Trowell & Etchegoyen, 2002). The roles of mothers and fathers in the psychoanalytic literature, however, as Mariotti (2012) points out, have largely been considered from the point of view of the child, rather than the parent. Very little has been written about the experience of becoming a father through donor conception. So what then are the experiences of men who are not able to become biological fathers?

Do men care about whether they can be fathers?

"Infertility" is defined by the National Institute of Clinical Excellence (NICE, 2004) as "the failure to conceive after two years of unprotected sex". It is thought to impact around one in seven couples (HFEA, 2010). This definition is a social, rather than a biological one, but, as Greil, Slauson-Blevins, and McQuillan (2010) point out, once diagnosed, further investigation into the causes of involuntary childlessness quickly becomes medicalised and gender-specific. They suggest that "no matter how medical practitioners may define infertility, couples do not define themselves as infertile or present for treatment unless they embrace parenthood as a desired social role" (p. 141). Unlike other medical conditions, infertility is not signalled by the "presence of pathological symptoms, but the absence of a desired state" (p. 141). Infertility has been referred to as a "non-event transition" (Koropatnick, Daniluk, & Pattinson, 1993), meaning that it is a significant emotional landmark in a person's life, but is not accompanied by any visible event happening.

Veevers (1980) found that having children is a social expectation, irrespective of racial, religious, ethnic, sexual, or social class divisions. Both social pressures and individual goals to procreate, which may seem like personal choices, sit on the back of what Dawkins (1989) describes as powerful biological imperatives: the need to ensure survival of the species by replicating our genes. Despite this, there has been a long standing cultural presumption that it is really only women who strongly desire to have children (Mason, 1993). There is ample research to suggest that this is a myth. Hadley and Hanley (2011) found that many men very much want children, and that like women, they are also profoundly distressed upon discovery of their infertility. Wischmann (2013) suggests it may just be that men show their feelings differently and less directly. It is important to recognise, however, that even when a man or woman wants to have children, this desire is rarely a straightforward one and is likely to be accompanied by contradictory, negative, and very mixed feelings. In couples facing infertility in one or both partners, such ambivalence may become exaggerated and lead to open or hidden splits between the couple around whether and how they wish to build a family via other routes.

Another common myth holds that infertility is usually a woman's "fault" (Andrews, Abbey, & Halman, 1992) and that male factor infertility is very rare. There is no evidence to support this belief. Figures suggest that 30% of couples presenting with difficulties in conceiving have problems that are attributable to male factor infertility. A further 30% of couples have difficulties related to female factor infertility and in 40% of presenting couples, problems appear to be joint or unexplained (Miles et al., 2009). According to Mason (1993, p. 3): "men are shadowy figures when it comes to infertility". She describes how lack of public recognition and discussion of male factor infertility probably fuels a widespread misperception that male factor infertility is rare, despite the even distribution between male and female contributions to couple infertility. This belief has continued to dominate thinking so profoundly that as recently as 1993, Snowden and Snowden commented that fertility clinics typically completed an exhaustive battery of tests to exclude female factors before investigating men, despite the greater ease of testing men.

There are a number of medical conditions that affect the quantity, quality, or motility of sperm and may lead to clinical sub-fertility. With time, these men may still be able to achieve fertilisation, either "naturally" or through a variety of fertility treatments designed to facilitate the meeting of sperm and egg. Less commonly, men may be diagnosed as "infertile", such as in instances of azoospermia, where no sperm are produced. There are some medical and surgical procedures to try and correct conditions associated with infertility, but in the absence of these working, the men are unable to achieve fertilisation or use assisted reproductive technologies using their own gametes. Infertility treatments then set out to overcome the problem of involuntary childlessness, rather than address the underlying medical causes. This research focuses on the experiences of this latter group of men, where donor conception using *in vitro* fertilisation (IVF) or intrauterine insemination (IUI) with third-party donated sperm may be the only options available to couples who wish to experience a pregnancy and birth. This solution circumvents the male partner altogether and concentrates treatment on the female partner (Berger, 1980). So what is this experience like for men?

The discovery of infertility: the loss of the ideal and unborn self

My choice to begin the men's stories at the point of their discovery of infertility, may give the impression that this was the start of their journeys. This would of course be wrong. For most, diagnosis came at the end of months or years of trying, waiting, and hoping to conceive naturally, followed by extensive and intrusive medical tests and examinations. Each of the eight men told a different story of how they found themselves in a clinic room, receiving the news that they would be unable to have a child who would be genetically related to them. This moment was however the landmark that joined them all, so perhaps is a good place to begin.

The men all described powerful emotional reactions to the news that they would not be able to have their own genetic child. All of them had wanted and imagined having children, and the discovery of their infertility stirred up a number of challenges and feeling of loss.

"I didn't feel a true man"

Raphael-Leff (2003, p. 45) talks about infertility as a disturbance of "generative identity". To a greater or lesser extent, all the men in this study commented on feeling the diagnosis to be an attack on their sense of manhood and to represent the loss of an "ideal" self they had wanted to see themselves as and a future they had imagined would be theirs. Various authors have commented on the tendency for biological fatherhood to be seen as an indication of "masculinity" and "sexual potency" within our society. Gannon, Glover, and Abel (2004) explored social constructions of male infertility and suggested that there is a tendency to mistakenly equate male factor infertility with impotence and emasculation. They suggest this has contributed to male factor infertility remaining hidden and unspoken about, leading to men feeling isolated and stigmatised. Crawshaw, (2011) suggested that in our culture, fatherhood is seen as an expression of "manliness", demonstrated by the ability to impregnate. Mason (1993) similarly found that the concept of "manliness" was more closely associated with impregnating a woman than being a "father". Humphrey (1977) suggested that childless men tended to associate the notion of "father-hood" with masculine identity, whereas women's perceptions of "motherhood" were more associated with contentment and the achievement of life goals.

In this study, it seemed that society's conflation of fertility and masculinity had been internalised by many of the men. Dylan identi-fied how "gentle social messaging" linking sexual potency, masculine strength, and fertility, had infiltrated every sphere of his life and had remained unquestioned by him until his own fertility was brought under inspection. Many spoke openly about how the discovery of infertility had made them doubt their sense of themselves as "real" or "true" men. This seemed most acute for the men who experienced developmental delays at puberty, leading to investigations that had highlighted conditions associated with infertility.

> *Dylan*: All my kind of peers were growing and becoming men if you like, and because all of that was delayed in me, there was something in my head that was kind of thinking: "you're not a proper man, kind of thing, you're missing a piece".

> *Gary*: As a man, as a bloke, everyone wants to be able to feel they can have children and if you can't, then I think there's definitely a feeling of: "oh you're not a true man".

For men where the discovery came unexpectedly in adulthood, they described the impact more as a "dent" to their sense of masculine identity. Their concerns seemed to relate more to a sense of personal disappointment and "guilt" about denying their partner and parents by failing "essentially to do what you're put on earth to do" (William).

> *Sam:* Not being able to get Yasmin pregnant ... there was a massive amount of guilt around that.

Dave, Graham, and Jed did not feel as strongly that their masculine identity was compromised by the diagnosis. They felt they had grown up with a family discourse of manliness that placed less emphasis on the importance of sexuality and fertility. They all, however, had a sense they were letting their families down by not being able to continue their genetic line.

A recurring theme in many of the men's accounts was a feeling that they were alone with their difficulties. Watching others around them becoming pregnant and enjoying growing their families with apparent ease was painful and caused many of the men and their partners to want to distance themselves from these friends.

Talking to other men and couples who were going through the same challenges seemed to help considerably. Perceptions of themselves as "abnormal" or de-masculinised were often quashed when they met other "manly", "normal" men going through similar ordeals. They realised they were not alone.

> *Josh:* actually it's meeting a guy who has had a child who is DC who seems perfectly normal, actually more than normal, a decent, nice guy.

The loss of the imagined future

The men recounted how the discovery of infertility had forced them to re-evaluate their expected life-journeys. Some men spoke of the imagined future that had been unfairly stripped from them.

> *Graham:* I had a picture of myself in the future for a long time and suddenly that's not going to be anymore.

Sam spoke of having to: "let go of that kid I had in my mind's eye that was basically a little replica of me". This evocative description perhaps typifies the essence of "reproductive" failures: the inability to replicate one's self and genes.

Many of the men experienced the discovery that they would not be able to have genetic children of their own as a form of bereavement.

William described how he loved kids:

> *William*: The thought of having my own children was very important to me, and then to have that snatched away from me was … yeah … I would term it a bereavement.

On learning of their infertility, most of the men described feelings of "depression", "powerlessness", "anger", and "guilt". This was consistent with the findings of other researchers such as Hadley and Hanley (2011) and Peterson, Gold, and Feingold (2007). For some of the men, infertility had stirred existential questions about the meaning of life, provoking a heightened awareness of their own mortality. Two men had questioned the point of "going on" and described having had some suicidal thoughts.

Martin and Doka (2000) found that men and women characteristically deal with and demonstrate their grieving in different ways that are in line with social gender roles and expectations. They claim that socialising in early childhood discourages boys and men from showing their feelings openly. As a result, they suggest, men tend instead to develop problem-solving, pragmatic solutions to dealing with emotional concerns. As has been found in other studies, the men in my research described feeling profoundly distressed by their infertility. Many of them, however, found it difficult to talk about this openly and were left struggling with their feelings alone. As Burns and Covington (1999, p. 8) put it: "when it comes to infertility, typically women weep, and men watch".

Making decisions: the long road to fatherhood

All the men described the arduous process of tests, treatments, endless waiting, raised hopes, and repeated disappointments involved in the route from first diagnosis to becoming a father.

> *William*: Five years of worry and decision-making and then IVF and then the pregnancy and then the long labour …

> *Sam*: We felt like we were going down a road that took us to this family and suddenly we found our road was a dead end, or it didn't even exist. We were lost … and that was what the donor conception part of it, that's what it gave us, that suddenly there was a road, but it look a lot longer.

Describing his emotional journey, Sam goes on to say: "I don't know how many times I built that bridge, I kept trying to build it, it kept falling down".

In the two extracts above Sam shifts from talking about the path he and his partner trod together, as a couple, to the solitary journey he felt he undertook emotionally. This oscillation was reflected in each of the men's stories. The majority of the men talked about initially experiencing the infertility as their own personal loss: one that they felt their partners neither understood, nor had entitlement to mourn.

Graham: My partner was saying that she was having as tough a time as I was, and I kept thinking: God well you're not, I know which shoes I would like to be in. I would rather be the fertile one, you know, and have a partner that was infertile!

For some this initial resentment of their partner's expressed grief was replaced by a greater appreciation of what they too had lost and the struggles they were undergoing.

Sam: I didn't really believe that she had the same level of loss that I did, but of course she did, because we didn't have the genetic kid that we wanted or that we envisaged.

For some, the experiences brought them closer to their partner and consolidated an appreciation that they were in it with each other.

Dylan: We were kind of on edge, but on edge together, so it was alright.

All but one of the men described the moment of discovery of their infertility as a vivid "flashbulb" memory that they remembered with crystal clarity and described in minute detail in the interviews.

Jed: I was driving home and it was about two hours away, the doctor's office, in a fairly rural area at the time and I remember pulling off into a park. There was a park and a waterfall and it was winter and it was icy and snowy and I remember pulling off into this parking lot next to the river, which was the central attraction to this small park, and just cried. I was just terribly devastated.

For most men, this flashbulb memory was then followed by a period of fragmented, "blurred" recollection.

Sam: I don't really remember very well because I stared at my feet quite a lot and shut down mentally I think, I went into autopilot.

Some men described this as a time of "numb inertia". Josh talked of a sense of "walking around in a daze", neither looking for, nor finding solutions. In common with other men, he commented that: "you kind of switch yourself off emotionally from the whole experience". It seemed as if physiological infertility became equivalent to a kind of psychological castration, which left men feeling a sense of despairing stuckness.

The decision to undertake donor conception, rather than pursue adoption as a means of creating a family, seemed largely to stem from a desire for the baby to be genetically related to at least one of them. There was a preference of both partners to be able to experience the process of pregnancy and birth together.

> *Dylan*: We also really wanted to go through the process of being pregnant and growing the baby.

When it comes to donor conception, Blaser, Maloigne-Katz, and Gigon (1988) found that in most instances, treatment is initiated by the female partner. The majority of the men in this study also identified that it was their partner who had been the driving force in initiating donor conception to create a family and the men, initially reluctantly, followed behind. Sam described how: "Yasmin pretty much took over, she started doing everything."

There was a sense of some of the men finding it difficult to protest or deny their partners the possibility of a genetic child and a fear of the possible breakdown of their relationship if they did, as well as a feeling of guilt that they were denying their partner. Ultimately, it seemed that pragmatism was the primary factor for men agreeing to donor conception.

> *Dave*: It was the only option if Louise was going to have a natural birth and absolutely that's what she wanted and I wanted her to have it as well. There was no other option. If she wanted to biologically have a child, she was going to have to do it with someone else's sperm.

Raphael-Leff (2013) talks about parents who, if when facing irreversible infertility fail to emotionally process their pain associated with what she describes as the "presence of absence", run the risk of passing on a psychological legacy of loss and disappointment to their children.

Jed described the need to "grieve for your own loss" before embarking on "building a family". He spoke of the importance of his own genetic heritage in making him who he was, but expressed a need to relinquish this so as not to pass on a "sense of loss to my daughters".

Re-defining the meaning of fatherhood

As the men went down the road of donor conception, many consciously or unconsciously seemed to re-define their ideas about what it meant to be a "father", moving from a biological to a social construction of parenthood. They shifted from a position of wanting to create a baby with their own genes, to an understanding of the importance of creating the "person"; differentiating the "doing" of the act of conception from the "being" of the "daddy on the ground" (Jed). As Gary poignantly stated: "it takes a second to be a father, but a lifetime to be a daddy."

> *Josh*: That's actually not being a father just because you've gone out there and given your sperm, that just proves that you can do the act or whatever. Being a father is picking them up from school, feeding them. Just being there. That's being a father, isn't it?

The donor conception procedure disembodies the "biological father", while creating a "social father". Ehrensaft (2000, p. 390) describes how: "as we watch sperm transformed into men and men reduced to sperm, we witness both the construction and the destruction of the father".

All the men in the study were involved in some way with "making the baby", whether through choosing a donor, administering hormone injections, or attending medical appointments, as well as being there at the birth. Greater involvement seemed to act as an important way for the men to engage with the process and was associated with an increased sense of control and easier early bonding with their child.

> *Dylan*: Giving injections and stuff like that. It was kind of exciting when we were in the middle of doing it . . . and the kind of physicality of having to give Leila an injection and stuff it was kind of like: "it's happening!"

The fact that the process of donor insemination physically "bypasses" the male partner, can result in men feeling excluded and an "unnecessary piece of the puzzle" (Sam). Fertility clinics that are focused on women and "Mother and Baby Units", leave little space for men. This practice persists despite long-standing research demonstrating its negative impact on men's well-being (Mason, 1993; Wischmann, 2013). The men in this study talked about how medical and support services around infertility and parenthood sometimes worked in a way that they experienced as excluding them and left them feeling irrelevant and nameless.

> *Graham*: The consultant writes to my wife and I'm actually admitted to the clinic under her name. You don't ever get referred as a man.

Those men in the study who perceived that medical professionals viewed them as an "equal" partner in the treatment, ·seemed to then find it easier to go through the donor conception process and bond with their child. They commented on how being involved at every step helped them come to terms with their infertility and donor conception and strengthened their relationships with their partner and child.

Donor insemination transforms the moment of conception from something that is private and intimate between a couple to something "artificial" and public, no longer under personal control. The clinical, medical, and impersonal atmosphere of fertility clinics helped some men to distance the procedure from fantasies of sexual impregnation by another man. These fantasies sometimes included the doctor carrying out the procedure as well as the disembodied figure of the donor.

> *Jed*: There was a male doctor involved in the fertility treatments. What did I think about that? You know to cut right down to it, here is this guy who is going to get my wife pregnant and I'm not, you know? Sure all of these thoughts occurred to me but I didn't take them seriously, I felt that the care was all very professional. Of course part of it is the kind of building, which is very clinical, very professional, and there are times that you want that distance . . . it wasn't impersonal but you want it to be very . . . this is *professional* this is a *procedure*.

On the other hand some men experienced the clinics as emotionally cold and excluding and would have welcomed greater acknowledgement of them and their feelings and being more included in the process of creating this new family.

The joys and challenges of becoming a dad

Once conception had been achieved, some men remarked on their relief at being able, for the first time, to enter the "mainstream". Along with couples that had conceived naturally, they attended "normal" scans, antenatal appointments and classes, as well as the birth of their baby.

Sam: We purposely left [asking about the gender of the baby] as a surprise 'cos you just start getting back into the routine of stuff, once you've conceived and we just started going for the normal scans. In a way it's kind of normal, now we're going through the stuff that everyone else goes through. It's been more normal than I thought it was going to be to be honest.

Many of the couples were driven to take the more "natural" path (Dylan), wherever possible, as an antidote to the "artificial" interventions they had undergone. For example, Dylan and his partner fought for a natural birth over the Caesarean section that was being suggested. He felt that this, in addition to the choice to breastfeed, would facilitate their bonding with the baby.

The birth of the children stirred a complex mixture of feelings. Joy, excitement, and relief sometimes ran alongside anxiety, a sense of exclusion, and a difficulty in feeling entitled to claim the baby as their own. These issues were sometimes heightened when it came to decisions around whom to tell about the donor conception. As with any new birth, people enjoy looking for real or imagined similarities between baby and parents. Comments from family friends such as "Oh he's the spit of you Davey boy!" felt difficult to manage. Dave enjoyed being seen as similar to his son, however this was tempered by some discomfort that he was withholding the truth.

Bonding

There are powerful and sometimes unhelpful social expectations that the bond between both mothers and fathers with their babies should be forged instantly and that there is something wrong if this does not happen. There is a substantial body of research to suggest that, regardless of the means of conception, for many families attachment and bonding may take time to develop and this is completely normal. Fathers commonly feel excluded from the early intimacy of the mother–baby dyad (Fägerskiöld, 2008), sometimes failing to realise how crucial their role as fathers can be in supporting the mother and offering a different relationship to the baby. It is not surprising perhaps that in families where the father is not genetically linked, but the mother is, the sense of exclusion can be magnified. Some men in the study did speak of the bond between them and their child happening immediately at birth, but for the majority, this took time. Dave was typical of the men when he said:

> *Dave*: I'll be honest and say that the love for my children has been relatively slow burning and has just sort of grown as they get older.

The absence of falling in love at first sight caused anguish and anxiety for some men:

> *Josh*: I always knew I wanted to have a parent . . . I mean I wanted to *be* a parent, but I didn't know, when our children were going to be born, how I would feel and actually when Zack, my eldest son, was born, I felt nothing for him at all. I felt no emotional attachment to this child at all. That scared me.

Josh had not had a relationship with his own father when growing up. He had been told that he had fathered many children with different mothers. In this extract, Josh inadvertently makes clear his longing for a father himself. His description of his father hinted at a fantasy that he was a hyper-virile character who, like the donor, sired but did not raise his children.

The fathers in the son

Studies of child-gender preferences in naturally conceived families suggest that men tend to "favour" sons (Dahl & Moretti, 2008; Goldberg, 2009) and spend more time with sons than daughters (Manlove & Vernon-Feagans, 2002; Raley & Bianchi, 2006). An unanticipated finding of this study, that cannot be taken as generally applicable without further investigation, was that the men consistently reported finding bonding with their sons more complex and problematic than with their daughters. There seemed to be different "fathers" who were consciously and unconsciously fantasised and perceived within the donor-conceived son at different times. Mirrored in the faces of their sons, the men alternately imagined: the donor; their own father; the child themselves as a parental figure; and only with time, themselves as the father. Some men imagined that their sons would be born as hyper-masculine, or as boys of oedipal age (three to five years old), who might further threaten the men's sense of masculine identity and undermine their confidence in being a good-enough "alpha role-model" for their sons.

Dylan: I don't know why but I envisaged them coming about as five years old or you know, kind of toddlers, kind of really loud, shrieky boy toddlers, that wanted to play football and do "man" things.

Sons appeared to more clearly represent the donor: a more "virile" and "potent" man, who had successfully impregnated their wives, and thus were a painful reminder of what they had been unable to achieve.

William: As soon as I picked her up I was you know, completely smitten with her and remain so. With Jack ... I was overjoyed too but it's been less, it's been less ... it's taken me longer to bond with him, and it's getting easier 'cos he's started smiling and cooing and all that malarkey, but I suppose I look down at Jack and I do see, ... I see the donor, which I'm finding harder than I thought I would.

Why might these fathers experience greater difficulty in coming to terms with the birth of a son than a daughter and feel a greater sense of exclusion from the mother–baby dyad in the early months after birth? Thinking about this from a psychoanalytic perspective, Freud pointed out that some of the young child's earliest curiosity in his unconscious life is about where babies come from. Between the ages of about two to three years, the boy gleans a basic sense of the facts of life and has to come to terms with the idea that his parents have a procreative sex life from which he is excluded. During the "phallic" stage of development, which Freud defined as occurring between the ages of three and five, a desire is awakened to possess his mother and of rivalrous feelings in relation to his father. His awareness that his father is bigger and stronger, arouses unconscious fears of retaliation by his father. Ultimately, he must also acknowledge his mother's choice of his father over him to share this intimacy with and the sense that his father is capable of procreation in a way that he is not. Freud referred to this dilemma as the Oedipus complex. The boy compensates himself for this humiliating realisation by reassuring fantasies that he will be able to have children himself when he grows up. He attempts to resolve his oedipal conflict by later identifying with his father. The man who is diagnosed as infertile is deprived of this possibility of comfort and resolution and may experience this as a form of attack on his manhood that re-awakens childhood feelings of helplessness, rage, and inadequacy. This model of psychological development relates to the unconscious and does not reflect the actual parental relationship or family situation. It remains to be explored how growing up with a dad who is understood not to have been procreative may be reflected in conscious and unconscious fantasies.

The choice to try to resolve childlessness by donor conception gives rise to fantasies about the donor as a more fertile man who is possibly also imagined as a more sexually potent male. Even though the man consciously knows there is no sexual contact between the donor and his partner, the impregnation of her by this man may nevertheless feel like a powerful act of intimacy, from which he is excluded.

After the birth, there is normally a period when mothers become intensely preoccupied with and absorbed by their baby (Winnicott, 1958). This may heighten the father's feeling of exclusion, echoing earlier, childhood fantasies of exclusion from the parental union. Perhaps for men who have become fathers through donor conception, these feelings may be more intense in relation to a baby boy than a girl. In the visual appearance of the baby boy, who should have mirrored *his* genes, been the product of *his* own unborn self, he sees another father. This baby boy becomes the mother's new love. This may re-awaken for the father a sense of inadequacy about not being able to procreate, similar to that felt in childhood competition with his own father. Other fantasies may also emerge, that his son will also turn out to be more of a "man" than him and threaten future feelings of emasculation as he grows up. Some of the men in this study referred to fantasies that the baby boy would emerge as a vigorous young child, rather than a baby. Perhaps this reflects some combined representation of the donor, the father's own father, and the oedipal boy that he feels reduced to.

Feelings of threat, exclusion, and ambivalence towards the baby boy and his partner, are likely to be experienced guiltily and silently by the donor-conception father. They may co-exist alongside feelings of overwhelming joy and love for the baby and gratitude towards the donor. As the father's bond with his son develops, such feelings of threat, loss, and ambivalence seemed to fade for the men in this study. It seems quite possible, however, that they may be re-evoked at future stages of the child's development.

Understandably, it took time for the men to see themselves as the father reflected in the faces, behaviour, and personalities of their children. It was notable that when men began to identify the distinctive personality of their child developing and also to recognise aspects of their own mannerisms in their child, this bond began to strengthen. Following Josh's comment above about his lack of early bonding with his first son, he went on to tell me about the strong and loving relationship that had developed between them both.

> *Josh*: We're actually, we're incredibly alike, we really are. Clearly we're not genetically linked, obviously, but we're just soul-mates, you know, the way we think, the way we . . . so maybe it's sort of discovering him.

Josh was able to see Zack as a person in his own right and notes their similarities and the close bond that has grown between them.

When selecting a donor, many families strive to find a good "match" to the non-genetic partner, with the belief that this will increase the likelihood of successful bonding.

> *Gary*: Because when they were trying to match me with another donor, you know he's a really good looking boy and we're really happy. Also something that people said as he was young, it was like "oh well he looks exactly like you" . . . and that gives you more chance to bond with the child.

Gary also describes the joy of noticing his own character traits beginning to be mirrored in his son:

> *Gary*: He says "hello" to people in the park and I say "hello" to people, so it's a classic case of nurture or nature.

Dave explained his pleasure in noticing the "really brown eyes" that he, his son, and his mother all shared.

Despite all the hurdles they had had to jump on the way to fatherhood, all the men expressed feelings of joy and gratitude for the "brilliant" and "normal" family they had attained. Many spoke of their children as "special" and the ones they were "meant" to have. William and Gary maintained they would not change their infertility as:

> *Gary*: If we had had our own children, we wouldn't have Tommy and Tommy is brilliant to have.

Disclosing to the child and discussing the donor conception with others

One of the biggest challenges facing recipient parents is the matter of if, how, and when they might tell their children about their donor origins. This can be a fraught topic and one that couples may well differ over (Daniels, Lewis, & Gillett, 1995). Public and professional opinions and advice have evolved over time. Historically, medical professionals advocated total secrecy within families, advising parents that "under no circumstances should they, or need they, ever tell the child the method of conception—in fact they should forget about it themselves" (Bloom, 1957, p. 207). Professional opinion has transformed, and most medical and mental health professionals and support groups now advocate disclosure (Montuschi, 2006). Josh, however, explained how he had still been advised by a doctor: "If I were you I would have this procedure then forget it ever happened".

The recommendation to disclose to children follows research, for example by Feingold (2011), who found evidence that secrecy and non-disclosure may cause psychological damage to the child and undermine trust and honesty within families. Brewaeys (2001), noted secrecy within families associated with donor conception had a negative effect on the father–child attachment relationship, particularly when fathers had not adequately grieved the genetic child they would not have. Lycett and colleagues (2004) also found evidence of more positive parent–child relationships in disclosing than non-disclosing families. Berger (1980), meanwhile, suggested total secrecy also prevents the "working-through" of conflicts between parents.

Despite this, research suggests that although the number of parents telling their children about their DC conception may have been growing (Crawshaw, 2008; Freeman, Jadva, Kramer, & Golombok, 2009), "the majority of children conceived in this way remain unaware that the person they know as their father is not a genetic parent" (Golombok et al., 2011, p. 230).

We may hypothesise that for men who have very strong fears of an internally emasculating father, donor conception treatment or being open about having had children this way, is very challenging. Perhaps professionals who continue to recommend denial, non-disclosure, and personal forgetting of the fact of donor conception, are projecting their own fears of their internal father on to prospective donor users in an unhelpful manner, even though the advice may be consciously given with helpful intent.

For parents who do wish to disclose to their children, however, it is perhaps unsurprising that the choice of when and how to tell brings a number of challenges and worries. It would seem informing offspring at a younger age of their donor conception origins has bene-fits for their psychological adjustment (Golombok et al., 2011), while those who discover their origins accidently, or later in life, appear to show increased rates of anger, feelings of betrayal, and distrust (Jadva et al., 2009). Golombok et al (2011) recommend children are told in pre-school years. This information can then become part of their story early on and they grow up always having known (Montuschi, 2006). Burns and Pettle (2002) and Hunter, Salter-Ling, and Glover (2000) found parents who told their child at an early age felt it somewhat easier to do than those who delayed. They also identified men tended to be more worried than women that telling would threaten the rela-tionship between them and their child. MacDougall and colleagues (2007) found that although men were concerned about disclosure, they experienced positive feelings of relief once it was done. In this study, despite men's initial anxiety about disclosure, those who had already told their children, all felt they had made the right choice and were relieved it had been done. Some felt increasing the amount the DC was discussed in their family actually reduced the chance that it may be used against them in the future.

In The UK the Donor Conception Network offers information and workshops to support parents in telling and talking to their children (Montuschi, 2006).

The effects of the lifting of donor anonymity

In 2005 the law in the UK changed, and the anonymity of donors was lifted. Using identifiable donor gametes raises the likely future iden-tification of both the donor and any half-siblings and opens up the possibility that their child might invite these biologically related strangers into their lives. While a few of the men welcomed this as a possibility, it also represented a source of concern. The prospect of the donor entering into their family lives aroused both anxiety and ambivalent feelings towards the donor.

On the one hand, the men all expressed feelings of immense grat-itude towards the donor for giving them the opportunity to be fathers.

Josh: I don't know how I feel. I am incredibly grateful. "Thank you very much 'cos you have given me two of the most important people in my life", and if he was here today I would actually hug him.

This appreciation was coupled however, with "raw", painful feelings.

> *Graham*: The way we think about that is grateful, relieved, grateful, happy, that's how we generally felt about it . . . but initially it's quite hard to use the word donor . . . because it was a lot of rawness still that you carry around.

Gratitude was also accompanied with a threat that this man may re-enter their lives and claim their children back.

> *William*: They have to abstain. It is a very conscious decision to make and now that anonymity is lifted . . . they have to be aware that in eighteen years' time you might get a knock on the door saying "Hello! I'm your genetic offspring." So it's not . . . a small thing to do. So I am full of admiration for anyone who would do that and I feel . . . nothing but sort of gratitude . . . in that he has enabled me to have a family. But that's tempered, I suppose . . . by a slight wariness. I am aware of the fact that Jack and Lily might want to go and track him down and I don't know quite how I would feel about that.

Whose business is it?

Currently there is no legal requirement for parents to inform their children that they are donor conceived. This creates a dilemma for recipient parents about whether or not to tell their children. In contrast to research suggesting that most families still do not disclose to their children (Golombok et al., 2011), all the men in this study felt it was their responsibility not to withhold this information from their children. They all feared, however, the possible repercussions: that their child might reject them in favour of a biological "father", whom they would at some point be able to identify and find. The House of Commons Science and Technology Select Committee (2005) expressed concern that lifting anonymity might reduce the likelihood of disclosure to children. This research supports the findings of Blyth and Frith (2008) and Crawshaw (2008), who found no evidence that the lifting of donor anonymity had reduced parental disclosure. The men's worries about possible rejection following disclosure seemed to have been overridden by the desire for and belief in the importance of openness and honesty.

In this group of men, Gary seemed to be struggling with this decision the most and was the only father who had not yet made a firm decision to tell his son about his donor conception origins. He worried that the disclosure would damage the emerging and developing bond between them and had an urge to maintain his son's belief that he was his biological father.

> *Gary*: I'd feel really heartbroken if I have to say "you're not mine" as such. "You are mine, but you're not mine" it's total opposites, you know, very difficult.

Choosing the "right" time and way to tell

In line with research by MacDougall and colleagues (2007), the men in this study and their partners, chose a mixture of disclosure strategies. Most had employed a "seed-planting" approach, whereby they used storytelling to begin informing their children while they were preverbal, so that they "always knew". Others opted for a "right-time" strategy, waiting until they felt their children were old enough to understand the information, but young enough that they did not feel they were "keeping it" from them.

William spoke of his uncertainty about the "right" time to tell his children:

> *William*: I think we just have to sort of choose our moment really, when they're old enough to realise what we are telling them but not so old that they're like "why didn't you tell me earlier?"

Dave wanted his children to know when they were still toddlers and talked about his discomfort in how to find the right words to do that:

> *Dave*: He was probably about eighteen months so … that's a little bit weird, 'cos it contains words like sperm and stuff which you do think like if somebody random came into my house they'd think, "what are these people teaching their children?"

Josh recalled the different responses of his sons to the information as they grew and developed.

> *Josh*: They're kind of like growing into it, the older they get. There was this book … it was all about this girl. I read it to my two boys and Zack, my eldest, got it, he really understood it. Chris went "what do you mean they haven't got the same jeans? … why would they be wearing the same jeans?" Took it very literal and fell asleep. Zack and I burst into tears and

then we had just a really, really lovely moment 'cos he was sort of understanding.

For Josh, his son's realisation did not signal rejection, but an intense moment of closeness.

"You're not my real daddy!"

For the majority of the men, the decision about whether or not to tell their child was coupled with a fear that one day their children would turn around and reject them with accusations that they were not their "real" fathers.

> *Gary*: If you were having an argument you know and then he would say "you're not my real daddy" sort of thing and that would be awful . . . that's the number one isn't it, then you just have to walk out there . . . But that's looking at arguments when he's fourteen, fifteen, sixteen, that's when it all comes out.

It might be helpful for these fears to be considered in the light of "normal" child development and necessary separation from parents. Freud (1909c), described the "Family romance", whereby children imagine that they are really another (more idealised) person's child. He thought that this was a consequence of the child's resentment of the boundaries created by parents saying "no" to the child. It is therefore a normal part of child development for such doubt to be expressed to parents. For a donor recipient parent however, such utterances may be experienced as particularly painful and rejecting. It may sap a parent's confidence in their child's love for them, arousing anxiety that their child will reject them in favour of the donor. It would seem helpful for donor recipient parents to understand these "normal" developmental processes and be aware of the psychological stresses they may pose. Fear of rejection might be a factor contributing to parents choosing not to inform their children of their donor origins. It is more likely, however, that attempts to deny, disavow, or repress the facts of the donor's existence would seem to run the risk of actually stirring such anxieties in recipient parents. Being fully conscious of and thinking about the psychological consequences of the donor's real and imagined presence in the family is potentially a way of containing these anxieties and may be a useful focus for therapy if men chose to pursue this.

The strangers that lurk in the shadows

The lifting of donor anonymity seemed to raise fantasies both about .the donor and any half-siblings he may also have helped to create, that might be at large in their communities. These seemed to be brought to mind in everyday situations for many of the men. Graham described the repeated shock of imagining seeing his child in the faces of strangers everywhere he went.

> *Graham*: We'll be at the swimming pool or in the queue at Tesco's and another sort of six-year-old is running around and he is the spitting image of Peter and you think, it's a slim chance, but you do see some children, and there is something about them. We were at the museum yesterday, and this child, and I almost walked up behind to say "Peter". Completely different clothes and everything, but the face . . . oh! That *could* be a sibling.

Clearly the decision about whether to use a known, rather than an unknown, donor brings different challenges. Put off by the idea of an unknown stranger, Sam chose his brother as the donor. He was aware however of the potential blurring of roles this could create within their family and the distress he would feel if his son were to run up to his brother and call him his "daddy".

The power of the donor is perhaps also reflected in the fear that the donor will eventually return to claim their child. On a practical level, it remains an uncertainty about whether children will want to search out their donor and what kind of relationship between the child, the parents, and the donor might then follow. But what is feared is an imagined or fantasised return, where the presence of the donor diminishes the sense the recipient parent has of being the legitimate father.

Talking to friends and family

Many of the men worried about sharing the information about their infertility with family or peers, for fear of humiliation or rejection. William described how scarce and skewed the coverage of male factor infertility is, which he thought contributed to a lack of public understanding and exacerbated men's feelings of isolation and reluctance to talk.

> *William*: Male infertility is relatively sort of um obscure and rare in its coverage, in being talked about

A "boys don't cry" attitude at school left Gary convinced that he could not share his anxieties around developmental delay at puberty with his peers.

> *Gary*: Fourteen years old at an all boys' school. You'd never say that sort of thing, no. You probably wouldn't have a little shoulder, it would be "oh there he is!" No I definitely didn't. You would have been called "Jaffa" you know, seedless sort of thing. People never really spoke at school like that anyway, you know. You talk about football.

Gary seemed to be in internal conflict. On the one hand was his desire to be open and a belief that keeping it "all bottled up" could lead him to feeling "bitter". On the other hand he continued to find it difficult to talk.

Both Sam and Josh described difficulties in being able to express and share their experiences of both infertility and donor conception in a straightforward way to friends and family. They spoke of indirect ways they had disclosed to peers and how this had fallen on "deaf ears".

Sam described his disappointment when a male friend encouraged him to "keep that to [him]self". He explained:

> *Sam*: Yasmin did [a run] to raise money for [a DC charity], and this is again an insight into the way that men deal with the situation. Everybody knows why she did that, it was really obvious, but whenever we met up with blokes in particular they would ask about [the run]:"how did the run go?" which is a way of asking, "how is the fertility treatment going?" basically.

Josh described how difficult he found it to tell even close friends, lest they would "reject or think badly of [him]".

By contrast, some of the men's initial reluctance to discuss their infertility or donor conception with friends was replaced by surprise and relief that most of the friends they had told had been supportive and had welcomed conversations.

> *Dylan*: I was pretty overwhelmed really by how supportive they were, particularly the guys. I kind of thought they wouldn't want to talk about it . . . but all of them from your standard guys to the guys who are really big, butch men were really happy to talk

All of the men described the dangers of secrecy and of suppressing emotions—for themselves, their families, and for other men experiencing male factor infertility and donor conception. Despite their initial trepidation in opening up, almost all the men commented on how when they had been able to do this, talking honestly had helped them to both come to terms with their infertility and donor conception, and to repair their damaged sense of self.

Dylan spoke of talking, particularly to his partner, as painful but reparative:

> *Dylan*: I just didn't want to have to talk about it . . . 'cos it reminded me . . . that it was real . . . and I suppose that it was probably talking to Leila that you, as time goes on, you feel a little bit less like it's a raw wound kind of thing . . . maybe you grieve a little bit and then it becomes something you are naturally more comfortable talking about.

Many of the men described the benefits of being given the space to talk. Throughout his interview, William repeatedly spoke of the value of being offered an "emotional sounding board" by friends, family, and counsellors.

Some spoke about who "deserved" to know, suggesting there was a filtering process in how the information was shared:

> *Dave*: They're not important enough in my life that they need to know. I don't feel anybody has a kind of right to know this.

Many of the men used variations on the phrase: "it's private, not secret". This gave me the impression that while men believed it was appropriate to talk about the donor conception, there were limits to what, when, where, and to whom disclosure should take place. This was something that was the subject of on-going negotiation with their partners.

Dylan, Dave, and Jed spoke about who they thought had "rights" over this information and the sharing of it. Dylan noted that there was a point at which he and his partner would have to relinquish control of the information, which would become the property of their children:

> *Dylan*: I guess at some point the information stops being ours and starts being theirs.

Breaking the silence

Jed, Sam, Dave, and Josh spoke of the importance of "breaking the silence" around male factor infertility and donor conception at wider

societal levels, in order to reduce stigma and increase public awareness. These men engaged in and advocated social action as an active
attempt to gain some mastery over their experiences and to reach out
to help other dads who were going through this. Between them, they
had written plays; published pieces about controversies in donor
conception; set up and run support groups; and had been involved in
fund-raising events for donor conception. A few of the men cited the
desire to enable a more open and public debate about male infertility,
donor conception, and men's health issues generally as a reason for
having engaged in this study.

Seeking support: real help or "social services for foetuses"

Several of the men experienced the compulsory pre-donor conception
counselling session as more akin to an "examination", designed to
assess their suitability to "go ahead and have a family" (Graham).
They perceived the experiences as a "hurdle" to get past, rather than
a space to consider hopes and concerns.

> Dylan: It was actually framed as "come and talk to us". And I went: right
> this is an exam; we need to prep for this. It just comes across as a bit like
> social services for foetuses.

By contrast, three of the men spoke of the value of more open-
ended therapy and of talking to counsellors who were independent
from the tangled emotional relationships in their families and social
networks:

> Sam: There was no way we could have got, gone down this road without
> that support and without just getting all of this stuff out . . . all the
> emotion, all the guilt, all the stress, all the anger, and um you can't do that
> with friends or family. The last thing I wanted was for someone to turn
> round and tell me it would be all okay. It wasn't okay.

Talking to the counsellor acted as a vent for releasing painful feelings, enabling movement and growth. At the point of discovering his
infertility Sam particularly valued having a space to talk and work
things out for himself, in an arena free from guilt and without practical suggestions or false reassurance.

Not all the men felt the need for therapy, but suggested it would
have been helpful for this to be on offer at different stages. For the

men who had experienced therapy, either alone or with their partners, the benefits had been striking. They expressed a preference for therapy that combined help finding practical solutions with an open and supportive space to discuss feelings.

Infertility and donor conception workshops, support groups, and on-line chat forums, usually accessed through charities such as the Donor Conception Network, also provided the opportunity to hear other men's voices and experiences. This helped to "normalise" their experiences and reduce the sense of stigma.

> *Dave*: That's been massively helpful . . . I obviously met people who were thinking about doing it you know, just random, just normal people that were doing it and you know it wasn't anything weird if you know what I mean. I just think it is great that they're out there banging the drum and normalising it a little bit.

Summary, conclusions, and recommendations for clinical practice

Becoming a parent involves difficult psychological, emotional, and relationship challenges for everybody. Parenthood via donor conception undoubtedly involves additional layers of complexity.

Despite the initial reticence of some men in this study to undergo donor conception, they all celebrated the families they had helped to create. As has been seen, however, the birth of these men's children did not mark the end of the emotional journey. As one man remarked:

> *Sam*: It's not over by a long shot. It never will be over, for me, or for Yasmin, or for our kids, but it's just a different route.

On-going and changing challenges and concerns persist and still continue to present themselves. The sadness and sense of loss about not being able to procreate seemed to leave a lasting legacy that lessened considerably after having a family, but for most, the barbs still pricked at key moments. Whether or not, and how to tell their children and others about the donor conception remained an issue that required thought and negotiation with their partners. Deeply ambivalent feelings and fantasies about the donor; the possible intrusion of this man and other half-siblings into their future lives; the threat that their child might reject them as not their "real" dad, all remained poignant anxieties that had to be wrestled with.

The men's accounts highlight how the creation of families does not occur in a neutral or non-judgmental environment. We get a sense of the power of society's expectations that couples who marry or make a commitment to each other, ought to have children and that male infertility is equated with lack of virility. This social discourse forms the unconscious backdrop to our lives. These messages only came into focus for the men in this study when they were forced to confront their infertility and the choice of whether to pursue donor conception to create a family. Such external pressures combine with a child's earliest fantasies and enquiries about how children come into the world, to create an internal template about how procreation should happen "naturally". We could see from these men's stories, how failure to live up to or conform to this model, and the prospect of using assisted reproductive technologies, generated for many of them, significant anxieties and fear of both internal and external condemnation. The advent of assisted procreative technologies, such as donor conception, challenges deeply embedded social and personal beliefs. Highlighting these expectations and acknowledging their impact, may help to reduce tensions and anxieties for individuals, by encouraging them to re-think their assumptions about the nature of families and how they are created, and to separate the act of procreation from the job of parenting. Perhaps it is timely for society to also make adjustments in the assumptions made about how children "should" come into the world and to re-consider the meaning of parenthood.

All the men believed that it would help to reduce stigma and feelings of isolation for the issues around male infertility and donor conception to be much more widely debated in the media. In contrast to the commonly held belief that men would prefer not to talk about these very personal and private issues, the men in this study welcomed the opportunity to "break the silence" and make their experiences heard through this research. It is possible that these men were not representative of men in general, as they were, by virtue of having volunteered for this research, more willing to talk. Some participants feared rejection or humiliation at the prospect of opening up to family or friends, particularly other men. Most of those who did talk, were pleasantly surprised by the support they received. A non-judgmental and open sounding-board for discussing their feelings with partners, family, friends, others in the same position, and professionals, was appreciated and seen as helpful in reducing the toxicity and loneliness of their experiences.

The "professionalism" of fertility clinics sometimes helped to dampen the powerful negative feelings stirred up by the donor insemination procedure. The men were in agreement, however, that the focus on their female partner, as reflected in registration only being under their partner's names; the lack of male toilets in some clinics; the failure in some instances to properly include men in treatment plans and discussion, all contributed to the men feeling side-lined and undermined. Registering both partners and re-naming clinics in a more gender-neutral way, would seem to be helpful.

The obligatory session of counselling prior to DC treatment was perceived by the majority in this study as an "examination" to test their paternal capabilities. This was felt to be unhelpful and the men did not feel able to openly discuss or voice any conflicting thoughts or worries about going through the procedure, for fear that they would be deemed "unfit". The timing, lack of clarity about the purpose of these sessions and the location in the fertility clinic, all contributed to this being a squandered opportunity for emotionally processing their feelings.

It would be helpful for the purposes of the counselling to be explicit and for sessions to be offered in separate locations, independent of the fertility clinic.

The three men who had gone into longer-term therapy, either alone or with their partners, felt they had gained enormously from the experience. They found therapy that combined a space to talk openly, with the opportunity to consider practical issues, most helpful. Access to therapy during the perinatal period has been recognised by the Department of Health as offering benefits to children and parents both as individuals and in terms of couple and parent–child relationships. Keylor and Apfel (2010) and Raphael-Leff (2003) specifically assert the importance of offering supportive therapy for individuals and couples experiencing infertility and embarking on procedures such as donor conception. The opportunity to access psychological therapy, before treatment, during pregnancy, after the birth, and at later points in the child's development, would be strongly welcomed by the men in this study.

The informality of on-line forums and support groups and workshops offered by charities such as the Donor Conception Network, were greatly valued. These were particularly helpful when men were contemplating donor conception and later when thinking about how to talk to their children about their origins. For some men, talking to others facing similar dilemmas helped to normalise their experience and was sometimes easier to make use of than formal therapy or counselling.

The donor conception road to parenthood had, for all the men, often been difficult and at times painful, but they were nevertheless all very clear: they were glad they had made the decision and grateful that they had been given the opportunity to have a "normal" family life.

> *Graham*: I had a picture of that person who would be a donor conception father, and that just didn't feel like me. But here I am now, and it *is* fatherhood. It's everything you wanted. It's all the "oh dears"; and "I'm absolutely exhausted"; "look after Peter"; and "Peter put your shoes on". It's like that every day. And then there is like all the good, funny bits, happy bits. It's just normal life.

References

Andrews, F. M., Abbey, A., & Halman, L. J. (1992). Is fertility-problem stress different? The dynamics of stress in fertile and infertile couples. *Fertility & Sterility, 57*(6): 1247–1253.

Berger, D. M. (1980). Couples' reactions to male infertility and donor insemination. *American Journal of Psychiatry, 137*(9): 1047–1049.

Blaser, A., Maloigne-Katz, B., & Gigon, U. (1988). Effect of artificial insemination with donor semen on the psyche of the husband. *Psychotherapy & Psychosomatics, 49*(1): 17–21.

Bloom, P. (1957). Artificial insemination (donor). *The Eugenics Review, 48*: 205–207.

Blyth, E., & Frith, L. (2008). The UK's gamete donor "crisis": a critical analysis. *Critical Social Policy, 28*(1): 74–95.

Brewaeys, A. (2001). Review: parent-child relationships and child development in donor insemination families. *Human Reproduction Update, 7*(1): 38–46.

Britton, R. (1989). The missing link: parental sexuality in the Oedipus complex. In: R. Britton, M. Feldman, & E. O'Shaughnessy (Eds.), *The Oedipus Complex Today* (pp. 83–102). London: Karnac.

Burns, L. H., & Covington, S. N. (1999). *Infertility Counselling. A Comprehensive Handbook for Clinicians*. New York: Parthenon.

Burns, J., & Pettle, S. (2002). *Choosing to be Open about Donor Conception: the Experience of Parents*. London: Donor Conception Network.

Crawshaw, M. (2008). Prospective parents' intentions regarding disclosure following the removal of donor anonymity. *Human Fertility*, 11(2): 95–100.

Crawshaw, M, (2011). The impact of infertility on a man's social relationships. [PowerPoint slides]. Presentation at the European Society of Human Reproduction & Embryology, Seville, 22–23 September.

Dahl, G. B., & Moretti, E. (2008). The demand for sons. *The Review of Economic Studies*, 75(4): 1085–1120.

Daniels, K. R., Lewis, G. M., & Gillett, W. (1995). Telling donor insemination offspring about their conception: the nature of couples' decision-making. *Social Science & Medicine*, 40(9): 1213–1220.

Dawkins, R. (1989). *The Selfish Gene*. Oxford: Oxford University Press.

Ehrensaft, D. (2000). Alternatives to the Stork fatherhood fantasies in donor insemination families. *Studies in Gender and Sexuality*, 1(4): 371–397

Fägerskiöld, A. (2008). A change in life as experienced by first-time fathers. *Scandinavian Journal of Caring Sciences*, 22(1): 64–71.

Feingold, M. L. (2011). Building health donor conceived families. American Fertility Association Library. Retrieved 14 November, 2012, from http://www.theafa.org/article/building-healthy-donor-conceived-families/.

Freeman, T., Jadva, V., Kramer, W., & Golombok, S. (2009). Gamete donation: parents' experiences of searching for their child's donor siblings and donor. *Human Reproduction*, 24(3): 505–516.

Freud, S. (1909c). Family romances. *S.E.*, 9: 237–241. London: Hogarth.

Gannon, K., Glover, L., & Abel, P. (2004). Masculinity, infertility, stigma and media reports. *Social Science & Medicine*, 59(6): 1169–1175.

Goldberg, A. E. (2009). Heterosexual, lesbian, and gay pre-adoptive parents' preferences about child gender. *Sex Roles*, 61(1–2): 55–71.

Golombok, S., Readings, J., Blake, L., Casey, P., Mellish, L., Marks, A., & Jadva, V. (2011). Children conceived by gamete donation: psychological adjustment and mother-child relationships at age 7. *Journal of Family Psychology*, 25(2): 230–239.

Greil, A.L., Slauson-Blevins, K., & McQuillan, J. (2010). The experience of infertility: a review of recent literature. *Sociology of Health & Illness*, 32(1): 140–162.

Hadley, R., & Hanley, T. (2011). Involuntarily childless men and the desire for fatherhood. *Journal of Reproductive & Infant Psychology*, 29(1): 56–68.

House of Commons Science and Technology Select Committee (2005). Human Reproductive Technologies and the Law: Fifth Report of

Session 2004–05, Vol. I. Retrieved 14 November, 2012, from http://www.publications.parliament.uk/pa/cm200405/cmselect/cmsctech/7/7i.pdf.

Human Fertilization and Embryology Authority (HFEA) (2010). *Fertility Facts & Figures 2008.* . Retrieved 17 November, 2012, from http://www.hfea.gov.uk/docs/2010-12-08_Fertility_Facts_and_Figures_2008_Publication_PDF.PDF.

Humphrey, M. (1977). Sex differences in attitude to parenthood. *Human Reproduction, 30*: 737–749.

Hunter, M., Salter-Ling, N., & Glover, L. (2000). Donor insemination: telling children about their origins. *Child & Adolescent Mental Health, 5*(4) : 157–163.

Jadva, V., Freeman, T., Kramer, W., & Golombok, S. (2009). The experiences of adolescents and adults conceived by sperm donation: comparisons by age of disclosure and family type. *Human Reproduction:* 24(8): 1909–1919.

Keylor, R., & Apfel, R. (2010). Male infertility: integrating an old psychoanalytic story with the research literature. *Studies in Gender & Sexuality, 11*(2): 60–77.

Koropatnick, S., Daniluk, J., & Pattinson, H. A. (1993). Infertility: a non-event transition. *Fertility & Sterility, 59*(1): 163–171.

Lamb, M. E. (2004). Introduction. *The Role of the Father in Child Development* (4th edn) (pp. 1–32). Hoboken, NJ: Wiley.

Lycett, E., Daniels, K., Curson, R., & Golombok, S. (2004). Offspring created as a result of donor insemination: a study of family relationships, child adjustment, and disclosure. *Fertility & Sterility, 82*(1): 172–179.

MacDougall, K., Becker, G., Scheib, J. E., & Nachtigall, R. D. (2007). Strategies for disclosure: how parents approach telling their children that they were conceived with donor gametes. *Fertility & Sterility, 87*(3): 524–533.

Manlove, E. E., & Vernon-Feagans, L. (2002). Caring for infant daughters and sons in dual-earner households: maternal reports of father involvement in weekday time and tasks. *Infant and Child Development, 11*(4): 305–320.

Mariotti, P. (2012). *The Maternal Lineage: Identification, Desire, and Transgenerational Issues.* Sussex: New Library of Psychoanalysis.

Martin, T. L., & Doka, K. J. (2000). *Men Don't Cry ... Women Do: Transcending Gender Stereotypes of Grief.* Philadelphia: Taylor and Francis.

Mason, M. C. (1993). *Male Infertility—Men Talking.* London: Routledge.

Miles, L. M., Keitel, M., Jackson, M., Harris, A., & Licciardi, F. (2009). Predictors of distress in women being treated for infertility. *Journal of Reproductive & Infant Psychology*, 27(3): 238–257.

Montuschi, O. (2006). *Telling and Talking Series for 0–7 year olds, 8–11 year olds, 12–16 year olds and 17+*. Nottingham: Donor Conception Network.

National Institute of Clinical Excellence (NICE) guidelines (2004). *Fertility Assessment and Treatment for People with Fertility Problems*. London: RCOG Press.

Peterson, B. D., Gold, L., & Feingold, T. (2007). The experience and influence of infertility: considerations for couple counsellors. *The Family Journal*, 15(3): 251–257.

Raley, S., & Bianchi, S. (2006). Sons, daughters, and family processes: does gender of children matter? *Annual Review of Sociology*, 32: 401–421.

Raphael-Leff, J. (2003). Eros and ART. In: J. Haynes & J. Miller (Eds.), *Inconceivable Conceptions: Psychological Aspects of Infertility and Reproductive Technology* (pp. 33–47). East Sussex: Brunner-Routledge.

Raphael-Leff, J. (2013). Enid Balint lecture: Psychic "Geodes": the Presence of Absence. 18th Enid Balint Memorial Lecture 2013. *Couple and Family Psychoanalysis*, 3: 137–155.

Snowden, R., & Snowden, E. (1993). *The Gift of a Child: A Guide to Donor Insemination*. Exeter: University of Exeter Press.

Trowell, J., & Etchegoyen, A. (2002). *The Importance of Fathers: A Psychoanalytic Re-evaluation*. Sussex: New Library of Psychoanalysis.

Veevers, J. (1980). *Childless by Choice*. Toronto: Butterworth.

Winnicott D. W. (1958). Primary maternal preoccupation. In: *Collected Papers: Through Paediatrics to Psycho-analysis*. London: Tavistock.

Wischmann, T. (2013). "Your count is zero". Counselling the infertile man. *Human Fertility*, 16(1): 1–5.

CHAPTER SIX

When baby makes three or four or more: attachment, individuation, and identity in assisted conception families*

Diane Ehrensaft

U sing examples from clinical work with parents and children in assisted-conception families, this chapter explores the anxieties, conflicts, and psychological defences of parents as they intersect with the developmental tasks and emotional experiences of the children. Coining the term "birth other" to refer to the outside party in conception—donor, surrogate, or gestational carrier, the resurfacing of early primal scenes and oedipal dramas on the part of parents is connected to psychological strategies and defences, particularly denial, to ward off anxieties generated by introducing an outside party into the most intimate arena of family life—conception of a child. The parental negotiation of conflicts is then associated to three developmental tasks for the child: confronting one's sense of uniqueness; establishing a sense of belonging; forging an identity based on assisted-conception origins. Lastly, developmental facilitators are outlined to enhance success in each of these tasks respectively: age-appropriate narratives of the child's origins; family reveries (shared fantasies about the birth others and their position in the

*First published in 2008 in *Psychoanalytic Study of the Child*, 63: 3–23. Reproduced with the permission of Yale University Press.

family); a child's family romances that include the birth other. The intent of this discourse is to sensitise clinicians to the psychological issues in their work with children and parents faced with internal or interpersonal challenges when baby was conceived with the help of an outside party.

"Mummy, mummy, when I grow up, I want to be a mummy just like you. I want to go to the sperm bank just like you and get some sperm and have a baby just like me." Emily, age six, is dreaming of a mother-hood just like her own mother's. Emily's reverie is emblematic of the next generation's growing understanding and acceptance that babies can be made from science rather than sex and that fertility clinics, syringes, petri dishes, even turkey basters have replaced the stork in bringing babies to the family's doorstep. As is often the case, the children are one step ahead of their elders in absorbing sea changes in the culture—in this case, dramatic innovations regarding fertility, conception, and birth.

Currently, if a man or woman discovers that his or her body does not work to make a baby or finds that he or she is missing another body with whom to make a baby (as is the case for single parents and gay and lesbian families), new alternatives to adoption are available to build a family. In the words of one reproductive endocrinologist, "No sperm, we get sperm. No eggs, we get eggs. No uterus, we rent a uterus."

Medical science has sailed ahead to find new ways to help men and women have babies of their own using assisted reproductive technology, leaving in its wake a conundrum for psychoanalytic theoreticians and practitioners.

Bedrock concepts—the primal scene, oedipal configurations, psychosexual development—have been challenged as babies are no longer universally the product of sexual intercourse between a man and a woman and when an outside person, either a sperm donor, egg donor, or surrogate or gestational carrier, is introduced into the most intimate realm of family life—the creation of the baby.

Just as D. W. Winnicott posited that there is no baby without a mother (1960), in the context of assisted reproductive technology, there is no baby without a mother or mothers, father or fathers, and all the other individuals (donors or surrogates) who helped make that baby. On the basis of two decades of clinical work with children and parents from families formed with the help of assisted reproductive technology, I would like to focus on anxieties, conflicts, and psycho-logical strategies and defences of the parents as they are interwoven with the developmental tasks and psychological experience of the child in assisted-conception families. My lens of observation is informed by—while simultaneously challenging—some basic psycho-analytic benchmarks, including part- and whole-object relating, the primal scene, oedipal dramas, and the family romance.

Taking notes on surrogacy and gestational carriers, I discovered I had mistakenly typed in "birth other" instead of "birth mother". I had been searching for a single, cogent term for the outside person who either donates gametes or offers the use of her womb to prospective parents. With typographical error, or perhaps a Freudian slip, as the mother of invention, I have coined "birth other" as a succinct term for the outside person who offers gametes or uterus so that someone else can procreate and will be using that term throughout (Ehrensaft, 2005).

The so-called nice man or woman who helped us have you

A trip to the fertility clinic offers infertile individuals or couples the option to undergo medical treatments to conceive a baby of their own or to choose to use sperm or ova donated by an anonymous or known donor or a surrogate or both to aid in conception or gestation. Such a trip also affords perfectly fertile single persons or gay or lesbian couples the opportunity to receive the missing gametes or to make use of another's womb to have a genetically related baby of their own. That outside person, the "birth other", is typically referred to as the "nice" man or woman "who helped me (us) have you". Embodied in that one four-letter word is the requisite parental gratitude toward this person who donated body substances or allowed the use of her womb. No room is allowed for the alternate set of feelings that might surface, much to the chagrin of the parents—ambivalent or outright hostile feelings toward the nice man or woman.

The unexpected negative or uncomfortable parental feelings run the gamut from sexual threat or desire to envy or hatred of the "birth other" as a potential kidnapper of the baby's love or affection. Marian, a pregnant single mother, revealed in her therapy session vivid sexual fantasies about the sperm donor, a gay man she met only briefly to establish whether he would be the right choice for her donor insemination conception. She imagined the conception as a result of a night in bed, rather than a procedure in a doctor's office. Echoing the experiences of many couples who have grappled with the presence of a "third" in the conception of their children, another mother whose friend donated eggs so that she could have a baby admitted that she,

> felt like the odd woman out in the donor egg process, as my old friend from college was my donor, but this meant that her eggs would be fertilized by my husband's sperm. They are making the embryo/baby while I wait, then I'll carry their embryo that I didn't contribute to making. (Cooper & Glazer, 1994, p. 233)

In fantasy, this mother is forced to watch her husband in a romantic tryst with another woman while she sits on the sidelines and even participates in their lovemaking by carrying their child. It is as if she were walking in on them in the act of coitus, much to her surprise and dismay. In her felt position as the "odd woman out", she recreates a primal scene experience in which she reverts to the "small child, credited as he is with no understanding or memory, [who] may be witness of the sexual act on the part of his parents or other adults" (Freud, 1924, p. 379). As exciting as this voyeuristic act or fantasy might be, it is also painful as the child comes to the realisation of an erotic union between two beloved people from which she will forever be excluded.

Since Freud's formulation of the concept, there has been ongoing debate as to whether the primal scene, based on the assumption of innate knowledge of procreation, is phylogenetic and universal or merely a social construction. Nonetheless, there appears to be general agreement that within Western culture children are intrigued by what goes on behind the bedroom door, particularly their parents' bedroom door. In this scenario, children are made simultaneously excited and uneasy by the entry of a third person, whether it be themselves or someone else, into this intimate scene. Over time, this disquiet dissipates but never disappears. We can locate the residues of the drama in our intimate adult relationships. Seldom do men or women experience anything more intense than the rage and distress they feel upon discovering a spouse or partner's love affair with someone else. It is this very drama that may find its way into assisted conception.

Bringing an egg or sperm donor or a surrogate into baby making can stir up archaic bedroom scenarios, stimulating fantasies of illicit extramarital sex or *ménage á trois*. The fantasies spill out in all directions, not just in parents' but in the children's and in other people's psyches, as well. Madeline, age nine, who had just been told a child-friendly narrative by her psychoanalyst mother about Madeline's friend Jocelyn's new baby sister, conceived by Jocelyn's father and a surrogate, piped up in response, "Okay, Mommy, I think I get it. Jocelyn's daddy did adultery."

Along with the stimulation of erotic fantasies, the presence of the birth other can create psychic havoc in another domain. In *The Eros of Parenthood* (2001), Noelle Oxenhandler identifies the universal parental fear of the kidnapper who comes to take their baby from them. The fear emanates from parents' strong attachments to their children, coalescing with their guilt for not taking care of the children well enough and their realisation that their children are placed with them only temporarily and will someday leave them. The internal fear, anxiety, and guilt are projected onto an externalised "evil other"—someone who will want the baby as much as the parents do and who will act on that desire by stealing the baby. For parents using assisted conception, that fantasised "evil other" easily takes the form of the "birth other". The stark reality that the birth other is no stranger to the baby but rather someone who either is genetically related to the child through sperm or egg donation or housed the child in her womb for nine months and, furthermore, may be a family member or friend only fuels the fearful fantasy.

Stephanie was an older mother who welcomed the offer of her much younger sister, Maggie, to donate eggs so that Stephanie and her husband could have a baby of their own. She entered therapy with troubling feelings that her gratitude toward her sister had devolved into wariness and suspicion since the birth of her daughter, Chloe. Each time her sister came to visit, Stephanie struggled to sweep aside morbid images of Maggie seducing Chloe to love Maggie best. Her anxious fantasies replicate the experience of many assisted-conception parents when they discover the "nice" man or woman surfacing in dreams and in reveries as the cloaked kidnapper who will usurp the parents as the "real" mother or father. As the child grows, any interest in knowing the identity of the donor or surrogate or deepening a relationship with a known donor or surrogate can send unexpected danger signals into the psychic system of the family, foreclosing thinking or dialogue about the "outside" party who now feels entirely too inside. As will be discussed shortly, fears about the birth other, now transformed into the baby-snatching evil other, ironically impede the very experience that will fortify rather than shatter parent–child bonding: the opportunity for the family to engage in collective reverie about the person who contributed eggs or sperm or offered her womb to be used to house baby for the nine months of gestation.

Strategies to assuage birth other anxieties

It appears that we have been able to take the reproduction out of sex, but it has been far more difficult to take the sex out of reproduction. If sexual feelings intrude, parents may call on a particular set of psychological defences to prevent such ideations from consciously surfacing. Erotic fantasies about donors or surrogates and about oneself or one's partner in relationship to those people create a great deal of discomfort and undoing of past developmental achievements. The sexualised images can be particularly disturbing for the non-genetic parents, who may already be struggling with a blow to their gendered selves as a result of the inability to fulfil their libidinal reproductive desires and to bring to fruition their anticipated procreative identity. In lesbian and gay families, the non-genetic parent may suffer not from infertility-related ego deflation but from the painful primal scene exclusion as their partner "gets together" with someone else to make the couple's baby. To assuage the pain and anxieties connected to these sexual rumblings about one's body or one's desire, mothers and fathers may find themselves turning to a defensive strategy that eliminates the threat by denying the personhood of the "real" man or woman who has been able to provide what the parent could not. This is a psychological defence to which I refer in the vernacular as "Honey, I shrunk the donor."

Richard and Catherine were quite open about their daughter Angela's birth history. She had been conceived with sperm from The Sperm Bank of California. They had come to consult about Angela's present difficulties. They reported that Angela was having some behaviour problems at school, becoming disruptive in class and unable to sit still and attend to classroom demands. In consultation, I raised the possibility that Angela's behaviour problems could perhaps be secondary to a primary learning difficulty, which in turn could be genetically based. After gathering information about Catherine's family history, I inquired what Catherine and Richard knew about the sperm donor that might shed light on Angela's present difficulties. Richard became noticeably agitated and responded tersely, "As we said, we went to The Sperm Bank and got some sperm. That's it." Backing up to explore Richard's experience with assisted conception, I learned that he had been deeply ambivalent about turning to donor insemination to conceive a child. Richard had discovered that he was sterile, most likely as a result of a case of mumps during his adolescence. He and Catherine had very much wanted children. When a close friend of theirs offered to be a sperm donor, Richard adamantly refused. He was consciously aware that he could not tolerate such intimacy between his close friend and Catherine. His stipulation was that if he and Catherine were to use a sperm donor, it would have to be an anonymous donor so as to create as many degrees of separation as possible between himself and this outsider who "was not shooting blanks". Catherine readily agreed. Nonetheless, even with that stipulation in place, any mention of the donor on Catherine's part sent Richard into a state of silent withdrawal. With time, Catherine discovered that if she avoided using the word "donor" and referred only to "sperm," Richard was able to maintain his equanimity. Rather than saying, "I hope the donor will make it to the clinic this week," she would say, "I'm worried there won't be sperm for us this month."

Upon the birth of their daughter, the word "donor" disappeared from their vocabulary altogether, and Richard and Catherine limited both their language and their thought to the sperm that had helped create the daughter they so dearly loved. Unfortunately, this defensive strategy cracked in the face of Angela's present assessment needs. Brought to consciousness was the realisation that it was not the vial of sperm but the profile of the donor that might provide useful information in addressing Angela's problems. In the consultation room, their unresolved conflicts concerning their daughter's donor conception surfaced as they were forced to acknowledge that the "split-off" donated sperm was attached to a whole person who was both part of and could also deeply affect their daughter's life.

Until that time, Richard and Catherine were caught up in a defensive strategy shared by many birth other families: do a sleight of mind and reduce the donor to a vial of sperm or an egg in a dish or shrink the surrogate to a disembodied uterus. This is not just to eliminate sexual threat but also to get rid of a potential interloper who might provide a threat to bonding with baby or even steal the baby away. So there is no other man or father, just a vial of sperm. There is no other mother, just some extracted eggs or temporary housing for the baby. Cultural support for this defensive strategy can come, albeit unwittingly, from medical professionals who speak to prospective donor conception parents about gametes disembodied from the people who supply them and, until recent shifts in policy directives advocating disclosure (Ethics Committee of the American Society of Reproductive Medicine, 2004), by reassuring parents that no one ever need know that it was not their own sperm or eggs that made this baby come to be. So external and internal forces come together to collude in the defensive scenario "Honey, I shrunk the donor."

Following the rubrics of Melanie Klein's developmental theory, in shrinking the donor or surrogate to a body part or substance, parents (and others) can find themselves leaving the more mature world of whole-object relating and inadvertently reverting to part-object relating. In her developmental theory of object relations, Klein (1935) describes the infant as relying on body parts to represent the whole, especially breast = mother. Such part-object relating is considered the most primitive form of relating to another human being. As the infant grows, she discovers that mother is more than a breast; she is a whole being outside the baby's omnipotent control who comes and goes and has a mind of her own. The achievement of whole-object relating is celebrated as the entrance to healthy interpersonal relationships and to sturdy personal development. Whether babies really engage in part-object functioning remains to be empirically proven, but we certainly find such reductionism reflected, among adults, in the new equation sperm = sperm donor, egg = egg donor, uterus = surrogate or gestational carrier (Ehrensaft, 2000).

Sometimes parents who have used assisted conception can err in the opposite direction as they hold the donor or surrogate in mind: "From this bean a parent did grow." Rather than reverting to part-object thinking and reducing people to a body part to eliminate the threat of the interloper, they take a body part and fashion a person. For example, Anonymous Donor #156 from the sperm bank can be psychically transformed into a "virtual" father, perhaps envisioned by the mother as a brilliant, successful, or talented person who will burst on the scene to make himself known to the child. In such instances, the parent is engaging in a reverie about the person who helped bring a baby to his or her life, a fantasy that can certainly function in the service of acknowledging the reality of the birth other as a significant being in the child's existence. At the same time, such reveries put the parent at risk for overcorrecting more primitive part-object relating (sperm = sperm donor, egg = egg donor) by creating more of a whole object than exists in actuality. Rather than a corrective emotional experience, the reveries begin to veer toward the delusional. A single lesbian mother who, through a medical error, received identifying information about her son's anonymous sperm donor put considerable effort into surreptitiously finding out the whereabouts of this man, with fantasies of appearing in his office one day to present him with a photo of his "son". In her fantasy, she imagined that the donor would be swept away into a passionate bond with "his" child and become the father that her child had never had. It was difficult for her to hold in mind the strong possibility that this man would not "go with the program" and might have his own thoughts, desires, and feelings, repudiating any notion of himself as father to her child. In essence, from the self-chosen status of anonymous donor this man had become the mother's subjective object (Winnicott, 1971), a person who, in fantasy, is under her omnipotent control.

The psychological manoeuvring that creates a whole person from body parts is more often found among families with no history of infertility but with a reproductive "missing" rather than an "extra" part—be that either a father or a mother. This includes single parents or gay or lesbian parents whose reproductive bodies are in good order but who must go in search of another body with which to work in order to have a baby—the body of the man or woman, donor or surrogate, who helps make their child because, until further notice from reproductive medicine, it still takes a male and a female to procreate. The creation of a subjective whole object from a part object reflects a parent's anxiety about reducing the donor to a vial of sperm or an egg in a dish and reveals the parent's desire to be able to fill in the missing piece of the family, to create a third, and to have some image of the person responsible for half the child's genetic makeup and who might even be a partner in fantasy.

Heterosexual couples with a history of infertility or disease that precludes conception for one of the two parents are not exempt from such constructions of whole parents where there are none. The genetic parent may fantasise about the bigger-than-life person who might just be the third parent or replace the inadequate second one who could not contribute to making the baby. The infertile parent might create an idealised fertile parent to have a concrete container in which to deposit his or her anxieties, envy, or sorrow. In these instances, the psychological construction of a whole person from an assigned number at the fertility clinic can generate emotional havoc both intra- and interpersonally as the interloper, the "real" man or "real" woman who could do what the infertile parent could not, springs to life.

In the struggle to take the sex out of reproduction in assisted conception, we witness a paradox between a reduction of people to parts and an illusion of whole people where there are none. Either defensive strategy is extreme, and neither is reality based. The reality lies somewhere in between—the birth other is a person who helps a family have a child. He or she is not a body part; he or she is not a parent or lover. Psychoanalytic exploration that brings the uncon- scious to consciousness is often necessary to address the part/whole- object reversals and to bring parents to this middle ground.

Shrinking birth others to body parts or fashioning them into partic- ipating family members from a number on a sheet of paper is part of a larger phenomenon that I refer to as "immaculate deception" (Ehrensaft, 2000, 2005). A most compelling example that illustrates this psychological defence, one that is aimed at eliminating the reality of the "birth other" and denying the facts of the assisted conception, comes from the report of a lesbian non-biological mother-to-be. She and her partner were having a child, conceived by her partner and a known sperm donor. She accompanied her partner to the insemina- tion, tucking the bag of fresh sperm under her armpit to keep it warm on the way to the doctor's office. This woman developed a new narra- tive to the birth story—she and her partner, rather than her partner and the donor, had conceived a child together, because, after all, she had hand-delivered the sperm that made the baby. Her tale is emblem- atic of creative birth concepts evolving from assisted-reproductive technology and qualifies as immaculate deception. It allowed this mother-to-be to delete the donor from the conception process. Simultaneously, she could reinvent herself as the only partner in the impregnation. She drew pleasure from the erotic imagery of the warm sperm close to her body, of her own physical intimacy with her part- ner as the sperm that was kept alive only because of the heat of her own body travelled up her lover's vagina. From that intimate, erotic closeness a baby was made.

Sometimes men with very low sperm counts mix their sperm with more robust sperm from a donor or even several donors. If a successful conception occurs, they can imagine that they, rather than the donor, are the genetic fathers of their children, even in an era of reliable DNA testing, which could easily establish the identity of the actual genetic progenitor. Not to take advantage of such incontrovertible evidence of paternity is to engage in another form of immaculate deception, avoiding reality and holding oneself in a limbo state of fantasy and reverie—maybe I am the "real" father.

Immaculate deception, involving fantastic or delusional narratives about one's child's conception, is a means of assuaging the internal unrest that may come from shame about infertility, internal dis-ease with these scientific birth techniques, worry about other people's responses, anxious anticipation regarding the children's reactions, and disquiet about genetic asymmetry—that one's partner and oneself will not have the same genetic relationship to their child. Undoing the fact of the birth other conception in fantasy is a defensive strategy for eliminating an imagined sexual predator. It is also an effective antidote to the fears about the evil other, the conniving kidnapper, aka birth other. Psychological constructions of a birth that did not take place in the lab or with the participation of a third party, now dubbed immaculate deception, are understandable defences. They protect the self from a torrent of feelings and anxieties that can potentially flood the psyche, either consciously or unconsciously.

Boiled down to their essence, these defences all qualify as variations on the theme of denial. Anna Freud, in *The Ego and the Mechanisms of Defense*, concluded that "the typical situations in which the ego has recourse to the mechanism of denial are those associated with ideas of castration and with the loss of love objects" (A. Freud, 1966, p. 173). If we link infertility or lack of a parenting partner and the presence of the birth other with castration (of one's reproductive self) and expand loss of love objects to include the loss of fantasied objects (baby conceived from a sexual union), as well as the fear of loss of real objects (baby snatched away by the birth other), it becomes understandable that denial surfaces as a major psychological defence to bolster one's parenting ego and to assuage the angst about parent–child attachment and parental authenticity when baby is conceived by "me or us and someone else". Immaculate deception and part/whole-object reversals are adaptive strategies, but they run the risk of undoing the very authenticity that the parents are trying to protect, presenting impediments to actual parent–child bonding and interfering with the developmental tasks for the child whose origins include the presence of a birth other.

Three developmental tasks: difference, belongingness, and identity

As parents discover psychological strategies to accommodate the presence of a birth other in their children's origins, the children are faced with developmental tasks of their own. In contrast to children conceived by "traditional means" (i.e., sexual intercourse), children born with the aid of assisted conception face three tasks specific to their birth other origins.

The first developmental task: children must grapple with their sense of difference. The traditional birth story does not pertain to them. They were conceived not of a sexual union between a mother and father but rather from a scientific procedure. By definition, sex will not have been a factor in their conception. Jody Messler Davies wrote about the erotic feelings that surface in psychotherapy: "Each of us is conceived out of the desire of two significant others" (1998, p. 810). If Davies is referencing the sexual desire that culminates in a sexual union, this statement no longer pertains. Instead, the amended quote, taking into account alternative forms of conception, should read, "Each of us is conceived out of the desire of one or two people and possibly the assistance of one or more people who participated in our conception or gestation not out of sexual desire but as result of providing use of their uterus or donating their gametes so that we could be born." While psychoanalytic thinking may continue to forget the changed circumstances, the children who know of their assisted conception do not.

It is not just a matter of science replacing sex; it is also the presence of the outsider in a most intimate area of life, one's own conception. By preconceived arrangement, a person who never intended to parent a child will have participated in that child's conception with the understanding that someone other than that person will be the mother or father, or maybe there will be two mothers, or two fathers. The children may have no access to half of their genetic heritage. In the future, they may have to concern themselves with unwitting incest if they should perchance become romantically involved with one of their half-siblings from the same donor. Even if it is inordinately unlikely that such a union should come to pass, the child, as well as his or her parents, may still be burdened with fantasies about such a forbidden and feared incestuous coupling. Combined with reflections mirrored back from intimate others or the surrounding culture, any of these factors can instil strong feelings of uniqueness and difference in the child's psyche—some positive, some negative.

Ramie, age six, has two mothers and an older sister. She was conceived with a "yes" sperm donor, someone she will be able to contact on her eighteenth birthday. She had been told this narrative of her birth from the time she was old enough to understand spoken language. Yet, only at age six, with advanced cognitive skills, did she grasp that she was actually made with sperm from a man and one of her mothers' eggs. She was seemingly shocked by this information: "You're kidding, Mummy. I thought I was all girl. I didn't know I had any boy in me." Ramie had developed her own theory of gender based not on biology and XX chromosomes but on her own family composition. She was different from all her friends because there was no father, only an "all-girl" family. Until she could understand the basic scientific rubrics of reproduction, it was completely ego-syntonic that she would be "all girl".

The second developmental task: children need to establish their sense of belonging. Their family matrix includes the person(s) who intended to have them, the person(s) who donated gametes or allowed use of their uterus so they could come into being, and, last, their siblings, which could include those in their immediate family, those who share the same donors, and those who are the sons and daughters of the birth other. Within this matrix, who is their "real" mother or father? How are they related to the siblings in their immediate family, who may also have had donors or surrogates or have been adopted, or, alternatively, are full genetic offspring of both parents (as happens when parents face infertility or disease after the birth of their first child or children)? How are they related to other offspring of their birth other? If they are in a two-parent family, the children may experience genetic asymmetry—both of their parents intended to have them, but only one of the parents is genetically related to them. If the donor or surrogate remains anonymous, they may suffer from "genealogical bewilderment", a blocked access to half their genetic heritage, which may affect not only their feeling of difference but also their sense of belonging.

Clinical observations and research studies indicate that parents' anxieties about their children's acceptance of them as the "real" parents do not coincide with any bonding difficulties. Children from assisted-conception families have been assessed as strongly bonded to their parents and secure in their attachment histories (Golombok and MacCallum, 2003; Golombok, MacCallum, & Goodman, 2001; Golombok et al., 1999; Murray, MacCallum, & Golombok, 2006). For example, Delaney had not been told until she was eight years old that she had been conceived with donor sperm. Before that, her father, who was unable to reverse his vasectomy to conceive Delaney, worried that Delaney would reject him as a parent if she were to find out that he was not her biological father. Through parent consultation during the course of Delaney's treatment for ostensible divorce-related issues, Delaney's father worked through these anxieties and, on the basis of his experienced strong attachment and ability to "lay claim" to his daughter, decided with Delaney's mother to explain to Delaney her donor insemination origins. Many years later, when Delaney returned to therapy in adolescence, she articulated quite clearly: "My parents are my parents, no matter what. It doesn't matter that I don't have my dad's genes; I love him just as much—actually, maybe even a little more than my mum." She refers to her sperm donor as her "bio". Further exploration of her fantasies and unconscious stirrings found no discrepancy between her reported account and her deeply internalised sense of security in relationship to her parents, particularly her father.

The third developmental task: children have to establish their identities, weaving in the fact of their birth other origins as they shape their own sense of self. Erik Erikson (1963) established identity *vs.* confusion as the fourth stage in his eight psychosocial stages of human development. Whereas the designated age for this stage is adolescence, the actual work starts well before puberty. In Western culture, it is assumed that knowing one's genetic roots is an integral piece of identity formation and that children denied their genetic heritage will be impeded in this psychological journey:

> Children who have no knowledge of their genetic history must live with a sense of bafflement about how they came to be and bewilderment

about who they are. Our current understanding about human nature and the psychological development of human beings indicates that a genetic void is not in the psychological best interest of a person. (Cooper & Glazer, 1994, p. 351)

This certainly applies to children in assisted-conception families, particularly those with anonymous donors who will never be known to them; yet no studies to date document greater levels of identity confusion among youth with birth other origins. However, many anecdotal and clinical accounts attest to a sense of a "missing piece" in constructing a whole image of one's self, a feeling that can carry well into adulthood. Karen, now about 40 years old, was told only when she was eighteen, after her father's death, that she was conceived with an anonymous sperm donor, leaving her with a sense of identity dysphoria: "I was being told that my biological father was a nameless, faceless person. All the experiences that I thought about my identity, I began to second guess" (Morrisette, 2006, p. 52). Later, she summarised her feelings, "I feel that to intentionally reduce a genetic parent to nothing more than a source of sperm or egg demeans our need for genetic identity, heritage, ancestry and connections" (Morrisette, 2006, p. 56).

Children may not only feel robbed of their identity, they may also have difficulty expelling the same thought that adopted children have, that "somebody gave me up". These thoughts can surface despite the carefully laid-out explanations by their parents regarding how much they were wanted and to what lengths the parents went to have their dearly loved child. A colleague reported that her six-year-old daughter, conceived with donor eggs, confronted her mother with a seemingly innocent but searing question: "So, Mummy why was it that the egg donor didn't want to keep me?" This was asked after many years of careful explanation about "Mummy and Daddy and the nice lady who gave her eggs so Mummy and Daddy could have you." My colleague's daughter's cognitive and emotional status led her to her own theories, negating her parents' best intentions. Those childhood theories are not always so easily shaken, even as the child grows in her cognitive and emotional understandings of her birth other conception. Unconscious traces of such theories can be found in later adolescent identity struggles. Adolescents, while fervently separating from their parents, are simultaneously using them as a mirror as they investigate all the components that have gone into the mix to make them the individuals they are. It is an exercise not just of the mind but also of the body. Whereas many talk of the parent serving as mirror to the small infant to reflect back a sense of well-being and aliveness, the mirror surfaces again with vital importance as the children reach adolescence and begin investigating their changing bodies and as they develop more sophisticated understandings of the genetic contributions to personality. When the parent cannot serve that mirroring function because that parent has no genetic link to the child, the son or daughter will have to look elsewhere for the reflections. The quest to establish one's adult-bodied self, in conjunction with changing cognitive capacities that foster greater interest in psychological meaning and motivation, may lead adolescents to either search out their donor or surrogate or grow curious about the path the birth other took to decide to become a donor or surrogate.

Sierra was not told until she was fourteen that her father was not her biological father and that she was conceived with the sperm from a red-haired Italian lawyer. Suddenly it made sense to her where her red hair came from and she was also relieved to discover that she no longer had to worry about inheriting a predisposition for colon cancer from her father's side of the family. Sierra also found it romantic that she had a donor from another country. She went on the Internet to learn as much as she could about the city the donor came from, which, in addition to his profession and hair colour, was about all she knew or would ever know about him. She made up a story: "Once there was a man in Arezzo. He grew the garden, and there was this beautiful flower that grew in it. That was Sierra." The search for an identity, a sense of "who I am based on the fact that half of my genes come from someone else who has not functioned as a parent, or that I came from the body of another woman, not my mother" can generate a strong desire to seek out the birth other, not to find a long-lost parent or replace the existing ones but to lay claim to one's own heritage and future.

Developmental facilitators: storytelling, family reveries, and family romances

The child's first developmental task, coming to terms with his or her uniqueness, requires sensitive explanation by the parents of the child's origins, an explanation that will need to change over time and be told repeatedly to accommodate the child's changing developmental status. The story begins as the imparting of information but optimally evolves into a dialogue with the child, leaving room for the full breadth of a child's reactions and feelings, both positive and negative. Some parents choose not to disclose their child's birth other origins to them. These parents need to be prepared for the "un-thought known" (Bollas, 1987) transformed into the "unthought blown" on the part of the child—in this case, the unconscious knowledge about one's origins never communicated but yet perceived or intuited. The knowledge may come from inadvertent transmissions or "slips" on the part of the parents or others who do know the truth of the child's birth other origins. Children or adults who have been told of their assisted-conception origins after many years of not knowing often report that "I always knew something was different about me, but I never quite knew what it was."

Caroline, age seven, who was brought by her parents for individual therapy because of post-divorce anxiety symptoms, was also, I discovered later, the product of a donor insemination conception. She had not been told this information, particularly because her father was very anxious that it would disrupt his bonds with her and that his ex-wife might also use it to leverage their daughter into a closer connection with her over him. So Caroline did not know; yet, at age seven, she engaged in play with me that consisted of two repeated themes: birthing a baby from under her shirt that was born only from her mummy, with no daddy involved, and placing a pink quartz stone in a heart-shaped box filled with sand and instructing me to put the "egg" on a high shelf for one week, after which time it would turn into a baby. I assessed her play in the therapy as indicating Caroline's unthought blown and also signalling her readiness to hear the true story of her origins, which her parents, after a year of psychological consultation and reflection, decided to tell her.

The second developmental task, establishing a sense of belonging, involves the family reverie (Corbett, 2001). The family reverie includes the thoughts and fantasies that family members share about the birth other, whether that person is known to the family or not. Often a couple that has fantasised about the donor as they wait for their child to be born suddenly become mute on the topic once the child arrives. The foreclosure of thought or discussion is fuelled by the fear of the conniving kidnapper and the anxiety about their own ability to lay claim to the baby. The reality is that the children will fantasise about the donor or surrogate whether a gag rule is imposed or not. The opportunity to share some of those thoughts with the parents while also hearing how the parents hold the birth other in mind allows the child to integrate a full and rich picture of his or her entire family matrix, which includes the people who made the child and the people who raise the child.

Caroline, who perseverated on her play themes of parthenogenetic babies and petri dish births, became less emotionally constricted and anxiety-prone once her parents imparted to her the story of her conception and shared their own feelings about her conception with an anonymous sperm donor. After two years of engaging together in family reveries—wondering what the birth other looked like, wondering if Caroline got her deep brown eyes and beautiful singing voice from him, and so forth, Caroline was able to create the following drama in her play in my office. She and her parents were climbing a high mountain together. Unbeknownst to them, a scraggly man in a spooky hut had staked himself out at the top of the mountain. Climbing ahead, Caroline reached the mountaintop first, only to be lured away by this evil man, who promised her candy and adventure. Fooled by the strange man, she was snatched away from her parents, never to see them again. She spent the rest of her life on the lonely mountaintop, longing for her family.

This scraggly man was indeed the conniving kidnapper, her anonymous sperm donor. At this point, her real life was not on a lonely mountaintop but in a close and positive relationship with each of her parents. But only now, after she had been told the truth of her origins and after she had the opportunity for collective fantasies with her family, was she at psychological liberty to engage in this cold and dismal fantasy, which in turn helped her dispel her fears and actually strengthen her bonds with her parents, particularly her father.

The third developmental task, identity formation, involves the family romance, to be differentiated from the family reverie. The family reverie is a group experience; the family romance is a solo performance. In the traditional family romance, the latency-age child begins to fantasise about another family to which that child belongs—perhaps he or she is really the child of a famous king or queen. The difference for children from birth other families is that there may be some reality to the fantasised parent. Just as the adopted child often calls forth the birth parents as the key players in the family romance (Warner, 1993), the child in the assisted-conception family may evoke in fantasy the wonderful donor or surrogate who gave her the gift of life and half her genetic makeup and may someday show up on the scene to claim his or her long-lost child. The nice man or nice woman who so generously gave eggs or sperm can easily be transformed into the rich and mighty (and fertile) king or queen who will bring the child riches and glory.

In a birth-other family, parents can grow queasy about the child's family romances, misassessing them as repudiations and reinforcing their fears that a conniving kidnapper might actually win their child's favour, at least in their child's inner life. In fact, the exact opposite transpires. The family romance is predicated on attachment. Only upon establishing trust and safety in a secure home can the child feel adventuresome enough to wander beyond the confines of the family, even in fantasy. Without that anchor, the space for the family romance can easily collapse. Parents in assisted-conception families will benefit from the assurance that the family romance is not a bond-breaker; it is merely the child's own private affair where he or she can begin to individuate and explore a world apart from the parent, using the birth other as a foil. Engaging in the family romance dovetails nicely with the birth other child's identity tasks—through imaginings about the birth other, the child can compensate for genealogical bewilderment and engage in internal mirroring and discovery of the self. In contrast to the family reverie, the parent's role in the family romance is to stay out, rather than step in, and to tolerate, if such fantasies are shared, the child's internal musings as self-explorations rather than attachment blows.

Deanna, age ten, was brought to therapy because of social constriction at school and anxiety symptoms at home. There was a great deal of marital tension, and the parents worried that their fighting was negatively impacting Deanna. As is often the case in beginning therapy contacts, only well into our initial parent sessions did Deanna's parents share, "Oh, by the way there's something we thought you should know. Deanna is an egg donor baby. We didn't think it was very important, but we decided we should just mention it." Actually, it turned out to be a key factor in Deanna's inner life as she worked to insulate herself from her parents' fighting and establish her own independent sphere of being. Ostensibly, her parents' fighting did not bother Deanna. By her own report, she loved her parents very much but was too busy thinking about other things. She described her parents' fighting as "like an old brown chair in the living room—you know it's there but you just walk around it." Therapy sessions revealed that Deanna's busy fantasy life was taken up with thoughts about her anonymous egg donor, a woman she will never know. Deanna was an excellent basketball player. She imagined her egg donor was, as well. Certainly neither of her parents could dribble or shoot a basket. Deanna was pleased with her long, swan-like neck. Both her parents had short, squat necks, so she must have inherited her lovely neck from her donor. She shared her family romance with me: she and her donor would meet in a café. They would fall into each other's arms, overwhelmed with emotion. They would be awed by how much they look alike. Deanna would be at Harvard then, study-ing biology. Her egg donor would already be a well-known scientist. They'd move in together and become a rich and famous duo. All her classmates who ignored Deanna at school would suddenly be clam-ouring for her affection and attention. They'd be begging to meet her famous egg donor. Deanna's family romance may have functioned both to repudiate and to shield her from her parents' fighting, erasing her parents and usurping them with the wonderful donor. Yet, all of her play and clinical material pointed to a more poignant explanation for her reveries. Deanna was daydreaming about herself—her first forays away from home, filled with fame and fortune. Still in latency, she was in the beginning stages of forging an identity based on the fact that her birth story involved her mother, her father, and someone else.

Deanna's family romance was in the service of forging her identity as an "egg donor" child. As she and her cohort move into adulthood, their developmental needs and experiences will get woven together with the interpersonal transactions between them and their parents to create either an integrated tapestry or an ill-fitting fabric for their established self as persons whose origins involved the participation of a birth other in a scientific rather than sexual procreative union.

Conclusion

When Freud first established his theories of psychosexual develop-ment, there was on record only one sperm-donor child, a child successfully conceived from the donated sperm of a medical student and an experimental insemination by Dr William Pancoast of Philadelphia during an obstetrical surgical procedure in 1884, a fact never revealed to the mother (Mundy, 2007). One hundred years later, the growing numbers of children conceived through assisted reproductive technology necessitate that we both change our narrative of conception and extend or correct our developmental theories to account for the new phenomenon that a mother alone, a father alone, two mothers, and two fathers can make a baby using donated gametes or borrowed wombs. We must also acknowledge that these parents and children exist not in a vacuum but in a social milieu that is often prejudiced against the new birth technologies, generating a collective negative consciousness that is inevitably internalised by parents who have in fact chosen to have their children using assisted conception, and perhaps also by their children through direct contact or unconscious intergenerational transmission.

We can expect more and more children and parents from assisted-conception families to come for treatment. As a result of their life circumstance, family formation with the aid of reproductive technology, both the parents and the children are at risk for a specific set of conflicts or psychological turmoil. Although by no means pathological, such experiences may be difficult to negotiate on one's own. The opportunity to explore feelings and bring unconscious fantasies and anxieties to the surface with the help of a clinician sensitized to the dynamics, defences, developmental tasks, and facilitating factors will give "birth other" families a greater chance to have a healthy go of it and will help all of us understand at a deeper level the emotional realities of "doing what comes scientifically".

References

Bollas, C. (1987). *The Shadow of the Object*. London: Free Association.

Cooper, S., & Glazer, E. (1994). *Beyond Infertility: The New Paths to Parenthood*. New York: Lexington.

Corbett, K. (2001). Nontraditional family romance. *Psychoanalytic Quarterly, 52*: 599–624.

Davies, J. M. (1998). Thoughts on the nature of desires: the ambiguous, the transitional, and the poetic. Reply to commentaries [on "Between the disclosure and foreclosure of erotic transference-countertransference"]. *Psychoanalytic Dialogues, 8*: 805–823.

Ehrensaft, D. (2000). Alternatives to the stork: fatherhood fantasies in donor insemination families. *Studies in Gender & Sexuality*, 1: 371–397.

Ehrensaft, D. (2005). *Mommies, Daddies, Donors, Surrogates: Answering Tough Questions and Building Strong Families*. New York: Guilford Press.

Erikson, E. (1963). *Childhood and Society*. New York: Norton.

Ethics Committee of the American Society for Reproductive Medicine. (2004). Informing offspring of their conception by gamete donation. *Fertility & Sterility*, 81: 527–531.

Freud, A. (1966). *The Ego and the Mechanisms of Defense*. Madison, CT: International Universities Press.

Freud, S. (1924). Twenty-first lecture: development of the libido and sexual organizations. In: *A General Introduction to Psychoanalysis* (pp. 329–347). New York: Pocket Books, 1972.

Golombok, S., & MacCallum, F. (2003). Practitioner review: outcomes for parents and children following non-traditional conception: what do clinicians need to know? *Journal of Child Psychology & Psychology*, 44: 303–315.

Golombok, S., MacCallum, F., & Goodman, E. (2001). The "test-tube" generation: parent-child relationships and the psychological well-being of in vitro fertilization children at adolescence. *Child Development*, 72: 599–608.

Golombok, S., Murray, C., Brinsden, P., & Abdalla, H. (1999). Social vs. biological parenting: family functioning and the social-emotional development of children conceived by egg or sperm donation. *Journal of Child Psychology & Psychiatry*, 40: 519–527.

Klein, M. (1935). A contribution to the psychogenesis of manic-depressive states. *International Journal of Psychoanalysis*, 16: 145–174.

Morrisette, M. (2006). *Behind Closed Doors: Moving Beyond Secrecy and Shame. Voices of Donor Conception, Vol. 1*. New York: Be-Mondo.

Mundy, L. (2007). *Everything Conceivable: How Assisted Reproduction Is Changing Men, Women, and the World*. New York: Knopf.

Murray, C., MacCallum, F., & Golombok, S. (2006). Egg donation parents and their children: follow-up at age 12 years. *Fertility & Sterility*, 88: 610–618.

Oxenhandler, N. (2001). *The Eros of Parenthood*. New York: St Martin's Press.

Warner, L. L. (1993). Family romancer resolution in George Eliot's Daniel Deronda. *Psychoanalytic Study of the Child*, 49: 379–397.

Winnicott, D. W. (1960). The theory of the parent–infant relationship. In: *The Maturational Processes and the Facilitating Environment* (pp. 37–55). Madison, CT: International Universities Press, 1965.

Winnicott, D. W. (1971). *Playing and Reality*. London: Tavistock.

PART III

AN EXPLORATION OF THE IMPACT UPON CHILDREN OF KNOWING HOW THEY WERE CONCEIVED

CHAPTER SEVEN

Telling and talking: a family affair

Olivia Montuschi

J ust over thirty years ago my husband Walter and I discovered that the only way for us to create a family where I would bear a child was going to be by using a sperm donor.

The news of Walter's infertility was given to him with the casual brutality of the time, "You haven't got a hope in hell of fathering a child. Don't go to any quacks, they can't help . . . Next . . ." We staggered out on to the busy London street our hopes and dreams in tatters.

We were in fact already a re-formed family as I had had a son in my first marriage and with the abdication of his father from parental duties, Walter had taken on a stepfather role. Having failed to give this child a "normal" family life, I so much wanted to get it right second time around. I also wanted Walter's child . . . his blue eyes, his patience, sense of justice . . . intelligence. But, how does one move on from this very strong desire to have the child of a much loved man to being able to accept using an anonymous donor. Just how much did we want to add to our little family and how important was it that any child we had was biologically Walters?

In retrospect, I can now say that quite by chance as it seemed then, we were taking preparatory steps that have become part of the philosophy of the Donor Conception Network and that we continue to advocate to others. We gave ourselves time to think what infertility and donor conception meant to us. We nurtured our relationship, which had become a little fractious due to baby-making sex and anxiety about tests results, and we quietly, separately and together, moved towards a place where it was possible to make a decision about donor conception. Today we would recognise this as a grieving and ultimately healing process. At the time it just felt like giving each other space. I also researched donor conception clinics—not an easy task in pre-internet days—so that we would know where to turn should we decide to go ahead. It took a nine month gestation, to make the decision.

I will say more about Walter's and my personal journey to donor conception parenthood over the course of this chapter, but the main purpose is to explore some of the questions above from the broader perspective of having had the privilege of talking to many, many other parents and prospective parents over the years. And in particular to reflect on the fears and anxieties faced by those using donor conception about revealing this fact to their children and others.

Donor conception: the development of UK practice

In order to understand approaches and attitudes to donor conception today it is helpful to see it in the context of the history of first sperm and later, egg donation.

The first documented use of donor insemination took place in Philadelphia in 1884 (Hard, 1909) but it had probably been used informally to circumvent male infertility for much longer than that. At its simplest it can be a very low tech procedure, often referred to as "the turkey baster technique" because of the use of such a piece of kitchen equipment in home insemination before disposable syringes became available. The first clinic in the UK offering sperm donation—or artificial insemination by donor (AID) as it was known then—was started in the 1940s by Dr Mary Barton and her husband Berthold Wiesner.

In 1945 Mary Barton published an account of her artificial insemination work in the *British Medical Journal* (Barton, Walker, & Wiesner, 1945).[1] The response was almost universal condemnation. Around the world, politicians and church leaders called for artificial insemination to be made illegal. The Pope declared it a sin and the Archbishop of Canterbury set up an enquiry and called for Parliament to make it illegal. Although heated debates were held, this did not happen. But nor was donor insemination (DI) made a legal activity. This gave it an uncertain status and it continued to be conducted in the utmost secrecy.

The secrecy of AID served not only to protect the interests of the donor, but also those of the woman receiving treatment, her (infertile) partner, and the doctor performing the procedure. Few records were kept and the identities of the donors were not disclosed. Doctors tried their best to match key physical characteristics of the donor (height, weight, colouring) to that of the infertile man. This increased the chance of any children born fitting into the family, thus reducing the risk of questions being asked.

Couples having children by AID or as it later became known, DI, rarely told anyone and put their own names on the birth certificate as legal parents of the child. Few donor-conceived people were told about their origins in a planned way and, even if they were, there was no way they could find out about the donor. Sometimes, donor-conceived people found out either following a family argument or during a deathbed disclosure by a member of the family. They often described this news as being devastating, or like being hit by a train.

The law catches up with practice

By the end of the 1970s a law to allow the husband of a woman having DI to be treated as the legal father, had been passed in fifteen states in the US (Ben-Asher, 2008). It was not, however, until the 1980s that attitudes to DI began to change in the UK. Concern arose following the development of *in-vitro* fertilisation (IVF) to produce human embryos and the birth in 1978 of Louise Brown at Oldham General Hospital. These developments triggered the appointment in 1982 of the Warnock Committee. Its remit was to inquire into human fertilisation and embryology. The Committee reported in 1984, the same year that the first birth by egg donation took place in Australia.

Warnock recommended a comprehensive scheme to regulate all procedures using sperm, eggs, or embryos and the recommendations were implemented in the Human Fertilisation and Embryology (HFE) Act, 1990, which came into force in August 1991. With it came the legal framework for donor conception of all types and a central register of all assisted conception procedures recording information about donors, recipients, and children conceived with donor help. Although the identities of donors were to be recorded on the register, they were not to be disclosed to recipients, parents, or donor conceived people themselves.

Clinic practices with regard to the secrecy surrounding donor conception remained very much the same. Couples using sperm donation were encouraged to "go home, make love, and who knows who the sperm that creates any resulting pregnancy will have come from". Donor assisted reproduction continued to be regarded as an unfortunate last option for couples to circumvent their infertility and have a child born to them rather than adopting or remaining childless. The emphasis was on meeting the needs of the couple to have a child while protecting the infertile partner. Little thought was given to the needs of the people who might be born since it was largely assumed that they would never be troubled by knowledge of their unusual origins. Donors were discouraged from thinking about the implications of their donation much beyond the £15 they earned from each clinic visit. Their function was over once the donation had been made.

Recipient parents were also encouraged to see donation as a pragmatic way forward rather than a very different way to create a family that might require some time, thought, and grieving for the child that could not be, before going ahead. Telling the child was definitely a minority activity but there were some parents, like Walter and I, who could see no good reason to keep this information secret. For them, the question was more "how do we do this?" rather than "shall we tell them?" as there were virtually no resources to help parents think about this task.

Donor anonymity challenged

A landmark court case brought by a donor conceived adult and a child in 2002, Rose and E, established that Article 8 of the Human Rights Act (right to family life) was engaged and that, "an AID child is entitled to establish a picture of (his) identity as much as anyone else".[2] As a result, the Department of Health launched a consultation about the ending of anonymity for donors and began the process of setting up a voluntary register for matching donors and offspring from the pre-1991 era by

mutual consent. Much to the disgust of the fertility doctors, who anticipated their supplies of donors drying up as a result, the decision was
reached in 2004 by Labour Health Minister Melanie Johnson that only
donors willing to be identifiable to offspring from the age of eighteen
could be used from April 2005 (Johnson, 2004).

The Donor Conception (DC) Network, which had been started by
five families in 1993, supported the change in legislation, leading their
sometimes reluctant members to a position where openness about
donor conception could be seen as a first step to breaking down barriers to donor conceived people knowing more about the person who
contributed to their existence. Abandoning secrecy about donor information was the natural next step after dropping secrecy about treatment. This meant helping parents to face their fears about
acknowledging the role of the donor and the perceived or anticipated
rejection in favour of this person. It is interesting also to note the
change in language that took place during the years 1991 and 2005. In
the early years donor offspring were always referred to as "children"
no matter how old they were. This felt patronisingly infantilising to
the many donor conceived people who were increasingly insisting
that they were adults whose needs and rights were being ignored. In
2013 it is very unusual to hear anyone refer to donor conceived people
as "children" unless they actually are referring to under twelves.

The five families who started DC Network all wanted to be open
with their children about being conceived with the help of sperm
donation but were looking for others who shared their perspective
and resources to help with the telling and talking. Each family had
come to their own decision that withholding information from their
children was not a sound basis for the development of trust in family
relationships. Soon after the organisation started, the families came to
compare the ways in which donor conception was both the same and
different to adoption. It felt very confirming that experience with
adoptive families had shown that honesty with children from an early
age prevented the shock of finding out that assumptions about genetic
connectedness in the family were not true.

In 2000 David Howe and Julia Feast published the findings of their
ground-breaking research into the long-term experiences of adopted
adults. Among other things, they looked at why some adopted young
people struggle in their adult lives with the factors around their adoption, while others seem freer to enjoy their lives, even though there

may be large gaps in their histories, and those histories may be of grief and loss. The conclusion they came to is that "it is not what happens to you that matters, it is the way you make sense of it that counts in the end" (Howe & Feast, with Coster, 2003).

Howe and Feast were clear that stable and supportive family relationships were a very important protective factor, but also, that there is something powerful in how people come to see their stories and make sense of their experiences. Adoptive parents who told coherent (plausible, objective, as complete as possible) stories of the young person's history tended to have very good relationships with their children.

It is easy to see how this might fit with donor conceived children. If parents have made peace with their need to use donated eggs or sperm then they are free to be able to tell a very positive family story to their child, thus helping them begin to create their own story. Parents may not be able to fill in all the gaps in their children's stories, but the heartening view is that this does not seem to matter as much as how they are able to help their children make sense of what they *can* tell them.

The children's books that DC Network went on to write and publish are called *My Story* (Infertility Research Trust, 1991) and the series of books entitled *Our Story* (Donor Conception Network, 2002a,b,c, 2008) and the film featuring donor conceived young people is entitled *A Different Story* (2003). This has been updated to include children conceived though sperm, egg, embryo and double donation, in solo mum and lesbian couple families as well as heterosexual couples: *A Different Story . . . Revisited* (2014).

Twenty years on

DC Network has undoubtedly contributed enormously to changing the climate with regard to openness about donor conception in the UK. However, what remains the same after twenty years are the fears that many parents have about sharing information with their child and with others. What is different is that donor conception is frequently talked about in the media, reflecting a culture that has moved towards openness as a generally accepted "good thing" and resources that are now readily available to support parents in making decisions and sharing information with children, family, and friends. Which leaves us with a discrepancy between how some people feel and what the law now supports and the prevailing culture encourages. How these discrepancies are managed by families is a theme that recurs throughout the rest of the chapter.

Thinking about genes, and the response to infertility

To return to the five founding families of DC Network, Walter and I included among them. Four of the families were heterosexual couples with children by sperm donation. The remaining family was a single woman with her three donor conceived children. We all came from different parts of the country and had very different backgrounds but one of our uniting features was that none of the men felt diminished as people or as men by their inability to contribute to the making of a baby. All had been shocked to learn of their infertility and had gone through varying degrees of disbelief, sorrow, and sadness but had emerged from this time with a conviction that becoming parents and making a loving family was far more important than genetic links. Their identity was secure enough to be able to think about the meaning of using a donor for their children and the whole family, rather than focusing on their own loss. Being open with their children was a natural corollary of such an approach.

Speculation about the individual psychology of these four men that allowed them to feel so secure is beyond my remit, but they would certainly seem to fall into what sociologist Professor Carol Smart would call a "glass half full" group of people. In a presentation in June 2013 of her "Relative Strangers" research (Smart, 2013) she noted that parents she had interviewed who fell into this group tended to negotiate the meaning of donor conception in a more optimistic way, minimise the significance of the step they had taken, put emphasis on the activity of parenting rather than the way they had become parents, and work hard to create resemblances and connections through shared values and experiences. Those who struggled with disconnection (the glass half empty approach) saw difference everywhere, resisted reminders in the media or social life of their infertility or the fact that there was a genetic disconnect in the family, and continued to have a sense of loss.

Smart's important research highlights the paradoxical and fluid way that most ordinary people talk about genes. The meaning for each person will be filtered through their personal beliefs and values and the way that information is conveyed in the media. Information on television, the internet, and in newspapers may appear "scientific" but if explained in terms of metaphor, as it often is, will contain a way of seeing that is rarely neutral. Smart quotes neurobiologist Steven Rose who said in *Lifelines: Biology Beyond Determinism* (Rose, 1997) "It is hard to know which had more impact on the future directions of biology—the determination of the role of DNA in protein synthesis, or the organising power of the metaphor within which it was framed."

Smart found that many donor conception families had very flexible attitudes to genes and often, almost certainly without consciously realising it, veered in their views from genetic determinism to seeing nurture as the dominant force in creating identity and bonds within the family. Far from interpreting this as a sign of confusion, Smart understands this duality as donor conception families just trying to do their best with what she sees as "the mystery of genetic connectedness" (Smart, 2013).

Modern anthropologists and sociologists have focused recent work on the "doing" aspect of families and kinship rather than issues of structure or lineage; that is the everyday family practices, family stories, and resemblances, the sharing of home, food, and family rituals. Anthropologist Janette Edwards has coined the expression "born and bred" kinship (Edwards, 2000) and this may be more helpful to donor conception families in thinking about the creation of bonds and shared identity. But I think it is likely to be the "glass half full" families who are best able to integrate this perspective into their family narrative and the "glass half empty" ones who will continue to feel the loss of "blood lines" of heredity. They are the families who may struggle most with "telling".

Whatever a couple or individual's attitude to the meaning of genetic connections, the first challenge to those who find donor conception their only route to having a family is to accept their identity as an infertile person. This is something that the four men in the founding families were able to do. Experience over twenty years of DC Network has shown that perhaps not many do so as easily. I am indebted to Marilyn Crawshaw of the University of York for introducing me to Erving Goffman's 1963 concept of "spoiled identity" that certainly seems to fit how many men and women feel about their infertility—certainly at first. The perceived shame and stigma of not being able to fulfil their biological reproductive function is internalised as personal failure. Women tend to be pitied and men have their libido threatened, the difference between sexual identity and fertility identity very often being confused, particularly by men and by others.

In the early days of sperm donation women often took the "blame" for the couple not being able to have a child in order to "protect" their partner from taunts about being a Jaffa (a type of seedless orange) or "firing blanks". This occasionally happens today. It is, however, increasingly realised that attempts to deny or disguise male infertility may add to a man's injured sense of self by not allowing him the opportunity to grieve his infertility and potentially move on to be able see himself as a sexually potent man and loving father despite his inability to contribute to conception. It may take the birth of a donor conceived child for an infertile man or woman to fully comprehend that a genetic connection is not necessary to love a child wholeheartedly and without reserve. As one DI dad said at a DC Network meeting,

> Before our daughter was born it was all about me and how unfair it was that I couldn't have my own genetic child. Now she is here I see it's all about her and because I love her so much I want to be straight with her about how she began.

Grieving, simply allowing time to pass, relationships to heal, pondering a future without being a parent, and "letting go of trying to create a perfect image of us" are central components of making good decisions about whether donor conception feels a comfortable way to create a family. Counselling can be an important contributor, providing time and space for talking with an emotionally uninvolved third party who can encourage reflection and the safety to think the unthinkable. Breaking the isolation felt by so many people contemplating donor conception by meeting others and talking with them about their feelings and experiences can be a game changer in giving confidence that donor conception parenting can be much the same as any other . . . plus a few extra responsibilities. The "Preparation for Donor Conception Parenthood" workshops run by the Donor Conception Network attempts to do just this, but facilitators also regard a decision by participants that donor conception is not the right way forward for them, as an equal success.

Telling the child

For potential parents who have gone through the processes described above, accepting the responsibility of being open with any child they have becomes a natural part of their journey towards having a family. It does not necessarily remove the fears about the actual "doing" but it does provide a solid basis for the commitment. For those who have not had the time and space to think about what infertility and donor conception mean for them and any child—perhaps because of being hurried by a clinic into proceeding with donor conception immediately following failed IVF cycles, or because of being afraid of thinking about it too much—then openness is not such an obvious path. Many parents accept the theory that "telling" is the right thing to do but, for a variety of reasons, do not manage to get beyond the intention. It may be that managing the transition from stigma (about infertility or the use of donor conception per se) to acceptance is too much for them. This may be rationalised into "there never seems to be a right time" or "we just could not find the right words". The gap between intention and action can be great. For others, the imperative to "tell" remains a mystery. "She is ours, we love her to bits, why would we tell her?" is the essence of many posts on internet fertility forums. But these days it is said increasingly defensively.

One of the fears that is shared by both those who intend and those who do not intend to "tell" is that of rejection—by the child as they learn about and understand the genetic disconnect and by others when they hear about the use of donor conception. Those who manage the transition from fear to putting "telling" into practice often experience a strengthening of integrity within the family as a result of feeling they have "done the right thing".

Conveying basic information derived from attachment theory (Bowlby, 1988) about how babies and their care-givers make relationships can help give anxious parents confidence. It can lessen anxiety significantly to know that beginning to talk to their under five-year-old about "how mummy and daddy needed some help from a nice man (or woman) to help make you" is not going to result in the child deciding that their donor is the "real" parent and mummy or daddy an imposter. The series of *Our Story* (Infertility Research Trust,1991; Donor Conception Network, 2002a,b,c, 2008) books for young children are enormously valued by parents as aids to starting to tell a child their donor conception story in simple, age appropriate language. The four *Telling and Talking Booklets* (Montuschi, 2006) for parents of children at different ages and stages, are intended to continue to support parents in adapting their language and responses to children's questions to make them developmentally appropriate.

Of course as children grow up they move on from using the language of their parents and develop their own words to convey their current understanding of donor conception and what it means to them. Some will go through a period of referring to the donor as a "real"' father or mother or use the term genetic or biological mum or dad. The use of the word "real" seems to be a rational and conventional linking of family relationships that is most often used by young teenage boys. Its use rarely conveys anything about the quality of the emotional relationship in a family and as these boys move on to the more complex thinking that is characteristic of the second half of their teens, their language often changes again.

The unexploded bomb that sits in the chest of even the most confident of parents is the anxiety that one day their child will use the genetic disconnect to challenge them about their authority as a parent. This does not occur in all donor conception families (it did not in ours) but it certainly does happen and sometimes earlier than parents might think. A story told by one DI dad in an early DC Network newsletter was about his six-year-old daughter who wanted a puppy. In a family debate he vetoed the idea and was turned on venomously by his daughter who said that her "seed daddy" would certainly have let her have a puppy. This particular phrase had never been used by her parents. Her dad wrote:

> I was immediately engulfed by two simultaneous responses. One was the realisation that, for the first time, we had a positive indication that C really understood what we had been telling her about her origins as a DI child. The second feeling was that I felt hurt and rejected, which of course was the intended result.

> I am being quite honest when I say that, because I recognised her remark as a textbook example of the difficult side of being open about DI, and because I was prepared for it, my pleasure at the confirmation of her understanding far outweighed my hurt. I wanted to, and did, just cuddle C and say that I loved her whatever she said about me when she was cross.

This lovely man, one of the founders of DC Network, had the maturity to be able to put aside his own hurt and understand the strong feelings of his daughter who had reached for any weapon she could in an effort to get something she wanted very badly. Knowing the warmth of the relationships inside this particular family I have always thought that maybe this little girl had felt secure enough with her dad to be able to challenge him in this way. She knew he would not fall apart, something that would have been terrible for them both.

While the imagining by a young child of the donor as an alternative, more benevolent, parent is unusual, parents need to be prepared for unexpected responses. The simplicity of the explanations in the *Our Story* books (Infertility Research Trust,1991; Donor Conception Network, 2002a,b,c, 2008) can lead to surprising assumptions. Our daughter, also age six at the time, thought that we must know her donor because otherwise how did we know he was a "kind man" (answer: because he wanted to help mummies and daddies have a baby).

But it is in the teenage years that parents envisage a real challenge to authority will come. "Yes, I am going out and you can't tell me not to. You're not my real Dad/Mum anyway". Yet there are good reasons to think that this will not necessarily happen. Reported instances of it are not numerous. And why might that be, given the need teenagers have to establish their own identity and difference to parents? One reason is because even teenagers know that this particular line of attack may not press the hurt buttons it is intended to activate. There are probably other lines of attack that would hurt more. Teenagers may pick on anything that they see as a parental weakness or where they can score a good argumentative point. They will cite parental unfairness, inconsistency, or out-dated values compared to those of their friend's parents. If parents do not feel their non-genetic link to be a point of emotional vulnerability, their teenage children are less likely to pick on it.

Parents will have had at least twelve years of family life in which to have embedded the fact of donor conception. By then it should be a fact of life, one not easily available as a term of abuse. Unalterable facts that cause no embarrassment do not make good sources of challenge or abuse: "You've no right to tell me what to do, you're only five foot three", does not make much sense.

All children, whatever their age, need to know that their parents will not crumble when faced with difficult decisions and challenges.

Parents in donor conception families need to know that the genetic disconnect *may* be used against them at some point and be ready to respond to the feelings behind the challenge rather than engage in a defensive way with the words themselves.

Telling family and friends

Fearfulness about being judged or even rejected by family and friends now seems in 2015 to be more prevalent than anxieties about telling children. This is partly because of the change in culture towards being open with children, but also because of the range of resources now available to help with sharing information with them. But if children know about their donor conceived origins then it is important that those close to them also know. As one mother of a two-and-a-half-year-old daughter said,

> We could just imagine her telling granny about "the nice lady who gave mummy an egg to help make me", so it was important to us that granny was told about egg donation long before this could happen.

No matter how old they are, most couples and individuals contemplating donor conception want to know that their parents, in particular, will not judge or reject them for building their family in this "different" way. They also worry that their children will not be treated the same as other grandchildren. It is very common to hear potential parents talk about "letting their parents down"—feeling that they have somehow failed them by not being able to provide genetically connected grandchildren. The need for parental approval may be strongest in those who have had difficulty separating emotionally from their parents. One of the tasks of any supporter or counsellor could be to help a potential recipient of donated eggs or sperm to focus on how they will tell their parents. Is this something they plan to inform their parents about, rather than consulting them, thus taking adult responsibility for their life choices and letting go of the need for approval?

Potential and actual parents of donor conceived children become hugely knowledgeable about their own fertility status and all the tests and treatments required to help them become parents. They are likely to have gone through considerable heartache over a long period of time, adjusting their hopes, dreams, and expectations as they go. Many couples and single women share information about what they are going through with just one or two people, or no-one at all until a pregnancy is achieved. Most relatives and friends, therefore, have a lot of catching up to do in relation to their knowledge, and particularly their understanding about donor conception and its meaning for all concerned. One woman I talked to said,

> I was shocked when my mother said that the child I was carrying would not be her real grandchild, but then I realised that at first I had thought that an egg donation baby would not be my real baby. Her thinking was an extension of mine. Like me she needed time to think about what family and parenting means. Hopefully she will realise that family does not only have to mean genetic connectedness.

One of the unexpected roles that potential and actual parents can find themselves falling into is that of educator. Also becoming unofficial counsellors when the people they turn to for support need *their* feelings to be listened to and taken into account when they first learn about donor conception.

When, who, and how much to tell are all matters to be thought about and negotiated. The good news is that it is only rarely that fears of significant disapproval or estrangement are realised. At a national meeting of DC Network in 2012 over a hundred parents and potential parents completed an exercise inviting them to reveal their fears about sharing information about donor conception with friends and family and the results of having done so. Almost universally fears were shown to have been unfounded. Instead, most people from all family types, experienced interest, warmth, support, and some curiosity from their relatives and close friends. A few people had to wait a while for relatives to adjust to the situation, but none experienced outright rejection.

Some members who took part in the exercise commented that the act of talking with friends and family had deepened their own understanding of what it means to become a parent by donor conception. Sharing information also resulted in a very rewarding strengthening of trust within a family or friendship. Taking charge of the information, making positive decisions about who should know, and how this should happen, seemed to help many people build confidence and feel in control.

The question of "difference"

At the heart of many parents anxieties about sharing information with their children and with others is the issue of "difference". Despite the integration of IVF into everyday life as a way of conceiving a child, using donor conception remains a "different" way for a child to come into a family. And while acceptance of donor conception as one of the many ways modern families are formed is a goal of DC Network, acknowledgement of the use of donated gametes is likely to remain an important part of preparing for the responsibilities of donor conception parenthood for the foreseeable future. Parents and potential parents have to face and decide how they are going to manage this "difference" at some point in their journey or have it hanging over them forever.

Difference, of course, does not have to be negative. Difference can be exciting, stimulating, a cause of celebration or it can be relatively neutral, something that just is and accepted as that. Difference is only worrying or dangerous if people feel threatened by it or someone is threatening them because of it.

How people manage difference will depend on many things. Their culture and background, how they were raised, and the experiences they have had will all be important influences. If their parents were fearful of change or difference in others and perhaps inflexible in their attitudes then this approach to life may be picked up by their children. This is not inevitable for people brought up in cautious families, who can find themselves challenging the narrow boundaries in which they were raised. Individual personality and temperament of course play a significant part, but an ability to face and go *through* difficulties rather than *around* them, being able to take the perspective of others, a flexible approach and confidence without arrogance are all qualities that are most desirable for a positive outcome.

If these are indeed the qualities needed by parents of donor conceived children it raises the question of what happens when people presenting for donor gamete treatment do not seem to exhibit them? Unlike adoption, where parents are carefully chosen for existing children, there has never been any question of selecting those suitable to conceive using donated eggs, sperm, or embryos. Emphasising the needs of adults, fertility medicine has always taken a pragmatic approach to baby-making with only a cursory "welfare of the child" clause to rule out people like convicted paedophiles or current hard drug users from receiving assisted conception.

The acknowledgement of "difference" is at the heart of telling children about donor conception. As a result of the guidance, enshrined in the HFE Act that parents will "tell" and modern easy accessible DNA testing, what may be more important than selection is the preparation for donor conception parenthood of those who proceed with treatment. Requiring potential parents to attend preparation sessions as a routine part of their donor conception treatment journey would first of all encourage clinics to recognise the difference between IVF with a couple's own gametes and moving on to donor conception. It would also help shift the culture to focus on "family" rather than "baby" making and support those who are reluctant to "tell" in understanding why and how openness can promote healthy family relationships.

The question of whether there are any circumstances under which it is not in the best interest of children to know about donor conception is a controversial one. In 2005 the American psychologist Diane Ehrensaft listed what she called the only three good reasons for not telling children at all or postponing telling to a different time. (Ehrensaft, 2005) These are:

- Issues to do with the child's ability to understand: a child with a significant learning or developmental problem may well not be able to take in information about his or her origins.

- Issues to do with the bond between parent and child: for instance, if a parent has been away from the child for a long time for any reason (e.g., working abroad or in prison), re-building the relationship should come before "telling". Where parents are separating or divorcing, "telling" should never be used as a threat to break a relationship between parent and child. Unless children are at real risk of learning about their origins from someone other than a parent, telling should ideally only begin when both parents agree and the emotional climate has settled down.

- Issues for the child outside of the immediate family: if wider family members or those in the community are likely to reject a child then it may be difficult for a child to feel any sense of pride about their origins. This situation can apply where a child is being brought up within a culture or faith that disapproves of donor conception.

It is sometimes argued that not sharing information with a child with a severe learning or developmental disorder is patronising and that the child will take in what is appropriate to their developmental level and nothing more. My own feeling is that the child has little to gain and possibly something to lose in misunderstanding the information, but I could be wrong. The key is probably, like so many things, in *how* it is done.

The issue of children being born into families whose faith or culture disapproves of donor conception is much more tricky. Again, it can be argued that if members of these communities choose to have a child by donor conception then they must either accept the responsibility to "tell" like anyone else, find another way to build their family, or remain childless. But these apparent choices are not necessarily real ones. Adoption will reveal infertility, often putting a woman at risk (whether she is to "blame" or not) of rejection by her spouse's family. Childlessness will again point the finger at a woman, who may be abandoned by her partner or rejected by her community in the same way as may happen if donor conception is revealed. Rocks and hard places come to mind.

What does seem important is that people from donor conception disapproving communities are given the same information about openness as anyone else. To treat them differently would be patronising, although compassionate counselling is also likely to be necessary.

What do donor conception parents think about the donor?

To return to Walter's and my story. The donor for each of our two children was chosen by our clinic doctor who had taken Polaroid photos of us both and each time assured us he would match us with someone appropriate. That we accepted, without any information whatsoever about these men, is indicative of the culture of the time. We had no choice as we wanted to proceed. Not only did it just not seem possible to ask questions, I am not sure we wanted to either. We had, very unusually for the time, decided from the outset that we were going to be open with any children we had, but we were not in the slightest bit interested in the donor.

Having mourned our imagined child—for Walter the one that would continue the family line he had traced back over three hundred years and for me the one carrying his characteristics—we were focusing on what we could bring as parents, *not* what the donor would be contributing. We had no information at all on which to base any fantasy and no prospect that the donor's identity would ever be known. Not that this was something we wanted. To be honest we did not really think about it, we simply wanted to have a family.

When the time came to talk with our first child we explained that "daddy's baby-making seeds weren't working properly so a kind man had lent some of his seeds to help make you" The term "lent" came from the only book available to help parents with donor conception narratives at the time, Robert Snowden's *The Gift of a Child* (1993). Our son never asked if we had to give the seeds back, but he did assume for a while that the kind man had given up his own ability to make a baby in order to help us. By the time our daughter was ready to hear her story the very first children's book *My Story* (Infertility Research Trust, 1991) had been published, but the whole issue was on the family conversation agenda by then anyway.

How parents view the donor these days, whether or not he or she is included in the story they tell their children, is both the same and very different from the time when Walter and I were making our family. What is the same is that heterosexual couples mostly remain reluctant to include the donor as a person in their family narrative. What is different is that recipient parents usually have a choice of donor, they may have a considerable amount of non-identifying information about him or her and donors, donating after 2005, are identifiable to donor conceived people from their eighteenth birthday. That the donor could actually become a real live person, potentially entering into the life of a family, is something that I suspect a lot of parents have yet to grapple with. These conditions apply if parents have had their treatment in the UK. If they have chosen to go abroad, particularly to countries like the Czech Republic or Spain, then completely different conditions apply. Doctors rather than recipient(s) will have chosen the anonymous donor and the information available may be as little as age and blood group.

People who have their treatment in such countries do not have to think about the donor as a person at all if they choose not to do so. What they risk is their child wishing to know about this person and judging their parent(s) for going abroad when they could have had an identifiable donor in the UK. The oldest UK resident children conceived abroad are in 2013 just entering their teenage years. As yet, no-one knows how they will feel about being conceived overseas or, for those conceived after 2005, how they will feel about having an anonymous donor when identifiable donors were available in the UK.

For those parents who conceived in the UK, it is single women who are keenest on including the donor and indeed potential half-siblings into the family narrative. There is no male partner to protect from slights about his fertility and as single women often only have one child by donor conception, many are keen to make contacts with genetic relatives by donation early in their children's lives. It is interesting, however, that single women who have children by double (egg and sperm) or embryo donation are often reluctant to explain about the egg donor. Their children ask from an early age about whether they have a dad (and indeed other children ask them) so devising simple ways of explaining about sperm donation is one of a solo mum's earliest tasks. However, they have a mummy so they do not ask about the egg donor and even if their mother tries to explain about it, the egg donation part is less well understood at a young age. It may also be that in contrast to the celebration about genetic connections with half-siblings via the sperm donor, some solo mums are anxious that talking about using an egg donor as well means revealing that there is no genetic connection between mother and child.

Heterosexual and lesbian couples tend to be more cautious, seeing themselves as two parent families whose integrity may be changed or challenged by including the donor too significantly. DC Network members, while happy to acknowledge that a donor was needed to help with conception, are much more likely to put emphasis on upbringing as shaping genetically inherited traits, thus diminishing the role of the donor.

But, as I indicated above, all parents who conceived in the UK since 2005 are going to have to adjust at some point to the fact that from their child's eighteenth birthday he or she could find information that would identify the donor. This may mean this man or woman entering the life of the young person and potentially the whole family, if not actually in person then in the ripples thrown up by the contact being made. Because of the possibility of pre-2005 donors re-registering with the Human Fertilisation and Embryology Authority (HFEA) as being willing to be identified, these connections could start to be being made any time now (they have not yet as I write).

It is difficult to assess the value for people conceived after 2005 of their future rights of access to information and how many will decide to pursue those rights. If adoption is anything to go by, not all will, and of those that do the majority will be well past eighteen. The significance of the rights may be simply that they are there—the choice *can* be made. For some donor conceived people to know that the identity of their donor is contained in an official record behind permanently locked doors, is frustrating and tantalising in itself.

Walter and I are often asked how we would feel if our daughter made contact with her donor (she is the one who is curious and has registered with the Donor Conceived Register, while our son is not). Because he is not her genetic father I usually refer this question to Walter but he is clear that he would not feel threatened in any way. His relationship with our daughter is secure. What both of us would be worried about is that the donor might turn out to be a disappointment for her; that she would not feel any connection at all, particularly if he did not look like her. We would like to think that we would be happy for her if she found the experience a positive one and she was able to satisfy the curiosity she has talked about. If he did appear we would be nervous about the unknown—also curious—but not concerned that it would change the relationship we have with our children.

Sperm donors thirty years ago were mostly students who donated for money. Today's sperm and egg donors are also paid—the HFEA calls it compensation—but they have to be so much more. Because of the possibility of contact from age eighteen it is vital that only donors who really understand the long-term implications of what they are doing are recruited. It is unclear if clinics, with their continued emphasis on "baby" rather than "family" making, really comprehend the importance of only accepting egg and sperm donors who are mature enough to put themselves in the shoes of a donor conceived person looking for information and/or contact.

Until very recently donors were shadowy figures whose views we knew little about. Luckily, some donors are beginning to let us know how they feel. Kriss Fearon, a pre-2005 egg donor who has re-registered with the HFEA as identifiable, is a frequent commentator on donor conception matters, particularly from the perspective of donors. She has been a trustee of the National Gamete Donation Trust and through them and her current MA in social research has had contact with many egg and sperm donors. She recently made the following contribution to my blog oliviasview.wordpress.com (Montuschi, 2011) as part of a conversation about how complex the issues for all parties to donor conception are,

> What's interesting about this is the gradual acknowledgement over time, in society as a whole (or perhaps just our little part of it) that this whole process has a lasting impact on all involved. For the dc parents who have to support their children with this throughout their life, not just put infertility in a box after the birth. For dc people, obviously, But because this is my specific area of knowledge and interest, I'm thinking particularly of donors, who once were expected to donate and forget (but who rarely do forget) and treated as if they have an unhealthy interest if they don't. Now, especially since donors became identifiable, it's accepted as a decision with lifelong consequences that donors could be dealing with decades later even if contact never happens. That this has an impact on donors' partners and children. Or, perhaps, there is an identity change from donor to biological father/mother, as people's perspectives about parenthood change through their life. Not as major as the identity issues that adoptive and dc people are faced with but potentially significant nonetheless.
>
> I like this, though. Like many of life's really important matters, it is something that you carry with you that is on your mind more or less often depending on what else is going on. Something you can pick up and carry on dealing with like knitting a half-finished scarf. It's not going anywhere! And I think that's healthy, to be able to come back to things later, perhaps with a different perspective.

As a parent it is not necessarily comfortable to contemplate a donor coming to think of themselves as a biological mother or father rather than the more remote term, "donor". However, I do think parents are going to have to take on board the reality that some children (young people, adults) and some donors will use this terminology and that some donors and offspring, if they do get together, may develop emotional bonds as well. It is already beginning to happen in the US and Australia, although I know of only one instance in the UK.

The following post was made by a former sperm donor on the Yahoo group of the Donor Sibling Registry (DSR) in the USA in July 2013,

> Since I was a toddler my family had the tradition of spending at least 1 week every summer up at a lake in the mountains [actual location

edited out]. I was continuing that tradition with my friends and family in my adulthood. Thanks to Wendy [Wendy Kramer and her son Ryan started the DSR] and the DSR that tradition has grown to include 6 of my biological sons and 2 daughters, plus their parents and siblings. In 2008 one of my sons joined us. In 2009 it was four kids. Flash forward to this year and we had 26 people in a huge extended family reunion. 13 kids, 8 of them biologically mine plus cousins and nieces and nephews. We had to rent 4 cabins this year to accommodate everyone. I must say when I am participating in the swimming, hiking, boating and horseback riding making it all feel so organic and normal to be surrounded by so much energy and love. The siblings and their cousins have all bonded so naturally.

Fearon is right, feelings and attitudes do evolve and change throughout a person's life and with societal change. If I am reading the signs right we are probably moving towards a future where the donor will become a recognised person in family life, if not actually a third parent. Scenes such as that described by the former donor above may become commonplace. If parents have done a "good enough" job they should have nothing to fear, with the donor simply becoming another interested adult in a donor conceived person's life. Donor conceived people will have the opportunity to get to know others connected to them genetically and regard them in whatever way feels comfortable for them all.

Further thoughts about the future

Despite the predictions above it remains very hard to know what the future will look like for donor conception families. We are all still feeling our way and it will not be easy. So much has changed and yet so much has remained the same since Walter and I decided that sperm donation felt right for us. But the next thirty years must surely bring new challenges as the era of secrecy finally comes to an end.

As recognition of donor conceived people's needs for information and an increasing culture of openness led to the ending of anonymity, the next natural step, with donors now stepping out of the shadows, may be a better recognition of donors and their families as people with needs. Increasingly UK donors are men and women who are already parents themselves. There is little guidance for these people on how to explain to their own children about their role in creating children being raised in other families. Currently their own children—half-siblings to those created through donation—are not permitted to put their names on the register held by the HFEA in order to be in touch with their half-sibs by mutual consent. And then there is the question of donors, recipients, and the children created between them having contact, either from an early age or later on, and just how this would be managed.

Of course this question already presents itself where known donors are involved. HFEA statistics are not kept on the proportion of clinic treatments that involve donors introduced by the proposed recipients, but these appear to be on the increase. Frequently these involve a family member as a donor, sister donating eggs to sister, for example. In such families there is a preference for at least some genetic connection and if handled well, with all parties having the opportunity to talk through their feelings and expectations with a counsellor, this can be a positive experience for a child and the families involved.

Single mothers by choice are leading the way in wanting closer contact with their children's genetic relatives. They seem to have a greater interest in half-siblings and their families but I suspect would view positively, if cautiously, contact with their donor if he showed interest in being in touch with them. However, single women who are part of DC Network largely choose to conceive at an HFEA licensed clinic because of the legal safeguards with regard to the status of the donor. Lesbian couples, on the other hand, have traditionally chosen a donor from amongst their friendship group, often a gay man, and have opted for home rather than clinic insemination. A series of court cases (2011 and others)[3] have, however, now thrown a different light on arrangements of this sort. Failing to crystallise the intentions and expectations of all parties and to document these, some lesbian couples have found themselves being taken to court by men who find they have unexpectedly strong feelings for a child once s/he has been born. They want more contact than the mothers had bargained for. Cautionary tales of this sort are leading more and more lesbian couples to seek the legal framework of licensed clinic treatment.

From this we can speculate about a future where medical clinics will no longer be involved in bringing together donors and recipients, although there will remain a need for legal safeguards. In the US and South Africa it is mostly agencies that recruit donors and this is beginning to happen in the UK with egg donation. Altrui, the first UK egg donation agency, puts a truly enormous amount of effort into bringing together the right donor with the right recipient and facilitating their relationship with a fertility clinic. As yet, no donor and recipient have actually met but they do have the possibility of exchanging information through a letterbox system. However, in the US a few egg donor recruitment programmes do bring donors and recipients together. Ellen Glazer, writing in the second edition of her book *Having Your Baby by Egg Donation* (Glazer & Sterling, 2013), refers not to donor conception but to collaborative reproduction, which, like me, she believes should be thought of as a psychosocial as well as a medical issue. With a perspective that I find very refreshing, she talks about would-be parents being "the architects of your family story and the proud owners of that story". She encourages readers to "look to the future, and, in particular, to your hoped-for child's feelings, as you make the decisions that will begin your child's story." Because the donor is an important part of this story, potential parents are encouraged to meet her so that they can speak with confidence about her to the child as s/he grows up. Sometimes donors and recipients e-mail and phone first and then arrange to meet somewhere like a coffee-shop. Other times Ellen, as counsellor to the egg donation programme, meets with them both. Donors and recipients are both encouraged to sign up with the Donor Sibling Registry in order to keep in contact with each other at a level that has been agreed on and is comfortable for all.

It would take a change in the law for a system like this to work in the UK, but with egg donation agencies now beginning to transform the recruitment model I can *just* imagine it happening in my life-time.

Permanently anonymous donation has ended but we still have to wait until 2023 before the first children who have the right to identifying information are entitled to make enquiries. For some parents this is just the way they want it—a donor who cannot make his or her presence felt for eighteen years. Ambivalence about the donor remains strong for many couples. For others, mainly but not exclusively single women for the time being, it feels wrong that their children cannot make connections with genetic relatives before age eighteen. Their frustration with the current restrictions on making these links sometimes leads to more informal methods of seeking contact with families who have children from the same donor. The internet provides infinite possibilities.

The era of secrecy in which potential parents are "medical patients" doing what the doctor tells them to do, is coming to an end. Recipients are no longer patients but are said to be empowered consumers, demanding "no choice about me without me", living in a digital information age. But children and families cannot be produced to order, or with any certainty. All the information in the world will not necessarily lead to happy family life, and most people are right to be cautious, timid, and thoughtful before entering the donor conception pathway to parenthood.

Whatever the future brings, what feels fundamental to the well-being of donor conception families is that parents are educated and enabled to have the confidence and comfort to choose an identifiable donor and share information with their children from an early age. If they are then supported in raising their children in a warm, authoritative, and responsive way so that there is open communication and flexibility within the family, then it is likely that all will thrive and manage the challenges of donor conception, whatever they are and like anything else, as they arise. It is the quality of the relationships that count in the end.

Notes

1. 1940–1960 Bertold Wiesner and Mary Barton Barton Fertility Clinic, Portland Place, London W1A 1AA.
2. Joanna Rose & E (a child) v the Secretary of State & the Human Fertilisation & Embryology Authority (2002) seeks clarification of Article 8 of the European Convention on Human Rights, www.parliament.uk publications and records legal challenges
3. See, for example, P & L (Minors) (2011) EWHC 3431. Also see commentary on disputes with known donors by solicitor Natalie Gamble in Bio-News 20 February 2012 www.bionews.org.uk/page_128449.asp

References

Barton, M., Walker, K., & Wiesner, B. P. (1945). Artificial insemination. *British Medical Journal, 1*(4384): 40–43.

Ben-Asher, N. (2008). The curing law: on the legal evolution of baby-making markets, Columbia Law School. *Columbia Public Law & Legal Theory Working Papers*, 19 February, 2008.

Bowlby, J. (1988). *A Secure Base: Clinical Applications of Attachment Theory*: London: Routledge.

Donor Conception Network (2002a). *Our Story for Children Conceived by Egg Donation*. Nottingham: Donor Conception Network.

Donor Conception Network (2002b). *Our Story for Children Conceived by Sperm Donation into Lesbian Families*. Nottingham: Donor Conception Network.

Donor Conception Network (2002c). *Our Story for Children Conceived by Sperm Donation into Solo Mother Families*. Nottingham: Donor Conception Network.

Donor Conception Network (2003). *A Different Story*. A film by Liesel Evans.

Donor Conception Network (2008). *Our Story for Children Conceived into Heterosexual Couple Families by Double (Egg and Sperm) or Embryo Donation*. Nottingham: Donor Conception Network.

Donor Conception Network (2014). *A Different Story . . . Revisited*. A film by Cat Litchfield.

Edwards, J. (2000). *Born and Bred: Idioms of Kinship and New Reproductive Technologies in England*. Oxford: Oxford University Press.

Ehrensaft, D. (2005). *Mommies, Daddies, Donors, Surrogates: Answering Tough Questions and Building Strong Families*. New York: Guilford Press.

Glazer, E., & Sterling, E. (2013). *Having Your Baby Through Egg Donation* (2nd edn). London: Jessica Kingsley.

Goffman, E. (1963). *Stigma: Notes on the Management of Spoiled Identity*. London: Penguin, 1990.

Hard, A. D. (1909). Letter to the Editor: artificial impregnation. *The Medical World*: 163–164.

Howe, D., & Feast, J. with Coster, D. (2003). *Adoption, Search and Reunion: The Long-term Experiences of Adopted Adults*. London: The Children's Society.

Human Fertilisation and Embryology (HFE) Act (1990). From the UK Statue Law Database, www.legislation.gov.uk

Infertility Research Trust (1991). *My Story for Children Conceived by Sperm Donation into Heterosexual Couple Families*. Sheffield: Infertility Research Trust.

Johnson, M. (2004). MP and Labour Minister Keynote address for National Infertility Day for the Department of Health. UK Government Web Archive, www.nationalarchives.gov.uk

Montuschi, O. (2006). *4 Telling and Talking Booklets for Parents of Donor Conceived Children aged 0–7, 8–11, 12–16 and 17+*. Nottingham: Donor Conception Network.

Montuschi O. (2011). Comment made by K Fearon on 17 July 2013 in response to post entitled "Saying Goodbye" of 3 July 2013 Blog Oliviasview.wordpress.com

Rose, S. (1997). *Lifelines: Biology Beyond Determinism*. New York: Oxford University Press.

Smart, C. (2013). Academic Conference. *Relative Strangers: Living with Donor Conception, New Families and Genetic Identities: Developments in Law, Policy and Research*. LSE London 20–21 June.

Snowden, E., & Snowden, R. (1993). *Gift of a Child: A Guide to Donor Insemination*. Exeter: University of Exeter Press.

Warnock Committee (1984). The report on the Warnock Committee on human fertilisation and embryology. *British Medical Journal (Clinical Research Edition)*, 289(6439): 238–239.

Understanding and managing relationships in donor assisted families

Ken Daniels

Introduction

Mr and Mrs A and their three offspring are a close knit family. Despite a few tensions between the offspring and some tensions between the teenage offspring and their parents, they communicate well and certainly see themselves as "family". While how they function as a family could be said to be "normal", the way that the family was formed was different. Their family history includes the involvement of two people the offspring do not yet know about—two men who donated sperm so that their mother and father could become their parents. This chapter centres on the information and research that is available to this and other families as the parents share information about the infertility journey and the involvement of the donors in their family.

A key component of all family functioning is the relationships that exist between the different members. Arising from these relationships are factors associated with communication and what I describe as the establishment and maintenance of boundaries between them.

As the family history is shared with the offspring, the relationships, communications, and boundaries will be reviewed and changes will occur. Before the children were ever conceived, the relationship, communication, and boundaries between the parents were the subject of considerable reflection. Mother and father had expected to conceive children who were biologically part of both of them and many challenges emerged for them when they discovered this was not possible.

Traditionally, when families were built with the assistance of donated gametes from third parties, the parents were advised that no relationships were possible with the donors, they should forget about the donors, and that communication between parents and offspring should not include any reference to a donor's involvement. Boundaries were to be firmly set.

Mr and Mrs A are part of a growing trend that sees the rejection of this traditional approach. But what emerges in its place? This chapter will draw on the growing body of research and knowledge that is available to assist families explore relationships, communication, and boundaries in a more liberated age, an age in which parents are not burdened with keeping secrets from their offspring concerning the family history.

This chapter will look at who constitutes family, genetic and social factors as they relate to families, and the involvement of a third party in the family. The central relationships in gamete donation families will then be considered by looking at the donor and the parents, the donor and the offspring, and the offspring and the donor's family. The chapter will conclude with a discussion of relationship management as a key to healthy and well functioning families.

Who is family?

A family has traditionally been thought of as a set of parents and one or more children. Those children have resulted from the merging of the mother's eggs and the father's sperm. Such families are encased by a biological boundary—they are "of the same blood". The strong influence of this blood tie or genetic link is reflected in many aspects of societal functioning. Perhaps one of the most significant of these is the way in which relatives and friends look for and comment on the physical similarities between the child and her/his parents. Because biologically linked families are the most common in our society, an assumption is often made that this type of family is the "normal" family. Anything that deviates from this could be seen to be abnormal and give rise to issues about how to view and respond to such families. There tends to be a strong societal expectation that couples who marry or make a commitment to each other, will have children.

Those who experience infertility, apart from all the significant issues that arise for them personally, encounter this pro-natalist view. Some infertile persons experience this view as being so powerful that they hold back from sharing the infertility information. The fact that pro-creation and sexuality are intimately linked will almost certainly contribute to some not wanting to be open about their infertility struggle. For infertile couples who are then advised or choose to use donated gametes or embryos as a way of overcoming their infertility (note it is not a cure), there are likely to be concerns about how relatives and friends might react. In the early days of donor insemination (DI) some authorities said that introducing sperm from a donor into a couple relationship was akin to adultery (Daniels, 1998). In addition, the secrecy that was advocated by many doctors had the effect that couples felt they were doing something that was wrong or not acceptable and that it had to be hidden. The word stigma has been used to describe the experiences of many who were first infertile, and second who used donated gametes. I have always had some concern with the view that such couples were stigmatised. I think it is perhaps more accurate to say that it is the couples themselves who may feel stigmatised, but in fact, when they do share their information with others they frequently find that the reactions are understanding and sympathetic. For the couples, however, there tends to be hesitancy about sharing for fear of a negative reaction. Interestingly enough, a significant contributor to the changing culture (from secrecy and shame to openness and acceptance (Daniels, 2004a))—has been the fact that most donor insemination and oocyte (or a cell that gives rise to an ovum) donation (OD) is carried out by doctors within a medical system. Being carried out as medical procedures has added credibility and social acceptance to an area that has been associated with moral uncertainty.

The question of how we view families who have utilised gametes from a third and perhaps fourth party is part of the landscape on which we paint the information that follows. Such families see themselves as family, despite one of the expected and traditional boundaries not operating. Who is family when a donor has contributed his/her gametes to enable that family to be formed?

The relevance and/or irrelevance of genetics in families

How significant are genetic or biological connections between parents and their offspring? Biological parents pass on their genes to their offspring and as a result the offspring are linked through a genetic relationship. Physical resemblance, for example, has already been mentioned as an important and obvious factor that is "inherited" from parents. Resemblance can add a sense of belonging and of "being family". However, genes do not explain everything about relationships. Having the same genes does not necessarily lead to offspring and parents loving each other. Parents as a couple do not share genes, but they share love, commitments, and aspirations. We need to recognise that while genetic connections are significant, there are also social or socio-cultural factors that play an important part in family relationships.

The arguments over the relative importance of either the biological or the socio-cultural (nature *vs.* nurture) have been intense and of long-standing duration. They have often been presented as opposites and in an either/or relationship. In adoption there are no biological links between parents and offspring, so the linkages are all socio-cultural. In gamete donation families, one partner has a genetic connection and the other a socio-cultural connection. (In situations where there has been double donation, egg and sperm it is similar to adoption in that there is no genetic link with either parent.) This is sometimes reflected in DI in the use of the term social father for the infertile male. If the father believes that the genetic connection is very significant, he may believe that his female partner will have a more important and perhaps more powerful relationship with their child. He may well see himself as being in a less important position.

Mr and Mrs A had a struggle with this issue as they contemplated using donated gametes and as the children were born. In relation to the arrival of the children they were faced with comments of others concerning physical resemblance and interestingly they also found themselves looking for traits or characteristics that belonged to either one or both parents.

Two pieces of research I have been involved in shed some light on what seems to happen for some parents as they seek to understand and manage this situation. In research in New Zealand with forty-one families, I and my colleague (Grace & Daniels, 2007) explored with the parents how they made sense of the importance of genetics and the lack of genetic connection on the father's side. We said,

> Parents generate a parallel construct whereby genetic inheritance is seen to be simultaneously irrelevant (to the constitution of the family) and yet at the same time relevant (in highly bounded domains, for example related to medically specified conditions). There was ambiguity as they attempted to separate procreation from reproduction. (p. 1)

The reality is that families do have to live with an ambiguous situation in relation to genetics. It is not important to how the family bonds and functions (the socio-cultural), but it is relevant if there are medical issues arising that may be linked to the donor's genes. Mr and Mrs A were able to clarify matters for themselves when they acknowledged (and were thankful) for the contribution of the donor, but spent most of their time and efforts focusing on the socio-cultural dimensions that built and sustained their relationships.

The second piece of work was undertaken in Belgium by a PhD student for whom I was one of the supervisors. Astrid Indekeu found in her interviews with couples at three different points in time—before birth through to toddler stage—that those parents who were intending to disclose the family history to their offspring moved in their thinking from a focus primarily on the biological, to one that reflected the importance of the developing relationship. Those parents who were not intending to disclose did not seem to want to acknowledge this as an issue and dealt with it by denial. They were therefore committed to a pretence that the offspring were genetically part of both parents. There are many potential issues and complications (often when the children are older) that can arise from adopting this position and I will explain some of these later in the chapter.

The involvement of a third party

The challenges associated with being told that you cannot have children are enormous. To be then told that the best way for you to have your desired children is to accept the sperm or eggs from someone else can add considerably to the challenges. For some, of course, it may be a great relief to know that the possibility to have children is there. The end goal is more important than the means that are used to achieve that goal. For most of the couples I have worked with over some forty years however, there are issues to be faced and managed. It is not a simple matter to accept the involvement of a third party into the very personal dimensions of your relationship. Communication between the partners about these issues is, in my view, essential as part of the process of moving into treatment. There are likely to be differences between men and women on this issue (Rawlings & Looi, 2006). For a female who needs an egg donor there is still the fact that they will carry the child. For a man who needs a sperm donor, he will not have any physical involvement in the conception and gestation of the child. He is in effect being replaced by the donor in terms of his role and contribution in this respect.

One of the ways of understanding and managing the range of feelings which are likely to arise in such situations is to think about the reasons for the infertility. We often talk about the cause of the infertility and locate the cause in one or other of the partners. This has implications for one partner being "responsible" or "to blame". I would suggest that a more useful way of conceptualising this is to think of the infertility arising out of the relationship of the two partners. The desire is that *the couple* wish to have a child/children and it is *the couple* who cannot realise this goal without assistance. They are in this together, the donor in this situation is donating to the couple to enable them to realise their goal.

Other implications of this approach are that it is wise for both partners to go to all appointments and treatments together. There is a risk that a male partner may feel "left out" or "redundant", as some men have described to me if only their partner is attending the clinic.

It would seem natural for the partners to wonder about what the donor might be like and what might be their motivation. On the other hand some may want to avoid considering these issues feeling that the less the donor is thought about or the less that is known about them, the easier it is to deny their existence and importance. It is not uncommon for most people to deny, or try to deny, the existence of issues that cause disquiet and ambivalence. Denial in such circumstances may seem to give some short term relief and we shall return to this in more detail later. In essence, the central issue to consider is whether we see the donor as an unknown friend who wants to help, or a person who is a necessary evil and potentially a threat and/or challenge.

There have now been many studies of sperm and egg donors. For a review of these see (Daniels, 2007a,b; Van den Akler, 2006; Van den Broeck et al, 2013). In my studies of sperm donors, I have found that they come from a variety of backgrounds and experiences and that their reasons for donating tend to be influenced by their age, marital status, and if they have children of their own. It needs to be noted that there are some significant differences between donors who donate anonymously and those who donate in the knowledge and with the understanding that any offspring may contact them in the future—again more on this later. It needs to be noted also that the policies that clinics adopt in terms of recruitment can influence the types of donors and their motivations. Clinic policies can also have an impact in terms of providing non-identifying information to potential recipients and allowing them to choose. Such a policy enables couples to have some control in an area where control is usually in the hands of health professionals.

Mr and Mrs A began their infertility journey by focusing on Mr A and apportioning blame to him. They were able to shift their perspective however, and having done this the issues arising from the involvement of a sperm donor did not seem to be so huge. There were certainly issues to be considered and a great deal of discussion went on between them. When they had made the decision to proceed they were assisted by their clinic's approach, which was to involve them both, to have them choose the donor, to see his sperm under a microscope, and to encourage the view that the donor was a partner (and certainly not an intruder) in their efforts to have children.

The offspring and the parent(s)

In this section the focus will be primarily on relationships and communication and not so much on boundaries. Confidence plays a very important part in parenting. For a parent that has used donated gametes, confidence is likely to be an even more significant issue. The experience of wanting children, finding there was a roadblock to this goal and then traversing the treatment journey may well have sapped the level of confidence. The excitement of then being pregnant and having the desired baby will almost certainly be intense. This type of family building is different—not better or worse but different—and this may also impact on the level of confidence, especially if there is uncertainty about how openly this can be discussed with relatives and friends.

My colleague in Germany, Dr Petra Thorn, had been taking groups for would-be parents who were considering using DI. In 2000 I joined Petra and we offered weekend courses over five years. Couples (it was mainly couples) came from all over Germany. For the vast majority of those attending, they met others in the same situation as themselves for the first time. Infertility and the use of DI can be a very isolating experience. For two days the couples addressed the issues, concerns, and hopes about building their family with the assistance of donated gametes. In addition there were presentations on the medical legal and psychosocial issues associated with the use of DI. There was also a time when the men met on their own with me and the women with Petra. Towards the end of the weekend a family—parents and two children conceived as a result of DI came and talked. This latter session was always very powerful and important.

Research was undertaken (Daniels, Thorn, & Westerbrooke, 2007) to evaluate the impact of these weekend workshops and the results showed that the level of confidence about using DI increased significantly. This increased confidence remained well after the seminars and had an impact on their relationships with relatives and friends (they were more open about their family building decision), on their relationship with each other as a couple (with more communication and greater understanding), and their views about the nature of their planned relationship with the hoped for children (more open and honest). Communication and confidence were central elements.

In summary, I would suggest that a key element for participants was that they shifted from being reactive to being proactive. In the reactive mode they were responding to events and pressures in an almost defensive way. When their confidence levels increased and they moved into a proactive mode they were able to "feel good" about their choice of family building. There was a move from feeling ashamed to feeling proud. The reality is that most people would not choose to use donated gametes. Given the lack of choice, how can this be turned around so that parents can be confident in their parenting? We found the workshops/seminars where participants learnt so much from each other (and still keep in touch) proved a central part in attendees becoming effective parents. Other chapters in this book describe how these ideas were taken up and developed in the UK context.

A major concern for many parents revolves around whether to be open with their offspring about the use of donated gametes. Traditionally, parents were advised and counselled not to "tell the child". Sadly, this approach is still adopted by many health professionals although the changes that have taken place in recent years have seen this change dramatically. One of the major contributions to this change has been the growing confidence of parents who do not want to be told by others what to communicate to their offspring. They do not want to be dishonest with their children. In my book on *Building a Family with the Assistance of Donor Insemination* (2004b) I talk about secrecy and donor insemination as being "an unhealthy partnership". Space does not allow for a discussion of why this is an unhealthy partnership but it is important to emphasise, in line with the theme of this chapter, that it is unhealthy in the impact it has on relationships of parents and offspring and, flowing on from this, the way in which secrecy impacts on communication. In an interesting piece of research, colleagues in the US (Berger & Paul, 2008) have outlined how "topic avoidance" occurs between parents and offspring when gamete donation (GD) is being kept a secret. The offspring in the study report on how this worked and how they were aware from the avoidance that there was a secret being kept. This often led to unhelpful fantasies.

Another piece of research that adds weight to this view was undertaken in a New Zealand study (Daniels, Grace, & Gillett, 2011). Seven families told me at follow-up interviews when the offspring were aged fifteen to twenty that they wanted to share the DI family history with the offspring. Five of those seven families reported that their offspring had raised questions with them that indicated they were aware of a "genetic disconnect" between them and their parents. Interestingly for a number of the five, the issue had arisen first through biology lessons they were having at school. The information they were receiving raised questions as they did not "match" with the parents' physical characteristics. A number asked their parents if they were adopted. The parents all reported feeling "wrong footed" and completely unprepared for such questions, giving very inadequate responses that were accompanied by feelings of guilt and shame at not being honest with the offspring. One offspring was reported by his mother as saying in response to her floundering "Mum, why are you looking away?"

Mr and Mrs A have not experienced such an issue, perhaps because none of their offspring have been exposed to such biology lessons. While the offspring above may not have said anything, they may have "sensed" the topic avoidance or lack of physical resemblance. One of the sad consequences of offspring not feeling confident enough to raise these issues with their parents is that they are left to fantasise about possible explanations. As one offspring told me, he was sure his mother had had a "one night stand" and he was the result. It was actually a relief for him when he was told about the family history.

I, and many of my colleagues, argue that children should come to know of the family history from a very early stage in their lives. One wise person once said that a child should never be able to remember a time when he/she did not know. Again my book written primarily for parents (Daniels, 2004b) has some fifty pages devoted to talking with and explaining the conception story. The most important message from that chapter is that the issue is not one of parents knowing how to tell their child how she/he was conceived. Rather, the focus should be on how parents share the family building history with their child/ren. The focus should not be on the child, but rather the family. "This is how we came to be—this is our story not your story". Telling the child as if it is his/her story risks marginalising the child and making him/her feel different and as a consequence a boundary has been set up.

We began this section thinking about the confidence of the parents. Confident parents are likely to instil and develop confidence in the offspring. Such confidence is likely to result from relationships that are based on love, honesty, and openness. Communication is always a key element in the management of relationships.

The donor and the parents

There has been a dramatic shift in the culture of gamete donation over the last twenty years and this is perhaps most marked in the way we now think about the three main parties, the parents, the donor, and the offspring. The relationships between the three parties are of critical importance to the health and well-being of the family.

Mr and Mrs A's offspring will be able to learn about their donor and should they wish, have the opportunity to meet him when they are eighteen or older. This is possible because of the policy (now encapsulated in laws in a number of countries) that donors have to be open to contact with the offspring should this be requested. New Zealand is one of fourteen countries (including the UK) that now have such a law banning donor anonymity.

Some clinics in different countries provide non-identifying profiles of donors to the would-be parents. The recipients get to choose their donor from these profiles. Many lesbian couples and some single women ask a friend to contribute the gametes, so in this situation the donor is a personal donor.

The boundaries that traditionally separated recipients and donors have started to become more flexible and this has enormous implications for all three parties. Many parents liked and felt comfortable with the previously solid boundaries of using non-identifying donors, as it meant that the donor could almost become a "non-person" and not exist. Of course this was the parent's perspective, but when one begins to consider the perspective of the offspring the picture can and does change. For parents the "non-existence" and anonymity of the donor seemed safe, but for many offspring whose voices are now being heard, they see this as them being excluded from information about and possible contact with the person who contributed half their genetic information. The anonymity deprives them of information about themselves that they see as theirs.

Some ways have to be found to enable a coming together, of the views and needs of parents and offspring. At the heart of this seems to be the question of how parents view the donor. In attempting to answer this I suggest it might be wise to turn the question around and ask how do donors view the parents and accompanying this, what motivates them to donate in the first place. I once had a student who had donated sperm over forty years ago. He said he did it for the money and he wanted to be anonymous. He did not think much about the people who would receive his sperm or the offspring who would result. That all changed for him when (now living in New Zealand) he had children of his own. He began thinking about other possible children he had helped create and in particular their need for information about him. He let the Harley Street Clinic know he was happy for contact if any offspring approached the clinic. They told him they did not deal with such matters and that he should forget about the whole matter. He wrote to the Human Fertilisation and Embryology Authority (HFEA) in London and received a similar reply. This of course was some twenty-five years ago.

Two studies of semen donors that I have been involved in, one in London (Daniels et al., 2005) and one in the US (Daniels, Kramer, & Perez-y-Perez, 2012) found that donors' thinking frequently changed over time. I have also written a paper summarising the studies of sperm donors (Daniels, 2007a) and one study of oocyte donors (Daniels, 2007b). These papers along with two more recent reviews (Van den Akker, 2006, Van den Broeck et al., 2013) give an excellent insight to the views and experiences of donors, which vary a great deal. It has become clear from these studies and other work about contact, that the views of donors tend to reflect some critical factors, their age when they donate, their marital status, and whether they have children of their own. In essence such donors are likely to be more mature and to understand more fully the issues for infertile couples and future children. Coupled with this, I believe we should be moving from the notion of a man or woman donating, to one of one family donating to another would be family. The donor's family and particularly the partner, needs to be part of the decision to become a donor.

Having presented this ideal picture, it needs to be recognised that a particular clinic's policies are likely to have a significant impact. How do clinic staff view and treat donors, are they valued and respected, or are they seen as a means to an end with the major focus being on the gametes, rather than the person and the gametes.

In a recently published paper (Daniels, Kramer, & Perez-y-Perez, 2012) of a study of 164 previous sperm donors—most of them resident in the US—94% said they were open to contact with the offspring. Many of them added, very powerfully, that they saw themselves as being responsive to a request for contact. They did not see themselves as driving any contact and they did not want to interfere in any way in the family of the offspring. For them a boundary existed, namely that their willingness for contact was in response to an offspring and not vice versa. A study of oocyte donors (Kramer, Schneider, & Schultz, 2009) indicated that 97% of those responding to the question-naire were open to contact with the offspring. Again there was a recognition that this was in response to the needs of the offspring.

The above information is presented to hopefully alleviate some of the fears and fantasies that parents may have.

Some parents have described the donor as being "a stranger in our midst" or "a silent partner". Both of these phases indicate to me a natural uncertainty as to how to see the donor.

Having worked in the field of donor conception for almost forty years, I have come to the view that it can be very helpful to focus on the formation of the family and the development of the family. The donor plays a vital part in the formation stage—conception could not happen without their involvement—but they are not involved in the development phase—that is the task and responsibility that is accorded to the parents. I tend to think of the donor as a partner in the formation stage. I use the word partner as it represents to me the active and vital contribution they make. This is not to suggest that the donor can be forgotten after conception. If one is preparing for the offspring's needs/wishes in the future and there is to be open acknowledgement of the family history, then there will be reference from time to time as appropriate (usually occasioned by the offspring), to the donor. For the sake of the offspring I think it is help-ful for the donor to be referred to by his first name. That name might be the actual name if known or a name adopted for some family asso-ciation. It seems to me to be very unhelpful to refer to the donor as "the natural father" or "the donor father". Father is a word most appropriately kept for the parenting role in development. To use the word father in relation to the donor is to invite confusion in the mind of a developing child. Father to the child means the person who is part of their life, who loves them and who engages with them in family activities. He is known to the child. To use the word father in association with the donor is to potentially suggest that there is another person—unknown to the child—who is like the father he knows and loves.

Confidence again surfaces as a vital part of managing views and thinking about the donor. Feelings of threat and apprehension do not reflect confidence and they put the parents on the back foot. Moving to the front foot means, acknowledging the reality of the donor in the formation of the family, but highlights the parents essential roles and contribution in the development of the family—being parents in the nurturing and care of their child.

The offspring and the donor

I have now worked with quite a number of adult offspring who have been very frustrated and angry that they cannot obtain information about, nor have contact with, "their" donor. Most of the frustration and anger is towards the systems and policies of clinics and governments that in their view, did not consider their interests and needs at the time their parents received treatment. I have also worked with other adult offspring who have been able to locate their donor and who, as a result, feel that their life history is now complete.

Because of the changing culture, policies, and in some countries, legislation, there are likely to be fewer frustrated offspring in the future. Donor anonymity is losing credibility either by legislative change or health professions working to provide a more open system. Some of the adult offspring I refer to above could be said to have been caught in a time warp.

Another important factor is when and how offspring were told about the family building history. Currently all counsellors, social workers, and psychologists that I know and interact with would encourage parents to share this information with the child as she/he develops. Many parents used to think it was best to tell their offspring when they were teenagers or young adults. Again many of the frustrated and angry offspring mentioned above were told or discovered the involvement of a donor when they were young adults on the basis that they would then be able to understand and comprehend what this meant. Growing up with this knowledge and being able to ask questions and explore issues as part of their developing understanding is much more preferable to revelation when one is a young adult (Daniels, 2004b).

It is also important to note that not all offspring want information or contact with the donor, that some might only want information at a certain stage in life, and that within the same family, siblings may have different views about wanting or not wanting information or contact. We have very little information about what motivates some to seek information and contact, while for others this is not an important issue. We do hear more about those who want contact, especially when they are thwarted in their attempts. I am often asked if there is a gender difference operating here. Do, for example, more female offspring want information and contact than males. There is no evidence that I am aware of that enables an answer to be given to this question.

We might well ask the question, "Why do some people want information and or contact". You will note that I keep referring to information and contact. These are quite separate issues. For some, information about the donor seems to be all that is sought, whereas for others contact is the desired outcome. The simple and general answer to the question would be that there is a feeling that something is missing. This missing component will be different for different individuals and will be expressed in very different ways. The missing component may be knowledge related to genetic, medical or physical factors. One young person said to me "I need to know where I got this nose from as it's not like anyone else in my family". Genetic information is likely to become more significant as a factor with advances in medicine. With medical information on the donor, a doctor's request for the family medical history can be answered. Another missing component may be related to personality issues. "Does the donor have the same quirky sense of humour as I do?" one offspring once said. There may be a desire to know about what motivated the donor and what her/his values are. The other area often mentioned is to discover information about the donor's family and we shall address this issue in the next section.

What is perhaps most important to recognise is that for offspring who seek information or contact there is a belief/feeling that there is a linkage between the two of them. For those who cannot explore that linkage there is likely to be frustration and even anger.

What has been obvious to me is that there is a process that most adult offspring go through in relation to this and that process may take place over many months. There are many emotional and social issues to be considered, mostly centring on boundaries, relationships, and communication. Offspring frequently talk with me about the kind of relationship that might develop with the donor, and wondering what they will say to this person when meeting them, and if there will be anything to talk about. Experience shows that there is always plenty to talk about and that a planned sixty minute first session is invariably not long enough.

As the culture of gamete donation has changed, more parents have shared the family history with their offspring. As a result it has been possible to undertake research with the parents, their offspring, and the families. A great deal of this research has resulted from the establishment of the Donor Sibling Registry (DSR) in the US. This registry has attracted over 39,000 members located in many different countries around the world. Members are parents, offspring, and donors. The DSR was founded in 2000 to assist individuals conceived as a result of sperm, egg, or embryo donation that are seeking to make mutually desired contact with others with whom they share genetic ties. To date over 10,000 contacts have occurred between half-siblings and/or donors. The large number of members has provided access to a previously unavailable number of persons and, to date, eleven papers have been published by researchers working in conjunction with the co-founder of DSR, Wendy Kramer. Other papers are in process.

From a scientific point of view, some caution needs to be expressed about such research. Most of the data has come from the completion of internet based surveys and therefore from persons who have access to the internet and who know of the surveys. Also for responding offspring, they must know about the nature of their conception. It is of course impossible to access the views of offspring about gamete donation if they do not know about their parent's use of donated gametes.

These limitations quite rightly lead to the need for caution about the generalisation of the results. However, the surveys give us access to the views of large numbers of interested parties that were not previously available.

In a survey of 741 donor offspring it was found that 82% wanted contact with the donor some day (Beeson, Jennings, & Kramer, 2011). In another US based study—which was not part of DSR—(Mahlstedt, LaBounty, & Kennedy, 2010) found that 80% of over eighteenth year olds in their study wanted contact with sperm donor while 88% wanted contact with the half-siblings. To look at the perspective of the donors, Kramer, Schneider, and Schultz (2009) found that 97% of 155 oocyte donors were open to contact with offspring and Daniels, Kramer, and Perez-y-Perez (2012) found 94% of 164 sperm donors were open to contact.

In studies of what adolescents conceived by DI were looking for (Scheib, Riordan, & Rubin, 2005) it was found that there were two main reasons for wanting contact, information that would assist with their own identity and health and family history. Just over half of this group thought they would want a relationship with the donor that they characterised as being like a friend, 18% thought they would see the donor as more familial, like an uncle, and 12% saw the relationship as being like a parent–child. In the study of adult offspring, Mahlstedt, LaBounty, and Kennedy, (2010) found that there was a desire on the part of the offspring to fill in gaps in their own identifies. Almost two thirds perceived the sperm donor as being a biological father, 29% as a donor, and 6% as a donor dad/father.

In a study that sought the experiences of offspring who had had contact with their donors (Jadva et al., 2010), 70% said this was very positive and 10% fairly positive, but only seven offspring had had such contact.

It was reported in one study (Beeson, Jennings, & Kramer, 2011) that offspring who wanted to make contact with the donor experienced a variety of reactions from their parents. Interestingly, only 29% had told their father they were searching for the donor. Offspring described feelings of disloyalty to their parents about their desire to search. In another important study (Freeman et al., 2009), involving 791 parents, it was found that 87% of them were seeking half-siblings and 47% seeking the donor. Parents were much more likely to be in contact with half-siblings than the offspring, but this was likely to be accounted for by the current age of the children—they were still quite young. This highlights an important issue concerning contact—who wants the contact, the offspring or their parent(s)? For me the driver of the contact or attempted contact should be the desire and wish of the offspring and not the parents. Another aspect of this study was that parents' assessment of how well the contact had gone shifted significantly. With half-siblings, 29% of the parents' expectation before contact was that the contact would go "very well", but after contact 69% said it had gone "very well". In relation to donor contact the shift had been from 36% before contact to 91% after contact. It needs to be noted that this was the parents' assessment.

Shifting to the perspective of the donor, Jadva and colleagues (2011) found that 35% of sperm donors had made contact, although most of this was with parents as the children were still young.

So what might be concluded from this overview of research findings in relation to this new and emerging field of relationships? There is interest and desire for contact. Reasons for this and type of contact envisaged varies. When contact has occurred parents and donors assess this in very positive terms. This is, however, an emotional area and as such will raise a variety of feelings for offspring, donors, and parents. Boundaries and relationships will need to be explored carefully. Donors in one study seem very aware of the need to clarify appropriate boundaries. Of course communication to clarify boundaries and relationships becomes a central part of exploring this area.

The offspring and the donor's family

Walking to work one day I was stopped by a man—whom I had never met— riding his bike. Clearly we had passed each other on many days in the past as his opening comment was "you are Ken Daniels aren't you?" The following discussion revealed that he had been a sperm donor a number of years previously and the clinic where he had donated had contacted him about possibly meeting the offspring. He was very happy to do this, but in discussing it with his wife he found she objected to any contact. The main reason was her concern about the potential impact on their teenage daughters. Some five years later I was at a social gathering and he approached me to say that he and his wife were now agreed that he could contact the clinic to indicate a willingness to meet the offspring. This example highlights that all parties in gamete donation have their respective families and networks of which they are a part. The donor's actions in particular have implications for his family that need to be considered.

It is highly likely that many donors in the past donated when they were single. Have they told their partners they are now with? What feelings and issues might arise, for instance, when a partner receives the information that "their man" has a child/ren in one or more families? The sharing of such information challenges the boundaries the female partner had thought existed. It would seem honest, appropriate, and wise for such information to be shared before long-term commitments are made. It is not hard to imagine the impact on a relationship if the first time this information is revealed is in association with the fact that one of these offspring wanted to have contact.

In the largest study of sperm donors (Daniels, Kramer, & Perez-y-Perez, 2012) 91% of donors had told their wives/partners about having been a donor. Most of these donors had also told or intended to tell their own offspring and this is encouraging.

Given that 88% (Mahlstedt, LaBounty, & Kennedy, 2010) and 82% (Beeson, Jennings, & Kramer, 2011) of offspring in these two studies wanted or expected to have contact with their half-siblings and that the donors were sharing the information with their children, it is highly likely that contact will take place. It is interesting that in the US based studies there were larger numbers of offspring who wanted contact with their half-siblings than with the donor. This may reflect the policies in the US where it would seem very challenging to find the identity of the donor. It may also reflect the number of parents, and particularly single parent families, who have only one child and who indicate they want to have a network for that child (Scheib & Ruby, 2008). This point emerges from the motivation of the parents who are seeking to make contact and not from the offspring.

For the offspring, half-siblings may be the children in the donor's family or may be other offspring who have resulted from their donor's contributions. The considerations are likely to be different for these two groups. For the donor's own children there will be the issue of how their father's donor history is shared with them as well as the level and extent of communication that freely takes place between the parents and the children, who may of course be adults by the time such conversations take place. These children will be challenged to adjust their thinking about their father, in the case of DI as well as adjusting to the presence of another individual who shares half of their genetic history.

A great deal of the literature to date has been devoted to the offspring, the parents, and the donors. This section suggests it is necessary to take a broader view of information about the contact between offspring and donors. This is an evolving field that, quite frankly, counsellors and others are scrambling to understand.

It is obvious that such understanding is a necessary pre-requisite to seeking to work with families who seek assistance in managing the challenges to the established boundaries and relationships.

One study that does shed light into this area showed that offspring who had had contact with half-siblings described this as a very positive experience. (60%) or fairly positive (25%) (Jadva et al., 2010). Most of the half-siblings remained in contact, but it was a shock for some to know that their donor's contributions had lead to up to thirteen half-siblings.

In the study of 164 sperm donors, Daniels, Kramer, and Perez-y-Perez (2012) found that donors said boundary setting was very important and that the most common challenge faced by offspring contact was the relationship issues within their own family.

In the professional arena it is now common to use the phrase "donor linking" to refer to the contact between offspring and donors. I have great difficulty with this term, first because it puts the emphasis on the donor. For me this whole movement towards openness is because of and should be focused on the offspring. My second objection relates to the fact that most discussion seems to centre on two people, offspring and donor. What I hope I have indicated in this section of the chapter is that there are many other parties who are associated with and impacted on as a result of contact. It would seem to me that when we have two families coming together, the boundaries and relationships between them become very important. Establishing effective communication around these issues will be fundamental to the evolution of healthy and well-functioning relationships. The use of gamete and embryo donation in so much as it challenges the traditional ways in which we have thought about family and kinship, requires us to think about and seek to manage the relationships that will emerge, for the betterment of all.

It might be thought that we have left Mr and Mrs A behind. We may have in terms of their current situation—determined in the main by age—but the material in this and the preceding situation, could be said to be about what is likely to occur for them as their family development continues. The raising of these issues is done to assist in thinking about the management of information sharing. Parents like Mr and Mrs A are, in a sense, on a journey into unchartered territory. The relationships that have been established and the love that is the core of those relationships will be the key to the family's future functioning. An important issue for Mr and Mrs A is that two donors have been involved in their family formation. This not only extends the numbers of involved persons, but also raises issues about possible comparison of the donors and the nature and extent of any contact that may take place.

Relationship management for healthy and well-functioning families

This chapter has had a major focus on the concept of boundaries and how they impact on our understanding and management of relationships within families that have used donated gametes or embryos.

Boundaries can be very fixed and firm, an example being the non-acceptance of incestuous relationships. Such a boundary is reinforced by the existence of laws and any breaking of the boundary can lead to punishment.

In many instances, boundaries can and do exist that have a moral association, an example being the relationship between husband and wife. A breaking of the boundary through a relationship with a third person by either party can be said to be a breach of the trust associated with the boundary that in turn may lead to dissolution of the relationship. Boundaries exist, either covertly or overtly in all families.

At a societal level there have been many changes occurring in our understanding and acceptance of what constitutes family—the boundaries have been shifting. The recent moves in several jurisdictions to legalise gay marriage is perhaps the most obvious example of the changing nature of marriage and family. The strong protest movement against such legislation is a reflection of the strength of beliefs—usually moral in nature—about the shift of boundaries.

Families built with the assistance of donated gametes present challenges to the traditional boundary of biological connection being the basis of what it means to be a family. Such families have moved from a dominant mode of thinking that says a family results from the merging of gametes of two parties who are in a continuing relationship who will conceive and nurture a child, to a notion where the parents deliberately involve a third party to achieve their goal of family. Immediately a boundary is changed/modified/shifted, that boundary changing may be subject to legal considerations, the most obvious being a country banning donor anonymity and, who is registered as the parents on a birth certificate being the most obvious. There may be moral considerations associated with a third party being involved in what has traditionally been viewed as the privacy and intimacy of the dyad that is committed partners. Many couples I have worked with over the years report this to be a factor that impinges on their thinking and decision making. There may be additional moral considerations in a single woman or a lesbian couple who are planning to use DI.

At a societal level there may well be at best, confusion and uncertainty and at worst, criticism and condemnation of this form of family building with its inherent boundary shifting.

The existence of boundaries is significant and should not be dismissed lightly. What becomes important is how these boundaries impact on the relationships that exist and the relationships that will be created as a result of the family building.

I would suggest that boundary issues need to be considered at different stages of the family building journey. The discovery or recognition that a third party is going to be needed to enable conception to take place will raise the boundary issues—along with many other issues—for the couple or single person, the meaning of this will need to be explored; who should become involved in the process—family and or friends—is likely to impact on those involved. The views of others at this stage, or any other stage—influenced perhaps by moral or societal views—are likely to be a consideration for those struggling with the challenges they are encountering. To then be advised that donated gametes may be an answer to their dilemma will raise further boundary issues. Would-be parents have talked to me at length about the feelings of inadequacy and failure that can be associated with not being able to produce viable gametes for their partner. For many infertile men, this includes a consideration of offering a divorce to their partner because they feel they have failed to fulfil their part of the expected behaviour or marriage—the fathering of children.

Given the decision to use donated gametes, the focus naturally turns to the expected and hoped for conception and child. This will mean for most, the involvement of health professionals, doctors, counsellors, nurses, and scientists. While now well accepted as a medical treatment, the use of donated gametes to treat infertility may still be accompanied by staff attitudes that suggest some ambivalence. Donated gamete treatment does not share the same status as more "high tech" treatments such as *in vitro* fertilisation and intracytoplasmic sperm injection. Also if health professionals are indicating, overtly or covertly, that parents should keep the use of donated gametes a secret from their offspring and perhaps others, then they are indicating that this is something to be ashamed of. We only keep secret what we feel ashamed of. The relationship experienced with health professionals can be crucial in influencing or even determining the boundary modifications that are required, along with the responses that are made. If one feels ashamed or very uncertain about the use of donated gametes to form the family, it might seem appropriate to pretend that the traditional boundaries exist—that the child is the result of the merging of the gametes of its parents.

In infancy and the early family life development it may be possible to maintain this deception. However, as the research I was involved in with Lycett and colleagues (2005) showed, the impact of keeping a secret in DI families in the UK had an influence on the relationships between mothers and their children. We reported that the keeping of the conception story a secret led to mothers in these non-disclosing families to report the children to be more of a strain than those in disclosing families. The non-disclosing parents also reported a greater number of and more severe family arguments than the disclosing parents.

What might be concluded from this is that the pretence of a biological boundary linking the family members impacted on relationships and communication between mother and child. It is interesting that the impact was with mother–child and not with father–child, given that the child was not genetically linked to the father.

As the child grows and develops there is likely to be a revisiting of the connections that make up the family. As already indicated this may be reflected in issues associated with family resemblance, what and how topics are discussed within the family and information about genetics and biology that may be learnt at school. Each of these areas may give rise to issues associated with the family boundary.

In the study referred to earlier (Daniels, Grace, & Gillett, 2011) my colleagues and I found that adult offspring reported believing or feeling there was a "genetic disconnect" between them and their parents. There is much anecdotal reportage from counsellors about the impact the discovery of the secrecy and particularly the challenge this has on the ability to trust the parents and others.

How might parents manage these issues? Please note that I refer to issues and not problems. A problem only becomes a problem if you define it as such. Issues do arise for families who have used donated gametes and some of these will be quite different from what other families' experience. Responding appropriately to these issues will, as I have suggested, be strongly influenced by the level of confidence that parents feel about their decision to build their family in this way.

Mr and Mrs A feel very confident about their decision making and they are therefore expecting that sharing the family history with their offspring—while challenging and associated with some anxiety—will be fine. Their confidence is based on the fact that the relationships they have established with their children are based on love and that this is the cement that joins them as a family. Secrecy and feeling ashamed do not lead to confidence in fact the opposite is the case. Confidence also involves moving from a reactive stance—I can only respond to situations—to a proactive stance in which I can take some control and power so as to determine as far as is possible, the way I respond to situations and issues which arise. This notion is summed up for me in the quote that I use on the cover of my book (*Building a Family with the Assistance of Donor Insemination*) (Daniels, 2004b). "It was not our ideal way of building a family, but it is our ideal family".

Infertility can be a very isolating experience. The opportunity to meet and share with others who have or are having similar experience is critical in lessening the impact of that isolation. Groups have been established in many countries around the world to provide support, education, and to lobby for improved services. In the field of gamete donation there has been the development of many significant groups and it is my view that these groups have played a very important role in changing the culture of gamete donation. Many excellent publications have emerged from these groups, but it is the sharing of experiences that becomes so important in reducing the isolation and feelings of being marginalised and different. It is in such encounters that fears, fantasies, and anxieties can be expressed, explained, and learnt from. It was quite a regular experience to hear participants in our workshops in Germany, say after the visit of a family built with the assistance of DI (parents and two children), "The kids seemed so normal". I am not sure what they expected, but the underlying meaning was that the family seemed little different from most families and this was a surprise.

Based on this confidence relationships develop as a result of loving and open communication. Again to paint the negative picture briefly, I cannot communicate with confidence about something that I feel very uncertain about or perhaps even ashamed of.

Another central issue in the management of relationships is to think about the donor. Where does she/he fit in this family? Is she/he seen as an outsider who potentially poses a threat to the future health and well-being of the family? Is he/she seen as a person who in reality has played a vital and important part in the creation of the family—without him/her there would be no children? You will note that the emphasis is on the creation stage, but this person has not been involved in the development of the family and the nurturing of the children. For the children there is only one set of parents, the ones they know, the ones who love and support them. In countries that have legislated that offspring can access information and contact their donor, the age when this can occur is generally set at eighteen. This is in recognition of the family developing as a family as well as the offspring being "sufficiently mature" to manage the new relationship that is likely to emerge from contact. As we have seen, there are issues for offspring as to how to view the donor, what role they expect the donor to adopt and emerging from this, what kind of relationship might develop.

How parents view and talk about the donor will have a significant impact on the emerging views of the offspring. The donor has gifted his/her gametes (even although he/she might have been paid) so that this family might exist. It is natural to be thankful for gifts and especially gifts of such significance.

Two families I worked with were seeking guidance on how to share the family building history with their adult offspring. They wanted me to ascertain if information about the donor was available from the clinics involved and if it was there for them to share with their offspring. I suggested that it was important to recognise three things. First, the sharing of the information with their adult offspring would be a very powerful experience and that time would be necessary to absorb this. Decisions about information were a consequential issue and not appropriately dealt with at the same time as telling. Second, the information needed to be seen as belonging to the offspring and it would be their decision as to whether information was wanted, and third, that if the information was wanted the parents could, if required, work with their offspring in seeking to find the information.

Another element in the relationship management area is what language to use. As I have already referred to, many families I have worked with in DI plan to refer to their donor as the "natural father" or the "donor dad", or the "real father". I would caution against the use of such language. For a child the word father is associated with the person he/she knows, loves, and shares with. To introduce the word father or dad in relation to an unknown person who is not involved in his life is potentially quite confusing. The donor is a donor. His/her involvement and contribution is at the biological end of family building.

This chapter has suggested that understanding the concept of boundaries can be very helpful to families who have used donated gametes. In such families some of the traditional boundaries change and these changes impact on the relationships that result. Communication between all of the involved parties plays a vital part in the functioning of the family formed in this way. Traditionally, the relationships, and communications were characterised by a denial or rejection of the involvement of a third party. In such circumstances the family boundary was seen as encompassing parents and offspring only. Over the last twenty years there has been a dramatic revolution regarding this traditional thinking. Having said that, there remains strong pockets of advocacy for the traditional position.

This chapter, and I believe this book, is designed to contribute to and advance that revolution. Being open and honest about the family building history and the involvement of a donor leads to healthy and well-functioning families. Secrets, based as they are on shame and guilt, lead to significant issues of trust and confidence in the family relationships and this in turn impacts on communication. It is my hope that this chapter and its contents will increase the confidence of parents who build their families in this way.

References

Beeson, D. R., Jennings, P. K., & Kramer, W. (2011). Offspring searching for their sperm donors: how family type shapes the process. *Human Reproduction*, 26: 2415–2424.

Berger, R., & Paul, M. (2008). Family secrets and family functioning: the case of donor assistance. *Family Process*, 47: 553–566.

Daniels, K. (1998). The semen providers. In: K. Daniels & E. Haimes (Eds.), *Donor Insemination: International Social Science Perspectives* (pp. 76–104). Cambridge: Cambridge University Press.

Daniels, K. (2004a). From secrecy and shame to openness and acceptance. In: E. Blyth & R. Landau (Eds.), *Third Party Assisted Conception Across Cultures* (pp. 148–167). London: Jessica Kingsley.

Daniels, K. (2004b). *Building a Family with the Assistance of Donor Insemination*. Palmerston North: Dunmore.

Daniels, K. (2007a). Anonymity and openness and the recruitment of donors: Part 1. Semen donors. *Human Fertility*, 10: 151–158.

Daniels, K. (2007b). Anonymity and openness and the recruitment of donors: Part 2. Oocyte donors. *Human Fertility*, 10: 223–231.

Daniels, K., Blyth, E., Crawshaw, M., & Curson, R. (2005). Short communication: previous semen donors and their views regarding the sharing of information with offspring. *Human Reproduction, 20*: 1670–1675.

Daniels, K., Grace, V., & Gillett, W. (2011). Factors associated with parents' decisions to tell their adult offspring about the offspring's donor conception. *Human Reproduction, 26*: 2783–2790.

Daniels, K. R., Kramer, W., & Perez-y-Perez, M. V. (2012). Semen donors who are open to contact with their offspring: issues and implications for them and their families. *Reproductive Medicine Online, 25*: 670–677.

Daniels, K., Thorn, P., & Westerbrooke, R. (2007). Confidence in the use of donor insemination: an evaluation of the impact of participating in a group preparation program. *Human Fertility, 10*: 13–20.

Freeman, T., Jadva, V., Kramer, W., & Golombok, S. (2009). Gamete donation: parents' experiences of searching for their child's donor siblings and donor. *Human Reproduction, 24*: 505–516.

Grace, V., & Daniels, K. (2007). The (ir)relevance of genetics: engendering parallel worlds of procreation and reproduction. *Sociology of Health & Illness, 29*: 1–19.

Jadva, V., Freeman, T., Kramer ,W., & Golombok, S. (2010). Experiences of offspring searching for and connecting with donor siblings and donor. *Reproductive Medicine Online, 20*: 523–532.

Jadva, V., Freeman, T., Kramer,W., & Golombok, S. (2011). Sperm and oocyte donors' experiences of anonymous donation and subsequent contact with their donor offspring. *Human Reproduction, 26*: 638–645.

Kramer, W., Schneider, J., & Schultz, N. (2009). US oocyte donors: a retrospective study of medical and psychosocial issues. *Human Reproduction, 24*: 3144–3149.

Lycett, E., Daniels, K., Curson, R., & Golombok, S. (2005). School aged children of donor insemination: a study of parents' disclosure patterns. *Human Reproduction, 20*: 810–819.

Mahlstedt, P., LaBounty, K., & Kennedy, W. (2010). The views of adult offspring of sperm donation: essential feedback for the development of ethical guidelines within the practice of assisted reproductive technology in the United States. *Fertility & Sterility, 93*: 2236–2246.

Rawlings, D., & Looi, K. (2006). *Swimming Upstream: the Struggle to Conceive*. Adelaide: Peacock.

Scheib, J., & Ruby, A. (2008). Contact among families who share the same sperm donor. *Fertility & Sterility, 90*: 33–43.

Scheib, J., Riordan, M., & Rubin, S. (2005). Adolescents with open-identity sperm donors: reports from 12–17 year olds. *Human Reproduction, 20*: 239–252.

Van den Akker, O. (2006). A review of family donor constructs: current research and future directions. *Human Reproduction, 12*: 91–101

Van den Broeck, U., Vandermeeren, M., Vanderschueren, D., Enzlin, P., Demyttenaere, K., & D'Hooghe, T. (2013). A systematic review of sperm donors: demographic characteristics, attitudes, motives and experiences of the process of sperm donation. *Human Reproduction Update, 19*: 37–51.

PART IV

POSSIBLE IMPLICATIONS AND SPECULATIONS ABOUT THE FUTURE

CHAPTER NINE

Donor conception and the loss of old certainties

James Rose

his chapter seeks to bring together the various themes that can
be discerned in the chapters above. The reader will recognise
that the contributions differ in their content and style. Whereas
some have already been published in various professional journals,
the chapters written especially for this book are descriptions of the
experience of individuals and groups of individuals who plan to use,
or have used assisted reproductive technology (ART) to create their
families. They help us to consider the assumptions that we commonly
make, consciously or unconsciously, about how children should come
in to the world and how they should be looked after as they grow up.
Every one of us has some kind of sense—a cultural sense—of the life
cycle from birth to death, and hence of our own conception and birth,
and live all our lives with the certainty of our deaths. The history of
the development and implementation of ART is a vivid testament of
this sense. Quite apart from the objective realities mentioned in the
various chapters above; there is, as Amy Schofield shows us, evidence
that there are powerful fantasies that complicate the easy acceptance
of ART by those being treated. Hence, we can see that these matters
may evoke strong moral feelings that can create in society an uneasy
reception to the possibility of donor conception (DC), which risks

complicating how people using donor conception come to feel about the process—before, during, and after. Having read the book, the reader may see the potential opportunities presented to people and, inevitably, how these will be absorbed into how our society understands reproduction and childcare overall. Probably there will continue to be some unconscious resistance to accepting these changes and it behoves us as a society to understand all the real and imagined implications of these remarkable innovations.

Summarising the themes emerging from the texts above should start by considering the experience of those going through the process of anticipating donor conception as described by Katherine Fine and Tamsin Mitchell in Chapter Four. This may have been preceded by the intuition or discovery of infertility. How this can be experienced in men is described by Amy Schofield in Chapter Five. Apfel and Keylor (see Chapter Two) refer to the same experience in women. They add a very important perspective that emphasises that to understand the cause of infertility must be to take a psychosomatic approach. They call for an end to what they call the myth of psychogenic infertility— or the purely psychic cause of infertility. The work of Ken Daniels, augmented by Olivia Montuschi's chapter, (see Chapters Seven and Eight) adds to this by bringing in a societal dimension. Diane Ehrensaft, (see Chapter Six) identifies what she calls developmental tasks that have somehow to be addressed by donor conceived children, with the assistance of their parents.

Thinking of these processes in an abstractly descriptive way can put us at one step away from the actual experience of those using ART. When we generalise we can lose a sense of the pain of individual experience. For this reason, the chapters provided by those directly involved in the DCN are extremely valuable in expanding our consciousness in this regard and in challenging our unconscious preconceptions about reproduction. One fundamental preconception identified by Ken Daniels is an assumed equation of reproduction with parenting, which arises from what he calls the "pro-natalist view". He says that these must now be separated in our minds or the consequence can be that fathers of children conceived by donor sperm, can feel isolated and rendered, as they imagine it, redundant as parents—when the very opposite is true. Making this separation is much easier said than done, which reflects the grip of our preconceptions.

Another preconception that we can have is that it is possible to be neutrally detached when involved in supporting users of ART. This, of course, applies to supporting anyone going through the reproduction experience, be it assisted or not, whether we are professionals or members of the families of those concerned. If we are not aware of possible practical and emotional difficulties that some face, we may become part of their problems. The recognition of this is provided by the importance of what Fine and Mitchell refer to as "telling and talking" in Chapter Four, a theme that is developed by Olivia Montuschi in Chapter Seven. While some may have essentially thought that "what you don't know can't hurt you", there is ample evidence above that secrets kept from children about the facts of there being a donor involved in their birth can be very corrosive of family life. Children become aware that there is something that is not to be discussed. It is an example of what Bollas (1987) has called "the unthought known" (see Ehrensaft above).

An implication of the existence of these societal preconceptions about reproduction is that they create a range of anxieties among some ART users about the "third" involved in the birth of their child. These anxieties are vividly described by Schofield, Vaughan, Ehrensaft, and Daniels in their respective chapters. For example, Ehrensaft describes how some ART users can come to believe that a donor will return at some stage to claim their child and displace them from caring for their children. Acting in what can feel like defiance of these preconceptions can lead to a sense of shame, a fear of retribution, and being somehow uniquely different from others and thus isolated. If these fears are not addressed, they may come to have an unexpected force with all its psychological consequences of depression and a sense of alienation. What is intriguing is the evidence that if these fears are addressed, for example, by discussing the facts openly with family and friends, these expectations do not transpire. Indeed, experience can turn out to be the very opposite of what is expected.

The identification of the psychic impact and power of these preconceptions enables us to posit that the process of ART has traumatic potential. This is not to say that it will in all cases be traumatic, but that without proper preparation and support, it very easily can be. For heterosexual couples, this process begins with the discovery of infertility. Vaughan (see Chapter Three), however, shows us that this does not apply for lesbian couples. In these cases, there is a different sort of loss to be accommodated. It can, of course, be said that the same is true of unassisted conception. All parents somewhere realise when they gaze on their new born for the first time that life will never be the same again. But the presence of our—or society's—preconceptions complicates the matter before, during and after birth for all concerned—parents, donors, and children—and society as a whole.

At the psychological level, it can be said that ART has the potential to complicate the development of the child's "family romance" that is part of the process, described by Freud, of separating from their parents. It is a normal process through which all must go.

As Freud (1909c) put it:

> The liberation of an individual, as he grows up, from the authority of his parents is one of the most necessary though one of the most painful results brought about by the course of his development. It is quite essential that that liberation should occur and it may be presumed that it has been to some extent achieved by everyone who has reached a normal state. Indeed, the whole progress of society rests upon the opposition between successive generations. On the other hand, there is a class of neurotics whose condition is recognizably determined by their having failed in this task.

> For a small child his parents are at first the only authority and the source of all belief. The child's most intense and most momentous wish during these early years is to be like his parents (that is, the parent of his own sex) and to be big like his father and mother. But as intellectual growth increases, the child cannot help discovering by degrees the category to which his parents belong. He gets to know other parents and compares them with his own, and so acquires the right to doubt the incomparable and unique quality which he had attributed to them. Small events in the child's life which make him feel dissatisfied afford him provocation for beginning to criticize his parents, and for using, in order to support his critical attitude, the knowledge which he has acquired that other parents are in some respects preferable to them. The psychology of the neuroses teaches us that, among other factors, the most intense impulses of sexual rivalry contribute to this result. A feeling of being slighted is obviously what constitutes the subject-matter of such provocations. There are only too many occasions on which a child is slighted, or at least *feels* he has been slighted, on which he feels he is not receiving the whole of his parents' love, and, most of all, on which he feels regrets at having to

share it with brothers and sisters. His sense that his own affection is not being fully reciprocated then finds a vent in the idea, often consciously recollected later from early childhood, of being a step-child or an adopted child. People who have not developed neuroses very frequently remember such occasions on which—usually as a result of something they have read—they interpreted and responded to their parent's hostile behaviour in this fashion.

We can see from Freud's account of the development of the relationship that children have with their parents that the family romance is both a normal and necessary development. From the account of the anxieties of those parents using ART, we can see this development being matched by the fear that the donor will return and displace the parents. We have seen too that the development of this anxiety can have many determinants. In addition, we can see that the existence of the donor can provide a hook upon which to dramatise the family romance. In other words, the fantasied father, or mother, becomes a dramatic figure in the mind's eye of the child and of the caring parents. Thus, in itself, this is to be expected and, if expressed verbally by the child, need not necessarily be a cause of anxiety. However, if we imagine a situation in which the child is not told about the existence of the donor, but can somehow feel it in the family atmosphere, the situation becomes more complex. The child may sense that there is a secret and consequently ask themselves, "what is it that is so awful that I can't be told?" This makes the need to be open about the child's origins with the child all the more necessary because talking about these feelings with them is the only way of defusing the corrosive effect of the secret upon family life.

This description of the potential events at the conclusion of the assisted reproductive process brings a perspective on the process from its beginning. We might say that in principle there is no end but we can identify stages in a temporal sequence. These might be said to be:

1. The awareness of a wish for a child.
2. The discovery of infertility.
3. Embarking on the process of assisted reproduction and the entry of a stranger into the family—a donor.
4. The birth of the child and the creation of a family.
5. The development of the family as the child grows to maturity.

Each stage has its own characteristic anxieties and any supportive system has to be aware of them and if necessary address them with those concerned. Katherine Fine and Tamsin Mitchell capture vividly the themes of anxieties in the early stages. In posing the question, "What does using donor sperm or eggs mean to me" for discussion in their groups, they show how present are the feelings of pain resulting from previous failed treatments; facing the process alone for single parents and the loss of the imagined longed-for child. Such experiences can leave painful blots on their emotional landscape. Loss can also be felt in respect to the giving up of a genetic link with the child. We can see here the experienced disruption of a family centred model (or preconception) of procreation. The emerging feelings about a donor as an idea, arising from the process of choosing a donor, suggest that there can be something of a struggle to incorporate the donor into the reproductive process as a person, rather than as a depersonalised function. There is another emotional task that links closely to this. It links with whether donor conception is seen as the last resort—something I/we have to do—or whether it can be seen as a treatment of choice—something that I/we want to do. Seeing it as a positive choice admits the alternative possibility of consciously deciding against child bearing as a life ambition. Both Daniels and Montuschi refer to this as the acceptance of the donor family by the recipient family—the point being the link or implied relationship between families. This may be easier for couples who are able to acknowledge that they are an infertile couple, even if it is only one of them who is actually in need of donated gametes.

Both Schofield and Ehrensaft (see above) suggest that, in this process of procreation, the participants can feel quite persecuted by the conflict between their preconceptions and their reality as they experience it. Indeed, while they in part create this reality, they will not be readily conscious of this creation. With satisfactory support, Ehrensaft suggests they can become much more in touch with their feelings and experience the process in a much more satisfying way than they thought imaginable at the outset. This arises because the anxieties created by their preconceptions turn out, in the light of experience, not to be true.

Turning now to the stage following birth of the child, Ehrensaft clearly identifies certain tasks faced by the child supported by their parents. Again, it could be said that they apply to all children, regardless of how they came into the world, but the presence of a donor (in Ehrensaft's terminology—the birth other) adds a new dimension.

These developmental tasks are listed by Ehrensaft as:

1. The child coming to terms with his or her uniqueness, requiring sensitive explanation of the child's origin by the parents. This is an explanation that will change over time as the child and their body develops.
3. Establishing a sense of belonging, involving the family reverie. The family reverie includes the thoughts and fantasies that family members share about the birth other, whether that person is known to the family or not.
4. Identity formation that involves the family romance (see above). This is to be differentiated from the family reverie. The family romance is an individual experience through which all children go, enabling them to separate from the parents.

A clear implication is that the process of "telling and talking" is one that continues throughout the child's development to maturity. It is not brought to conclusion by a once and for all revelation. To never mention the donor again may be little better than never informing the child at all—indeed arguably worse. When and how must be left to the parents' judgement and their knowledge of their child.

Turning now to how to use this thinking in the provision of support services to those using ART, Amy Schofield makes several insightful recommendations derived from her research. To quote her:

> All the men believed that it would help to reduce stigma and feelings of isolation for the issues around male infertility and donor conception to be much more widely debated in the media. In contrast to the commonly held belief that men would prefer not to talk about these very personal and private issues, the men in this study welcomed the opportunity to "break the silence" and make their experiences heard through this research. It is possible that these men were not representative of men in general, as they were, by virtue of having volunteered for this research, more willing to talk. Some participants feared rejection or humiliation at the prospect of opening up to family or friends, particularly other men. Most of those who did talk, were pleasantly surprised by the support they received. A non-judgmental and open sounding-board for discussing their feelings with partners, family,

friends, others in the same position, and professionals, was appreciated and seen as helpful in reducing the toxicity and loneliness of their experiences.

The "professionalism" of fertility clinics sometimes helped to dampen the powerful negative feelings stirred up by the donor insemination procedure. The men were in agreement, however, that the focus on their female partner, as reflected in registration only being under their partner's names; the lack of male toilets in some clinics; the failure in some instances to properly include men in treatment plans and discussion, all contributed to the men feeling side-lined and undermined. Registering both partners and re-naming clinics in a more gender-neutral way, would seem to be helpful.

The obligatory session of counselling prior to DC treatment was perceived by the majority in this study as an "examination" to test their paternal capabilities. This was felt to be unhelpful and the men did not feel able to openly discuss or voice any conflicting thoughts or worries about going through the procedure, for fear that they would be deemed "unfit". The timing, lack of clarity about the purpose of these sessions and the location in the fertility clinic, all contributed to this being a squandered opportunity for emotionally processing their feelings.

It would be helpful for the purposes of the counselling to be explicit and for sessions to be offered in separate locations, independent of the fertility clinic. (Current volume, pp. 107–108)

In the study, these comments apply to infertile men.

The donation of oocytes is a more recent development and there is increasing use of egg donation as a means of assistance. The situation described by Susan Vaughan (see Chapter Three) was clearly written to imply that most would find her proposal with her lesbian partner, that she become pregnant using her partner's egg and with anonymous donor sperm, somewhat surprising. This surprise perhaps reflects society's preconceptions about reproduction. The anxiety that egg donation seems to arouse is potentially more overt than the concept of sperm donation, maybe because the idea of sperm donation is much more familiar to the world at large. Perhaps this is also because it flies in the face of an unconscious preconception that sperm enters a woman's body and something magical happens that leads to the creation of a human being. The comparatively recent discovery that *there is an intermingling of a man and a woman's genetic material to create the new human being* enables us to realise that the emerging human being requires parenting because procreation is only the beginning and involves two parties.

Let us now turn to thinking about possible implications and developments in the future. In 2012, Arathi Prasad published a book entitled *Like a Virgin*, which was subtitled *How Science is Redesigning the Rules of Sex*. She suggests in this book that it is now possible to envisage that reproduction can be brought about without the active involvement of humans—save for the provision of genetic material. This is because the provision of an artificial womb can provide an environment for the gestation of the neonate. However, we can see that Prasad concentrates solely on procreation. She does not consider parenthood and creating a family. Whether or not this form of reproduction would ever practically occur must be uncertain. But the idea does enable us to imagine what the consequences might be. These imaginings will reflect our preconceptions about child bearing and parenthood, which will be based on our own cultural traditions.

For example, what do we think would happen to primary maternal pre-occupation? How would we think that parents might relate to a child who possesses no genetic material from them at all? How would this complicate the development of the family romance and reverie? Whatever the practical reality of such a situation might be, such speculations about society's reactions does throw our society's preconceptions about reproduction into sharp relief.

Another implication of these developments in technology is that some adults might be tempted to delay parenthood until later in life, for example, to a time post menopause if they had stored their genetic material in such a way that it remained viable. Some children might then have older parents than the current norm. What will be the consequences of such developments, instances of which have already happened with oocytes donation?

Could it be that the situation might seem to the participants to be much more akin to adoption? There are significant differences in that the adopted child experiences an early loss that is potentially disturbing for the child (Bartram, 2003; Canham, 2003; Edwards, 2000). Donor conception is not complicated by this kind of early loss, but the experience of donor conception inevitably involves loss for the family, as is vividly discussed by Fine and Mitchell above. All these developments might seem to threaten the old fantasy of the stork—which perhaps reflected a sense of reproduction as being essentially beyond our control, brought about by some higher authority, which had benign or retaliatory potential or intent.

Olivia Montuschi's vivid personal account of her and her husband's experience of donor conception is evidence of the power of our society's preconceptions about procreation. There is a thread running through the chapter, of the fear of the donor and of other people's imagined judgments. She places a strong emphasis on the importance of "telling and talking" in the process of family building. She notes that families built by adoption often have to cope with obviously disturbing losses and she adds that various studies conclude that: "it is not what happens to you that matters, it is the way you make sense of it that counts in the end" (Howe & Feast, with Coster, 2003).

Montuschi's position is that "telling and talking" between all involved, enables sense to be made of the experience of bringing a child into the world by all concerned. She also points out that, although donor anonymity has ended,

> ... we still have to wait until 2023 before the first children who have the right to identifying information are entitled to make enquiries. For some parents this is just the way they want it—a donor who cannot make his or her presence felt for eighteen years. Ambivalence about the donor remains strong for many couples. For others, mainly but not exclusively single women for the time being, it feels wrong that their children cannot make connections with genetic relatives before age eighteen. Their frustration with the current restrictions on making these links sometimes leads to more informal methods of seeking contact with families who have children from the same donor. The internet provides infinite possibilities. (Current volume, p. 106)

Olivia Montuschi's chapter is complemented by Ken Daniel's chapter on understanding and managing relationships in donor assisted families. He starts by introducing us to Mr and Mrs A, which sets the scene quite reasonably by implying that we are talking about a man and a woman having a baby. This might be said to represent something derived from what can be called the family ideal currently prevailing in our society. He calls this ideal the "pro-natalist view".

What follows from this are a number of questions, namely:

1. What drives this ideal? This may look self evident but it seems partly to have given rise to certain distastes in society towards DC. Before DC, the ideal seemed to state that only a man and woman who are emotionally linked should conceive. If another party is involved, it seems to have been a source of shame. Indeed the very apparent self-evidence of the ideal shows the reason for this shame. It seems to have led to certain policies and expectations that now seem to have come into question in the light of experience.
2. Does it, for example, give rise to a feeling that if you depart from this ideal somehow you are not part of society? There is plenty of evidence for this possibility in the chapters above.
3. The importance of boundaries around the family unit perhaps also arises from this ideal, which again have been questioned in recent years. For example, the idea that there should be no contact with donors who should remain anonymous. Thus the idea that something illegitimate has occurred in the event of DC seems to be implied, which has potentially disastrous consequences that have been explored. What follows from this is the question of "Who is the family?"

Some further issues that can be addressed from the experiences that Daniels describes, if there is a departure from this ideal are:

1. There are often expectations of condemnation by offspring, immediate family, and society that are not fulfilled: implying the existence of a hostile critic in the minds of some of those who use donor conception to create their families.
2. Medical involvement in donor conception lends a legitimacy and credibility that seems to detract from any possible feelings of shame. The clear early ambivalence towards donor conception perhaps contributes to the creation of the hostile critic rather than mitigating it. The donor becomes part of the family but there is a question of how this is to be managed. This indicates the primitive feelings contained and perhaps perpetuated by the family ideal: for example, guilt/shame arising from infertility, or the man offering his wife a divorce on the grounds of his infertility.

One of the important ideas in Daniels' chapter is the idea of separating procreation from reproduction. Thus, the (sperm) donor is part of the procreative process but the father is part of the couple that creates the child as an individual person and who grows to become an adult. This has the effect of placing a proper emphasis on the role of the father in relation to the donor and a separation of their functions.

The family pro-natalist ideal equates procreation with reproduction, which has many unhelpful consequences. It may even support some negative stereotypes of men, for example, they only eat, squirt, and leave. It will underplay their significance as fathers to their children. Thus, while the donor is part of the biological creation of an individual, the father is part of the couple that psychologically creates an individual by bringing them to adulthood, which is an infinitely more important task and much more difficult and testing. It may be that the equation of the donor with the father reflects a deeply unconscious wish to know "where I came from". To hide the fact of the donor in a secret is potentially deeply troubling for this reason. The impact of this family ideal is also vividly illustrated by the questions surrounding informing the offspring of their conception. A psychoanalytic idea that has a bearing is the concept (Bollas, 1987) of the "unthought known"—or an unconscious knowledge of an absence. This is often revealed by the creation of the maintenance of a secret about the fact of a donor. Ken Daniels, as others do, says there are children who report a sense that there is something that cannot be discussed—indicating a secret, which if maintained is inevitably disturbing for all concerned.

Ken Daniels' consideration of each of the participants in the drama—parents, donor, children/offspring, and society as a whole is very helpful and useful. He considers the nature of each individual drama for all and the resulting family. What are their motivations and the psychological consequences for each player? With anonymity of the donor ended in the UK, it is still too early to observe the possible ramifications of this for children brought into the world with the help of a donor. Then, there is the issue of the consequences of denying the existence of the donor and the intercourse situation. This must include both the psychological consequences and the consequences for physical health arising from genetic history. Indeed, being aware of the psychic reality of the *fantasies* about procreation, reproduction and the creation of the family quite apart from the objective realities will help us to understand the predicaments in which some people find themselves. This is an important part of the book's message.

As a brief summary of this book, it seems that the donor conception experience described in this book exhorts all those involved in the creation of a child to allow all parties to become identifiable people as a result of identifying them as part of the procreative process. This does not mean that they have to be intimately involved as a child grows up but it seems that their existence has to be acknowledged. This perhaps reveals something that is not commonly thought about, but that has deeply psychological significance and is revealed by a psychoanalytic perspective. It stems from the power of the family ideal—or the pro-natalist view—that may be quite unconscious but nonetheless is very present. This strongly affects the individual's experience because the ideal creates such expectations. Thus, we all have mothers and fathers and how they got together, lived together, and then brought us and other children into the world, were themselves descended from their ancestors will be the stuff of curiosity, fantasy, wish fulfilment, and give a sense of meaning to each individual. This is inevitable and quite healthy and natural and is thrown into very sharp relief by the advent of donor conception and assisted reproductive technology.

References

Bartram, P. (2003). Some oedipal problems in work with adopted children and their parents. *Journal of Child Psychotherapy, 29*: 21–36.

Bollas, C. (1987). *The Shadow of the Object*. London : Free Association.

Canham, H. (2003). The relevance of the Oedipus myth to fostered and adopted children. *Journal of Child Psychotherapy, 29*: 5–19.

Edwards, J. (2000). On being dropped and picked up: adopted children and their internal objects. *Journal of Child Psychotherapy, 26*: 349.

Freud, S. (1909c). Family romances. *S.E., 9*: 235–242. London: Hogarth.

Howe, D., & Feast, J. with Coster, D. (2003). *Adoption, Search and Reunion: The Long-term Experiences of Adopted Adults*. London: The Children's Society.

Prasad, A. (2012). *Like a Virgin*. London: Oneworld Publications.

Organisations and useful websites

Organisations

British Infertility Counselling Organisation (BICA)
Website, including Find a Counsellor facility:
www.bica.net
info@bica.net

British Psychoanalytic Council
Unit 7
19–23 Wedmore Street,
London N19 4RU
Telephone 020 7561 9240
www.psychoanalytic-council.org
mail@psychoanalytic-council.org

British Psychoanalytical Society
Byron House, 112A Shirland Road,
London W9 2BT
Telephone: 020 7563 5000
www.psychoanalysis.org.uk

British Psychotherapy Foundation
37 Mapesbury Rd
London NW2 4HJ
Telephone 020 8452 9823
www.britishpsychotherapyfoundation.org.uk
enquiries@bpf-psychotherapy.org.uk

Donor Conception Network
154 Caledonian Road
London
N1 9RD
Telephone 020 7278 2608
www.dcnetwork.org
enquiries@dcnetwork.org

Facing Parenthood
Individual, couple and family therapy: supporting issues of fertility,
pregnancy, birth and parenthood.
Based in North London: accessible to all via telephone and Skype
consultations.
7 Lansdowne Rd
London N10 2AX
Telephone: 020 8444 9160
www.facing-parenthood.com
ips@ipsnetwork.co.uk

Human Fertilisation and Embryology Authority
Finsbury Tower
103–105 Bunhill Row
London
EC1Y 8HF
020 7291 8200
www.hfea.gov.uk
admin@hfea.gov.uk

Useful websites

American Fertility Association

http://www.theafa.org/about-the-afa/

A counsellor-led not-for-profit organisation providing supportive and educational materials for anyone looking to build a family and experiencing infertility and/or the need for donated gametes. Inclusive of all family types, this organisation has some excellent short leaflets and podcasts on many aspects of family creation by donor conception.

Choice Moms.org

www.choicemoms.org

Donor Sibling Registry (DSR)

www.donorsiblingregistry.com

The largest and most comprehensive site for connecting donor offspring/donors/half-siblings. Started in the US by Wendy Kramer and her sperm donor conceived son Ryan, it has many entries for UK clinics. In addition to the registry there is an excellent section giving access to up to date research and many ways of connecting with and exploring donor conception issues with others.

Fertility Friends

UK based: the largest and best used public infertility/fertility forum

www.fertilityfriends.co.uk

Single Mothers by Choice

www.singlemothersbychoice .org

The two websites above are well-respected, long-standing American organisations for single women who are choosing to become solo mothers.

INDEX